HANG ON TO A DREAM

THE STORY OF
THE NICE

MARTYN HANSON

Helter
Skelter
Publishing

First edition published in 2002 by **Helter Skelter Publishing**
4 Denmark Street, London, WC2H 8LL.

Copyright 2002 © Martyn Hanson. All rights reserved.

A CIP record for this book is available from the British Library.

ISBN 1-900924-43-9

Design by Chris Wilson @ CWDGA.

Printed in Great Britain by The Bath Press, Bath.

Photos and images by courtesy of the Bazz Ward Collection except:

Unknown: pages 16, 18, 23, 26-27, 37, 107
Brian Walkley: pages 20-21; Nick Robinson: pages 51, 65
Dave Westrop: pages 56, 72-73, 90
Phil Burns: pages 100-101 (illustration), 181
Chris Suttle: page 118; Mark Glinsky: pages 119, 134, 152
Lee Jackson Collection: pages 142, 156, 159, 165, 169, 170, 172
Dave Bentley: pages 168 (ELP), 177 (KE), 178
Liv Whetmore: page 171
Paul Remmington: pages 176, 177 (BD & LJ)

Front cover photos: Bazz Ward Collection (BD & LJ);
Nick Robinson (KE); Dave Westrop (DO'L)
Back cover photos: Bazz Ward Collection (The Nice); Claire Hammond (MH)

Every effort has been made to trace the copyright holders of the images
in this book, but a number could not be traced. The copyright holders concerned
should contact the publishers directly.

For Dale and Leeanne

When I started out, there were a few people who came to my rescue and got me up and running. My first thanks goes all the way to the United States to my friend, David Terralavoro. For many years David has been editor in chief of the excellent ELP/The Nice magazine, 'Fanzine For The Common Man'. His diligence to this cause kept the 'prog rock' flag flying from the late '80s to the late '90s. Needless to say, he answered my call for help and it wasn't long before packages of material were winging their way across the Atlantic. This was at a crucial time because I had barely any material on the band.

My next helping hand was from Robert Ashmore. Robert had played an important part in the ELP book and I was keen to enlist his help again. I knew I could rely on him for two reasons. Firstly, he has an excellent analytical mind and, secondly, I knew he wouldn't flinch from telling me exactly what he thought. Furthermore, he was usually right! He suggested many improvements to the original script. It was also thanks to Robert that I embarked on tracking down the many protagonists in the story – he tracked some down for me too. In this aspect I would like to thank my old friend David Bentley for putting me in contact with Lee Jackson. From Lee I got to Brian Davison and from him I got to Bazz.

One of the last major contributors was Andy Wilson. He offered to compile the discography for me and has done a wonderful job. Andy also went over some of the original manuscript.

These are the protagonists who gave me some of their time in this project. I direct heartfelt thanks to them: Lee Jackson, Brian Davison, Bazz Ward, Ian Hague, P.P. Arnold, Billy Nicholls, Mike Kellie, Brian Walkley, Richard Shirman, Greg Lake, Carl Palmer, John McBurnie, Brian Chatton, Mike Vickers, John Mayer, Godfrey Salmon, Gered Mankowitz, Alan Skidmore, Chris Welch, Gail Coulson, David 'Cyrano' Langston, Sandy Sarjeant, Terry Goldberg, Jack Barrie and, last but not least, the legendary Warren Mitchell.

Of all the people I approached – there were only a couple I failed to trace – only two didn't offer to help. To be honest, I'm second guessing here because they didn't even reply to me. They are Keith Emerson and Andrew Oldham. It was especially a great pity that Keith didn't have any input. Obviously, he could have filled in some of the gaps by adding his own version of events. But it wasn't to be.

I also owe many thanks to my Mum, Carole, David Flavell, Jenny Lamb, Liv G. Whetmore, David & Beth Rutter for getting me round Hove quickly when I needed to, Adam Fenton, Frank Askew, Nigel Hobday, Bjorn Are Davidsen, Nigel Dudas, Paolo Rigoli, Pete Rimell, Sefan March, Tom Szakaly (of Noddy's Puncture), Lennart Stahle ('My Back Pages'), Liz McLean (P.P. Arnold Fan Club), Sue Pittard, Karen Stober, Ian Hartley, Sid Smith, Graham Allen, Jackie Cowdry (Royal Albert Hall historian), all at the Newspaper Library (Collindale, London), Nick Robinson, Nigel Pryor, John Arnold (ELP Digest), Chris Suttle, John Thurston, Chris Charlesworth, John Kearney, John Hellier (Small Faces Fanzine – 'Whaping Wharf'), David Parker, Mike Masterton, Nick Moss, Kevin Smith, Mark Glinsky, Phil Burns, Terry Smith, Christine Offer, Andy Garibaldi, Jonny Greene, Derek Araujo, Albert and Lynn Merricks, Mark Burridge, Nick Rossi, Barry Green, Claire & Adrian Hammond, Hugh Fielder, Vicky & Paul Hay, Dr Peter Clarke, Michael A. Tusa, Patrick from 'Song For Me', Jules from Manband Archives, David Westrop, Pat & Margot (the last three being members of the legendary 'Marquee 12').

Chris Wilson for his vision and enthusiasm.

Many thanks also to Sean Body for having faith in me and giving me the opportunity of writing this book.

Finally, I would like to especially thank Lee, Brian and Bazz for welcoming me into their homes. Without them, this book could not have been written.

A million apologies if I have left anybody out.

Martyn Hanson

CONTENTS

FOREWORDS	BY LEE JACKSON, BRIAN DAVISON AND BAZZ WARD	**6**
INTRODUCTION	BY MARTYN HANSON	**9**
CHAPTER **1**	DAWN	**11**
CHAPTER **2**	THE FIRST LADY	**19**
CHAPTER **3**	HAPPY FREUDS	**29**
CHAPTER **4**	"THEIR INFLUENCES ARE MANY BUT THEY ARE INDEBTED TO NO-ONE"	**41**
CHAPTER **5**	THE BIG APPLE	**53**
CHAPTER **6**	ROAD MAPS, A STARTING PISTOL & SPRAY PAINT	**63**
CHAPTER **7**	THE SCHOOL MOTTO	**75**
CHAPTER **8**	THE ENGLISH INVASION	**83**
CHAPTER **9**	EVERYTHING AS NICE AS STRAT MAKES IT	**95**
CHAPTER **10**	THE FIVE MIGHTY BRIDGES	**105**
CHAPTER **11**	SWITCHED-ON EMERSON	**115**
CHAPTER **12**	CHIMES AT MIDNIGHT	**121**
CHAPTER **13**	FOR MOTHER, BAZZ & THE BEAST	**129**
CHAPTER **14**	REFUGEES	**139**
CHAPTER **15**	THE BIGGEST SHOW IN TOWN	**147**
CHAPTER **16**	THE DEATH OF MOTHER	**157**
CHAPTER **17**	THE NICE ROAD HOME	**167**
CHAPTER **18**	YOUR FRIENDLY NEIGHBOURHOOD GROCERY STORE	**173**
APPENDICES		**179**
	WHERE ARE THEY NOW?	**180**
	DISCOGRAPHY	**185**
	BBC SESSIONS	**208**
	LIST OF GIGS	**209**
	REFERENCE SOURCES	**212**
	INDEX	**215**

FOREWORDS

IN RECENT YEARS I have been less inclined to talk about my time in The Nice. In fact, it was these feelings that held sway when someone claiming to represent an ELP website contacted me and asked for an interview. I turned it down with the reply: 'I'll give you the interview if and when The Nice get back together again.' My response was interpreted by the 'offended party' who claimed that my rejection was based on bitterness. This incident struck home to me how much has been assumed with regard to many of the things surrounding Brian and myself.

With this in mind, I remember well when Martyn first contacted me while writing the book you now hold in your hands. The idea appealed to me immediately. One of the most surprising things in the year it took for Martyn to write the book was how I started to remember things I had put to the back of my mind. I'd talk about a particular incident and this would trigger memories in other areas.

As the work progressed, it became more and more of an emotional roller coaster for me. I must confess, at times I found it quite draining to read what Martyn was writing. That's not to say that there were never feelings of regret or even reliving the past. But when one's past was as much fun as mine with The Nice and then suddenly you are faced with the systematic re-ordering of that most memorable era, it inevitably initiates a period of reflection. Imagine if somebody did the same for your life?

Not only that. There are things in the book that I wasn't even aware of. I remember one chapter particularly well. I came across so many things I had never heard before I phoned Brian up and he duly confirmed the incidents. When you think about it, there were always going to be times when there was only a single witness to events.

I think that Martyn's book places The Nice firmly where they belong. At the historic forefront of the musical genre that became known as 'Prog Rock'.

FEBRUARY 2002

BRIAN DAVISON

WHEN I HEARD THAT Martyn was to write a book about The Nice, I was very happy that the band was to receive recognition as one of the influential bands of its time. Inasmuch as we were, and still are in many ways, part of the story of modern music, for that to be recognised 30 years on provokes deep emotion. Particularly when remembering the tremendous unity the band had, while live and recording, once it became a three-piece.

I feel that we helped to open that music gateway that became known as 'Prog Rock' and believe that much of today's more experimental music carries echoes of the sound that The Nice were producing in its time. I hope you, dear reader, will enjoy reading Martyn's work; an account of the merry-go-round of a band's brief life.

JANUARY 2002

BAZZ WARD

I REMEMBER IN THE EARLY DAYS of The Nice somebody asked me what my function was in the band. My reply was: 'I don't play.' The retort was instant: 'What do you mean by that?' I told him by that I meant I did everything else. The burden on a roadie in those days was huge, not that we ever thought about it much. Even though I'd been a roadie for a few years before The Nice they were a quantum leap for me. Looking back, I did a lot of crazy things to make sure the show went on. At the Blenheim Palace gig, with Pat, Keith broke the switch for his rotary speaker. So I took it off and was holding the two live wires together to keep the motor going, and pulling them apart to slow it down. I could have been fried! I learnt my lesson after that and always made sure we had some spare equipment.

After Alan Smith and John Robson came on board, my main function was to make sure Keith's Hammonds were working. As you can imagine they took a heavy toll. When I couldn't fix them I used to take them to Boosey & Hawkes. The engineer there couldn't understand why I kept taking them in for repair. Then one day he saw Keith on the television and that was that. Luckily we found Bill Hough and Bill Dunne and they came up with some incredible innovations. Sometimes it was hard work to keep Keith at bay. He didn't have the technical knowledge and would ask for impossible things. I would invariably have to say to him: 'Keith, that won't work like that.' I then would have to reassure him, usually over the next few days, and he would finally admit defeat. However, this wasn't necessarily a bad thing as he always kept us on our toes. As the technical side progressed, some of his ideas were gradually worked out and incorporated into his system.

In those days there was camaraderie between the band and the crew. We all mucked in together. You have to remember that for the first year, both band and crew travelled in the same mini-bus. I remember one time in Sweden, I was so tired that Brian drove the van so I could get a few hours sleep on the floor. It was a team effort. Strat used to say that everyone had their part to play. When promoters took the band out for a meal after the gig, Strat would insist the crew went too, "We all go or none of us!" This fostered loyalty. I remember when The Nice were on the same bill as Traffic. Stevie Winwood offered to double my wages to go with them. They were surprised when I refused. As far as I was concerned I was already with the best rock band on the planet, how could money lure me away from my boys?

Yes, I did have a reputation for decking people. But when you have to do a job you can't take any crap from anybody. When the local 'jobsworth' tells you 'You can't have the Grand piano (that's in the contract) because it's only for REAL musicians', you have to be prepared to point out the error of his judgement, sometimes physically! I did slip up a few times though. On the second US tour I took my eye off the ball. We'd apparently upset the support band, Sweetwater Canal, who was miffed about where I'd put our gear. The upshot was a sabotaged Hammond. Bill Hough had gone to Canada and I was in the shit. Incredibly I traced him down by telephone to some remote place where he had gone to fix one of the Compton Organs (who he also worked for). I then had him relay a complete fault-finding procedure, and got it fixed.

There was something magical about the band. They swung like crazy and they had soul. They were free flowing and improvisational. Keith would go off and Lee and Brian knew exactly where to fill in and most nights differed greatly. They were so good it was frightening.

When I found out the band were splitting I was devastated. I nearly went with Keith in his new venture but in my heart I knew it was time to go. I did meet Keith in the Ship pub in 1975 but he was frosty. I suppose he felt I'd let him down but you know there were a lot of people let down in 1970. I really think that if they had stayed together for another year or so... well, who knows what might have happened.

I have always been in contact with Lee and Brian and it seems strange that, over thirty years after the band's demise, I'm helping them to get gear for the upcoming reunion.

Looking back, it was a great period of time for creative musicians and, sadly, it'll never be repeated. But I wouldn't have missed it for the world!

MARCH 2002

INTRODUCTION

TOWARDS THE END of the book I co-authored on ELP, I made a pitch to the publisher. "Sean, how about a book on The Nice?" I told him, confidently, that I had known most of the story on ELP but with The Nice I only knew about 75%! For a while I laboured under that illusion. It was only when I'd been on the project a few weeks that I realised that figure had been wildly optimistic. Long before the end of the project it was apparent I knew next to nothing.

In fact, it was the knowledge gap that made it one of the most pleasurable things I've ever done. I spent many hours travelling the country and many more listening as the story unfolded. It was rather strange hearing Lee addressed as Keith in the Jackson household. It was even stranger addressing my correspondence to him as Keith, while the letter inside began with 'Hi Lee'.

I remember the first time I went to see Brian. I spent an evening listening to him play where he reminded all and sundry present just what a great drummer he is. His sea-view cottage provided a wonderful setting to recall this history. Bazz was able to open up the story in a dimension that none of the band ever could. Some of the stories included here Lee and Brian had never heard. As Bazz related recently, especially in the early days, "The only thing I didn't do was play!" In this sense I think I had the best of both worlds in rooting out the story.

I knew when I started there were two very painful areas I was delving into. The first was the departure of Davy O'List and the second was Keith's decision to break the band up. Long before I got to the break up I realised the impact the band had made; most of which has been unsung. I know that at times it was very difficult for Lee, Brian and Bazz to go over some of this period. But I think they realised it was important to set the record straight. I thank them heartily for that.

Originally, I'd written a far bigger book but it was decided to omit some the ELP/Keith solo material – I simply didn't have the room to cover all of it. Initially, I was disappointed but on reflection it was the right decision. What is left is a lot more focused than hitherto. For those who require more detail about Keith's post The Nice career, I refer you to the ELP book , 'The Show That Never Ends'.

Consequently, without similar restrictions, I was able to deal with Lee and Brian's post 1970 period in detail. These areas have never been covered before, and I know there is a large degree of interest, especially in the Refugee period. But I hope that readers will indulge me with Jackson Heights and Every Which Way because they were fine bands. There are also summaries of all the other members and associates of The Nice post 1970.

I have included many Appendices and I hope they are of interest. However, I must state that the gig list is incomplete. There are gaps and, try as I might, I couldn't complete it. In those days, nationwide tours were not well established. The band, in the main, played one-off gigs and this is why some of them were impossible to trace, especially out of London (or those that didn't appear in the national music press). Bazz is certain that somewhere he has a little book with all of them in but, alas, he never did find it.

I just missed The Nice by dint of being born in the mid-'50s, so it was late 1970 by the time I started listening to more serious music. I was one of the legion of young ELP fans who only had a vague idea that The Nice had been successful but knew little outside their albums. Suffice to say this project forced me to reappraise where The Nice stand in not only Keith Emerson's history but in music generally.

The title came to me very early. In fact, even before I met anyone from the band. However, when I did meet them, I knew this was the only title it could have been. It is therefore apt, in the light of the reunion, that you have to stick in there because dreams, sometimes, do come true.

When I started out, I was merely writing a book on a group whose heyday was over thirty years ago and who, to a large degree, had been forgotten. However, it wasn't long before I realised that I was writing a book about not just a very important band but the dawn of a new genre of music!

MARTYN HANSON
JUNE 2002

CHAPTER 1

DAWN

"I know someone
who plays
great Hammond."

BRIAN WALKLEY
to **GARY FARR**

IN THE EARLY SIXTIES, the clubs and dancehalls of the UK were teeming with bands, all of whom were hungry for a taste of the glamour and excitement of the burgeoning music scene. Alongside these young hopefuls were just as many managers and fixers, hustling, cutting deals and taking their percentage, hoping that their act was going to be the next big thing. Gary Farr and The T-Bones were just one of the many groups struggling to make an impact in the already crowded 1960s UK pop scene. With maverick impresario Giorgio Gomelsky at the helm, Farr and the T-Bones were popular and worked extensively on their native South Coast as well as in and around London. They'd recorded a clutch of singles – their first in 1964, 'How Many More Times' (later covered by Led Zeppelin) - but none had found favour with the record-buying public of the day.

A large bearded man of Russian extraction, Gomelsky was a producer and director of documentary films on jazz and blues artists and was the first to see the potential of the then unknown Rolling Stones. Although the bulk of Gomelsky's time was taken up managing The Yardbirds, and his roster of up and coming artists, including ex-office secretary, Julie Driscoll, Long John Baldry and even a young mod called Rod Stewart, he found time to fix Farr and the T-Bones up with tours and radio sessions, as well as residencies in clubs such as The Crawdaddy and The Marquee. Sometimes, things happened by virtue of being in the right place at the right time. Brian Walkley, drummer with the T-Bones, recalls the time when the band were on the same bill as Stevie Wonder, The Temptations and UK Liverpudlian chart-toppers Gerry and The Pacemakers for the 'Ready Steady Go' pop television show. The show was beamed live to London and shown later to the rest of the country. Wonder was impressed when he heard the T-Bones, "Those cats have got soul. Where can I sing with them?" Conveniently, the T-Bones were on their way to the Marquee for their regular Friday night slot and the diminutive Wonder came along, jamming with the band for twenty minutes.

Yet, despite this kind of acceptance, vocalist Gary Farr decided the band needed a change of direction. After listening to keyboard players such as Georgie Fame and Graham Bond, he announced he wanted a Hammond organ player in the band. T-Bone drummer Brian Walkley immediately remembered a young organist whom he had encountered back in 1962. Brian told Gary, "I know someone who plays great Hammond." Walkley had once sat in with The Keith Emerson Trio, who played on a basement stage in a pub called Harrison's. He recalls that sessions with Emerson's outfit were a very free kind of arrangement and invariably it wasn't a trio. On Walkley's recommendation, Farr travelled to see Emerson perform, although by now the keyboard player had formed a new band called John Brown's Bodies. What Farr heard that night greatly impressed him.

****

Keith Emerson was born on 2nd November 1944 in Todmorden, in the North Riding of Yorkshire, not a little in part due to the intervention of Adolf Hitler. When World War Two came in 1939, it became a common occurrence for those living on the south coast of England to be evacuated to rural areas. As Keith's mother was pregnant this necessitated evacuation. As the war was drawing to a close the family moved back to Worthing, Sussex, in March 1945.

Keith was an only child and was brought up in middle class prosperity. It was quite a musical environment that the infant Emerson was exposed to. His father was a musician and Keith remembers vividly his initial musical experiences, "The earliest music I can remember was my father, who had a piano accordion, and they used to have musical evenings. They used to have lots of friends come round, one with a drum kit, another that sang, and right from when I was very small, I used to go to sleep to the sounds of a 'get-together'."

It wasn't long before his father acquired a piano and the young Keith would watch as his father tickled the ivories, his fascination with the instrument turning into a desire to play. Keith quickly progressed enough for his father to suggest lessons. However, when the local piano teacher came round he was surprised to see a very old lady indeed. Miss Marshall was 80 years old and took discipline very seriously. This was serious stuff as scales were thrown at him thick and fast. It did little to foster an affinity for learning but Keith kept at it for a number of years.

Although Keith was something of an introverted child, this did not prevent him from giving public performances, playing an unusual gig for an aunt. Speaking to The Guardian newspaper years later, Emerson revealed, "I played for my auntie's dance classes when I was 13 or 14, everything from tap-dancing to ballet. I learned a lot of styles, but I was painfully shy, hiding away behind the piano, and being driven mad by the sight of all those girls. I used to make loads of Airfix Spitfires [plastic kit models] while dreaming of being a star and a hit with the girls." Such sessions equipped Emerson with the ability to change styles and tempo at the drop of a hat.

Despite his father's musical inclinations, Keith's parents believed that that full-time education and a steady well-paid job was the way to go. Emerson's father never considered a professional musical career for his son, believing that music was little more than a pastime, to be conducted on a part-time basis.

The arrival of skiffle in Britain took Keith, like many other kids, by storm. But as the new music was largely guitar-based, the fact that Keith had a piano created a sense of isolation, "Skiffle was very popular and fashionable, it had a unique style and anyone could play it, regardless of musical knowledge. So I didn't know what to do then. What was I doing hammering away at the piano, while everyone else was crazy about skiffle. Then I was given a guitar for Christmas, and I learnt a few chords. The only problem was that I couldn't sing! The other problem was I ended up with a huge blister on my finger... and couldn't play the piano." Some timely advice from his father saved the situation, "You know the piano better than the guitar - at least you can entertain people with the piano." After that aberration he was soon back on course, but it didn't cure him completely of his fascination with the guitar!

As Keith got older he became more critical of the rigid dictates of the classical formula, 'Play it as Beethoven did.' There appeared no room for self-expression, and it was far too dictatorial. At the tender age of fourteen, Keith had the chance to go to London and study at the Royal Academy. He turned down this apparently golden opportunity because, as he had led such an insulated existence, he was scared of leaving home. By this time, he was playing piano during his school's morning assembly, having terrific fun in racing with the choir to see who finished first.

He briefly attended the Local College of Further Education but largely just to kill time. Before long, Keith had stopped having lessons and had found himself gravitating to jazz piano, playing his first gig at a rifle club dinner for a very useful £1 - a lot of money for a young lad! The burgeoning rock 'n' roll scene didn't make much impression on the young man, though he did sometimes listen to a number of boogie-woogie and country pianists who were very popular at the time. People like Russ Conway, Winifred Atwell, Mrs Mills and Joe 'Mr Piano' Henderson were regularly making the Top 10.

"People like Roy Orbison and Cliff Richard were making the hit parade at that time," Keith later explained. "I had the attitude that I was really a jazz purist. I thought that pop music was okay, but that it had no musical value. Jerry Lee Lewis and Little Richard didn't pass me by, because I dug their piano playing, but people like Cliff and Elvis did. Then suddenly pop music took a swing, it began to offer me a lot more. People like Georgie Fame crept onto the scene; rhythm and blues suddenly became popular. People started to get interested in musicians like T-Bone Walker, Howlin' Wolf, and they were going back to the roots of the music. Groups like The Animals were making hit songs out of it and there were different instruments being used."

When he listened to records, Keith would always try to unlock the secrets of their composition and structure – particularly that of classical music. Improvising around Bach or something similar, he would entertain school chums with an astonishing display of precocious talent. However, tackling Jazz wasn't so easy and taking advice from fellow players led him down a few blind alleys. It wasn't until he found books with the improvisations written out, that he began to understand what was happening within the music. Although somewhat mechanistic, this approach helped Emerson develop his own improvisational style.

All the time, Emerson was making incremental adjustments to his already considerable technique. Given that he did not have access to a record player, most of his musical explorations were done via the radio. One tune he heard on the wireless that made an impression on him was Floyd Cramer's 'On The Rebound'. At the time he was playing a stride technique and as such listened to a lot of Fats Waller, but he also studied the playing of André Previn, Oscar Peterson, Hampton Hawes and, at the light entertainment end of things, Russ Conway. However, when he heard the multi-talented Dudley Moore, he realised that there was less need to play bass patterns with the left hand if one had a bass player.

It wasn't long before Keith joined a swing band run by the local council. Incredibly, councils did things like that in those days. The band played mainly big band arrangements like Count Basie and Duke Ellington, which led him to form his first real band, The Keith Emerson Trio, in 1962. It was quite an eye opener for the young innocent: "These pubs I used to play at were really awful. Sailors would come in pissed out of their heads, there were whores all over the place - on one occasion one of them removed her knickers and pulled them over the bass player's head." The material consisted of the pop tunes of the day, which Keith liberally laced with as many styles and variations as he could manage.

Whilst still managing to hold down his day job as a bank clerk, Emerson embarked on a new musical direction after hearing Jimmy Smith's 'Walk On The Wild Side'. The sound of the record captivated him and was responsible for Emerson discovering a new instrument - the Hammond Organ. Thanks to wages from his menial day job, savings and a contribution from his father, he finally acquired one in 1964, an L100, from the local supplier, Portsmouth Organ Centre.

However, quite early on, he became frustrated with the limitations of this particular model and the amplification failed to meet the requirements of a young musician wanting to entertain the crowds in the busy Brighton bars. Emerson attempted to connect the organ to a Vox amp but the results left a lot to be desired. Feeling frustrated, he wrote to Hammond Organ (UK) Ltd. The reply, dated 5th January 1965, read: "Thank you for your letter of January 4th advising us of your purchase of a Hammond Organ model L100 from the Portsmouth Organ Centre, and that you have connected a Vox amplifier to it with separate speaker and are disappointed with the result. Unfortunately the Hammond Organ is so designed that it will not easily match up equipment not specifically intended for use with it, and therefore we can understand your disappointment in this respect." The letter ends with the company quoting two blues artists that Keith had mentioned in his original letter, both endorsing the instrument.

****

After seeing Keith Emerson play, Gary Farr was positive that he had something special and immediately offered the young semi-pro musician a job with the T-Bones. To Farr's astonishment, Emerson turned him down. Remarkably, Emerson was reluctant to leave the security of his job with the Midland Bank.

Tactfully, Farr left the job of persuading Emerson to join the band to Brian Walkley. For the next month, the drummer and friend and local musician, Godfrey Sheppard, tried to change Emerson's mind. Eventually, Keith relented and responded to Walkley's suggestion that he just 'give it a go.' Although Emerson still harboured reservations about going pro, Walkley suspected that things would be fine once he'd tasted life on the road with the T-Bones, "I knew he would be hooked when he played the Marquee club and saw the girls and all the trimmings. He loved that life, so he stayed and never looked back."

If Gary and the rest of the T-Bones were happy with their latest acquisition, T-Bone roadie John Ryan (later to become Dave Brubeck's road manager) was driven to distraction. The keyboard player would always supervise Ryan like a mother hen, as he shifted the Hammond into the van, making sure that the instrument was not scratched. Recalling the period, Brian Walkley dryly recalls, "That was the same Hammond that got battered in The Nice."

The band divided their time between the South Coast circuit and London, where they stayed in the Madison Hotel, Sussex Gardens, Paddington. Whilst here they would often meet up with some of the big pop bands of the day that also used the hotel as a stopping off point when visiting the capital.

Gomelsky arranged for the band to back their namesake T-Bone Walker at the Marquee Club on 15th October 1965. With only an hour or so of rehearsals with the great man himself, the gig was quite a challenge. The highlight for Emerson came when T-Bone said to him, "Take a solo!" The following evening, the entourage drove to Manchester's Twisted Wheel club to entertain the crowds in the North.

Thereafter, the T-Bones took part in the famous Marquee Tour which ran until 6th December and also included Manfred Mann, The Yardbirds, The Mark Leeman Five (with drummer Brian Davison), Paul & Barry Ryan and The Scaffold. This was the first time that the paths of Brian Davison and Keith Emerson had crossed – although it was not to be the last. Davison vividly remembers one aspect of the tour, "One of the funniest things on the tour was to see Keith and Manfred Mann race into the hall to be the first to get to the piano when we got to the gig."

Yet all was not well with the T-Bones. Gomelsky was concentrating on a more fruitful association with The Yardbirds, while band members Winston Weatherall and Stuart Parks had fallen out with the new incoming manager, Tony Secunda. In order to keep Gary Farr and The T-Bones as a going concern, it fell to Emerson and Walkley to audition the hopeful replacements in a London church hall. Out of the half dozen bass players they heard that day, one caught their attention.

The MANFRED MANN, YA BIRDS, MARK LEEMAN F GARY FARR and the T-BO and the SCAFFOLD gathere Wednesday for a dress rehe of "The Marquee Show," w was due to open last night (T day) at Stockton. Missing picture: Paul and Barry R and Goldie (who replaces and Charlie Foxx).

****

Keith Joseph Anthony Jackson was born in Newcastle upon Tyne on January 8th 1943, to parents Alf and Evelyn. There was always music in the house – it was common for households in that era to have at least one player in the family and the Jackson's were no exception. Alf played violin in a symphony orchestra but his musical career came to an end when he had an accident with a breach-loading gun while in the navy. Thus from an early age, the infant Keith developed an affinity with music.

He was still at school when he discovered the sounds of Radio Luxembourg. Night after night, Keith would tune in to the music stations to sample the delights on offer. There wasn't a great deal of music business hype in those days and what 'scene' there was evolved more organically. It was in this heady atmosphere that kids all over the country were inspired to take up an instrument and attempt to be a part of this happening. The sounds Keith heard captured his imagination and he was determined to get a slice of the action – no matter how lowly or humble that would be.

Like a lot of kids up and down the country, he built a home-made guitar comprised of cigar boxes and nylon wire – a real 'mother of invention' contraption. However, it wasn't long before he acquired a real one, paying the princely sum of twenty-five shillings (£1.25) for a nameless Spanish job that someone had brought back from a holiday. It was accompanied, of course, by the ubiquitous Bert Weedon 'Play In Three Days' book. Rory McEwan's country blues book also came in handy.

Things really took off though when Keith heard Elvis Presley's 'Hound Dog' and Bill Haley's 'Rock

Around The Clock', and was immediately hooked on rock 'n' roll. Shortly after, he saw the film 'The Girl Can't Help It' which featured many artists, including Little Richard. Keith noticed that the bass player in the film had an electric bass guitar. It was the first time he'd ever seen one - up until then basses always seemed to be of the upright, slap-bass variety.

This chance encounter with the celluloid screen proved to be decisive and reshaped Keith's musical ambitions. Not long after, he'd noticed a Gibson bass guitar in the window of a Newcastle department store. The appearance of such a fabled instrument was something of a mystery – particularly as they were not generally imported into Britain at this time. Keith surmised that an American sailor who needed some quick beer money had pawned the guitar. Although the instrument was right-handed, Lee determined to buy it, and managed to persuade his dad to lend him the money, £50, which was then a considerable sum. As Keith recalls, "It was the biggest sales job I ever did."

In 1958, Keith joined a skiffle group called The Satellites, named after the Russian Sputnik which had been launched into space the previous year. Keith's semi-pro career took off when he became a member of The Four Just Men (later known as The Dynamics). The band worked the potentially lucrative network of working men's clubs, which were thick on the ground in and around the North East. Keith recalls that the band wore gaudy yellow jackets, causing rival bands to refer to them privately as 'Mary Baker's Lemon Tops', after a popular brand of cake mix. "I only found out years later that they used to take the piss out of us!" laughs Keith.

His musical apprenticeship in the clubs had served him well and, by 1963, Keith had joined a Sunderland band called The Valiants. The group was significant for two reasons. Firstly, the band were off to tour Spain - a great opportunity for any musician. Secondly, because the group contained several members called Keith, the young Jackson decided to change his name. An avid reader, Keith had recently finished a book on the American Civil War and the Generals, Lee and Jackson. Feeling that he was a bit of rebel, from that moment onwards – at least professionally - Keith Jackson became Lee Jackson.

On a return visit to his home town, Lee made a bee-line for the Club A Go Go. The venue had established itself as the centre of Newcastle's fledgling music scene. Here, local talent would have the chance to mingle with many leading lights in the music scene. When Jackson saw the house band, The Alan Price Combo, it was his first real exposure to the blues. Lee's response to Price's music was succinct: "I like that!" By now, Jackson had joined The Invaders, who found themselves booked in as the support act for the up and coming Geordie blues combo, The Animals. They created enough of an impression for The Animals' manager to sign The Invaders to a contract. Jackson remembers that they didn't see their new minder for the next three months. When they did, having completely forgotten who The Invaders were, the hapless manager then tried to sign them up all over again! This was Lee's first indication of just how fickle the music business could be. The Club A Go Go was important for another reason. It was here Jackson received some advice from visiting Brit-Blues supremo, John Mayall – if Lee wanted a real career in music, then London was the place to be. For the time being however, Lee kept his passport well stamped with a tour in West Germany, playing in a band called The Van Dykes (actually known as The Von Dykes). Playing mainly Tamla Motown in dance halls, the gruelling schedule (45 minutes on, 45 off - from 4 in the afternoon until 3 in the morning) was a fantastic education for Lee: "That sharpened you up alright!" On returning to England, Jackson followed Mayall's guidance and moved down to the bright lights of London and regular bouts of unemployment.

Eventually, he got a job with Kenny Barnard and The Wranglers at the Ad Lib Club, a stint that was curtailed when the club was closed due to excessive noise levels. From here, Jackson went on to his easiest gig of all, one which didn't actually require him to play in public. In 1965 he became reserve bassist for Hedgehoppers Anonymous, managed by impresario Jonathan King and comprising serving members of the Royal Air Force. Their regular bassist was on leave and, fearing he might be recalled any minute, they hired Jackson for £35 per week.

After a period of understudying in the pop world, Mayall once again proved helpful to Lee. Bluesbreaker John McVie was hospitalised for an appendectomy and Mayall rang Lee asking him to stand in on bass. Although he only played a dozen or so gigs with the Bluesbreakers, he enjoyed the experience. Laughing at the memory, Jackson remembers that when the band came up to Newcastle, his sister was put in a bit of a position, "She would often find Eric Clapton crashed out on her sofa." Mayall was too tight to pay for a hotel, avoiding it when he could.

Hedgehoppers Anonymous, with Lee Jackson (in shades)

The stint with the Bluesbreakers provided Jackson with a useful education and added considerably to his standing and pedigree – he was later to also fill in on bass for the other elder statesman of the British blues boom, Alexis Korner. Yet despite such engagements, it didn't prevent periods of unemployment, leaving Jackson to scour the small-ads section of the Melody Maker. When unable to find work as a musician, Jackson turned his hand to other means in order to make ends meet. "I worked in the retail clothing trade with Austin Reeds and Burtons. I also did a spell in a pool of casual labour in a cigarette factory. I was assistant train-driver on the factory's internal line." Thankfully, the Melody Maker came to the rescue when he answered a musicians wanted advertisement for Gary Farr and The T-Bones.

With everyone impressed by Jackson's playing and his Mayall and Korner credentials, the young Geordie bassist was in. A guitarist proved harder to spot but they went along with Emerson's hunch about David 'Cyrano' Langston. The first gig of the revitalised Gary Farr and The T-Bones was on New Years Eve, 1965 – most definitely a case of out with old and in with the new.

CHAPTER 2

THE FIRST LADY

"I looked at the
English pop scene
and I dug it.
It's small and
everybody's friends
and together, so
I decided to stay."

P.P. ARNOLD

THAT KEITH EMERSON'S PRESENCE had a radical influence on the musical direction of the T-Bones is beyond question. Not long after Lee joined, Gary's brother, Rikki Farr - who later went on to organise the Isle Of Wight Festivals and acted as a mentor to his brother - toyed with the idea of bringing another guitar back in the band. Rikki never really liked Keith's style of playing, as he considered it too jazzy. Instead, he preferred someone like Jeff Beck, who had jammed with the T-Bones a few times before Keith joined, to return the group to its blues-based roots.

Change was definitely in the air. Brian Walkley loved the jazz and blues content in Keith's playing but felt the way the band were moving was becoming too 'clean' for his liking. For Walkley, they had become too much like The Impressions, an American band, in using a lot of close harmonies. Such a change necessitated a lot of rehearsing - far too much in Brian's opinion - and, as such, he felt much of the band's original spontaneity had been lost.

Gary Farr & The T-Bones in their earlier, smartly attired line-up, in 1965

Left-right: Stuart Parks, Keith Emerson, Brian Walkley, Winston Weatherall, Gary Farr

Walkley, who had played a crucial role in bringing Emerson into the T-Bones and thus the wider listening public, decided to leave the group, playing his last gig with the band on 1st February 1966. Soon after, Walkley quit the UK music scene and relocated to France. An indication of the high esteem in which Emerson held Walkley came just before the drummer left. Keith was talking about getting a band together that would have played a new kind of material. He asked Brian to be the drummer in a duo that would play classical adaptations, in which Keith would have played bass parts using the Hammond foot pedals. Walkley turned it down, as he bemoaned later, "I stupidly said I wanted to do something else." Brian also turned down Arthur Brown in Paris the following year.

One gig toward the end of his time with the T-Bones stands out in Brian Walkley's memory. They played Brunel University and were supported by The King Bees. Walkley noticed that Emerson was transfixed by their fifteen-year-old drummer. Brian remembered the look on Keith's face, as though he was making a mental note. The drummer was Carl Palmer. Recalling the period, T-Bone guitarist David Langston revealed that they considered the youthful Palmer as a replacement for Brian Walkley but were worried about his timing and didn't even consider asking him to audition.

In the spring of 1966, with Alan Turner taking up duties behind the drums, the band secured a residency in Biarritz, France, which involved a mighty workload playing two sets a night for three weeks. Langston recalled they would finish at 2am when the owner of the club gave them free drinks. Needless to say by the time they got back to their apartments - usually at dawn - they were well served and accompanied more often than not by some local girls.

The band played on the bill with Chris Barber at the Canasta Club. For a joke, Langston hid the drummer's stool which Emerson used when sitting behind the Hammond. As a result, for the first time Keith had to stand up to play and it quickly became Emerson's preferred stance during performance. Lee Jackson also recalls that this wasn't the only change to his live delivery, "Keith discovered that the reverb could make a crashing sound when he tilted the Hammond and brought it to ground level [but didn't regularly incorporate it into the act as he was still being careful with his instrument]." One of the gigs at the Canasta Club was filmed for a live TV show.

Barber was so impressed with the T-Bones he recorded with them twice back in the UK. The first time was at the Marquee Studios on 26th April 1966, where they laid down 'If I Had A Ticket' with Kenneth Washington on vocals (Farr did the backing vocals) and Barber on trombone. The single was released on CBS and credits The T-Bones on the label. They didn't play on the flip side. Although these releases failed to create any kind of impact, they are significant being the first commercially available records which featured both Emerson and Jackson together.

Later in the year, on 8th September, the group recorded several tracks at Advision studios in London. They cut 'Stormy Monday Blues' (by T Bone Walker), 'Silver Meter' (John Patten), 'Rock Candy' (Brother Jack Macduff), and an original piece by Barber called 'Trombone Long'. They were paid the princely sum of £40 by Chris Barber but the songs remain unreleased to this day.

One of the highlights of the year was when the T-Bones played at the Windsor Jazz Festival. They drove back from Biarritz where they were still playing a residency. Lee remembers the day of July 30th 1966 very well, as they watched England win the football World Cup before playing the festival that night. They went down well and got some good press. They then returned to France where they played again in the Canasta.

As the year went on, the T-Bones put more effort into their image. Whereas once the choice of clothing wasn't considered too important, the arrival of psychedelia saw emblematic fashions start to gain prominence. Lee Jackson bumped into Eric Clapton in London's Portobello Road. The pair were talking about their Bluesbreakers days when they happened upon a junk shop, just as a load of red, braided guardsmen's jackets were being delivered. They each bought one on the spot for £2 and within a few months these jackets were highly sought after fashion accessories. Emerson also got onto the fashion bandwagon, transcending his jazz purist roots for the sake of the band's image.

Emerson could take some comfort though, knowing that his fashionable threads weren't the only thing that was causing heads to turn when Gary Farr and The T-Bones played in concert. Most observers agreed that the organ solos stole the show! The word quickly spread that 'you've gotta come and see this organist!'

Less than a year after Lee Jackson made his live debut with the T-Bones, Gary Farr played his last gig with them in late 1966. Farr decided to quit "to become Bob Dylan" as Jackson put it. Although the singer went on to record a string of albums with labels such as Marmalade, CBS, Atco and A&M, success eluded him and sadly, in 1992, he died of a heart attack in his sleep.

Now simply called The T-Bones, the band limped along for a further few months but it would only delay the inevitable. With David Langston taking on the lead vocals as well as guitar, they headed up to Scotland to fulfil some contractual obligations. However, making £30-£40 per night wasn't going to keep body and soul together for long. Perhaps as a last ditch attempt to keep the show on the road, the group called in all the favours they could. Prior to his career with The T-Bones, Dave Langston had been a roadie with The Who and used to tape-up Pete Townshend's battered guitars. Langston made a call and wanting to help out an old buddy, Townsend gave the new band a song. So keen was Townshend that, in late December, he took them into IBC studios in Portland Street at his own expense to record 'Mary Anne With The Shaky Hand', with Townshend producing and adding backing vocals.

Considered to be unsuitable for The Who at the time, Townshend used the song as part of his attempt to extend into other areas such as promotion and management. Having finished recording, Townshend then hawked the tapes trying to get The T-Bones a deal with a label but it never happened. Townshend later recorded the track and it appears on the 1967 album 'The Who Sell Out'.

In the end The T-Bones imploded. The diminishing number of bookings, adverse economics, the absence of any push from management and the lack of any prospective chart material, all combined to consign The T-Bones to obscurity – a fate shared with so many other hopeful bands. Looking back, Brian Walkley points the finger at Giorgio Gomelsky for paying too much attention to The Yardbirds. Gomelsky himself wrote later on how close the two bands were intertwined, "The T-Bones replaced The Yardbirds' residencies when the latter moved on to bigger and better things. The 'big-time' eluded the T-Bones only by a hair's breadth."

Whatever the cause of their demise, The T-Bones played their last gig in early 1967. Lee moved into Keith's flat in London where the poverty of the situation forced them to raid the electric meter, just to keep body and soul together. The landlady only let Lee stay because Keith had told her they were brothers. So when Keith's mother Dorothy came to visit she would always call

Lee her second son - something she still does to this day.

The two 'brothers' scoured the small ads and kept their ear to the ground in the search for work. Jackson secured a job with a London nightclub houseband, and Emerson successfully auditioned for a role in The V.I.P.s.

Prior to Emerson joining the band, The V.I.P.s had travelled to London from their hometown, Carlisle, in search of the big breakthrough. They were looked after by Chris Blackwell, who managed the successful Spencer Davis Group (and later Traffic), and released several singles on the continent. Although they managed to get a No.2 single with 'I Wanna Be Free' in the French charts, the group never had a UK release.

The V.I.P.s were a talented bunch of musicians - bassist Greg Ridley ended up in Humble Pie, guitarist Luther Grosvenor (calling himself Ariel Bender) ended up in Mott The Hoople and drummer Mike Kellie was in Paul Kossoff's first solo band. Touring Europe relentlessly, they built up sizeable reputations in both France and Germany. However, their guitarist, Jim Henshaw, had left and they were looking for a replacement. Henshaw had also filled in on upright piano – providing there was one available – for a couple of numbers.

For the second time in his career, Keith Emerson profited by a band that specifically wanted a Hammond organ player. Originally, The V.I.P.s would have loved to have had Steve Winwood for the band but as this was clearly out of the question, they were forced to spread the net wider. Using his Marquee connections from his days with The T-Bones, Keith got to hear of the vacancy and he showed up at the Marquee club's recording and rehearsal complex where The V.I.P.s used to rehearse. Keith used the 'house' Hammond and, needless to say, he passed the audition. It wasn't long before the reinvigorated band were off to France for a succession of gigs.

This was a big culture shock to Keith, as drummer Mike Kellie explained, "He had never come across anything like us before." The V.I.P.s were sometimes known as The V.I.Pills, a jokey reference to the band's recourse to chemical stimulation as a means of coping with the gruelling live schedule. Years later, Keith admitted to The Guardian newspaper just how much of a sheltered existence he'd had, "When I first went on the road with Gary Farr and The T-Bones and The V.I.P.s, I wasn't into the rock and roll lifestyle. I didn't even like beer!" Emerson declined to join in with the prevailing culture within the band but despite such differences, when it came to the music, things were more harmonious. Looking back at Emerson's tenure with the band, Kellie judges that, "Keith fitted into the band very well while he was in it."

Kellie also recalls that when the band was playing at Hamburg's Star Club, Luther Grosvenor spiked Keith's bottle of Coca Cola, wanting to see what would transpire. Kellie watched with interest as Emerson behaved totally out of character - rocking the Hammond on stage and generally behaving like a lunatic.

Emerson has a different recollection of this event, citing that one of the prostitutes by the name of Bloody Mary, who frequented the Star Club, had given him something that she claimed would cheer him up. It kept him awake for three nights during when, though Keith was unable to drive at this point, he offered to drive the van to the next gig which was in France. It was a hair-raising journey, as Keith recalls, "I crashed the vehicle, almost ruining all the instruments. We ended up playing this club somewhere in a vineyard. All the farmers there were getting really drunk." Then a fight broke out in the audience. At first the band were transfixed by the situation. "We were watching it from the stage playing away, the lads are saying 'keep playing, keep playing'." It was then, according to Emerson, that he tilted the Hammond, making a hundred different noises to distract the troublemakers. As far as Emerson is concerned, this was the first occasion when he tilted the Hammond on stage. Although the 'organ wrestling' didn't become a part of The V.I.P.s stage act, it's clear that Emerson was thinking about how he might improve his stage presence. Organists such as Georgie Fame and Graham Bond fronted groups but, in rock and pop terms, the guitarist was the main instrumental focal point. An organist couldn't compete in the charisma stakes, surely. Or could he?

Keith got other parts of his act from another source. He was at the Marquee when he came across the extraordinary Don Shinn, an eccentric individual with an L100 Hammond organ and a habit of disappearing around the back of it to draw out weird sounds with the aid of a screwdriver. This was largely played for laughs and audiences thought Shinn's antics were hilarious. Shinn also played 'treated' adaptations of classical pieces and Keith was struck by the aplomb with which he pulled it off. "He was a really weird looking guy, really strange. He had a schoolboy's cap on, round spectacles, really stupid. He had an L100. The audience were in hysterics... He'd played an arrangement of the Grieg 'Concerto'... I guess seeing Don Shinn made me realise that I'd like to compile an act from what he did."

In March of 1967, The V.I.P.s released an EP in France with contributions from Emerson. 'Stagger Lee' and 'Rosemarie' were the stand out tracks (he also plays on a track called 'Late Night Blues'). Mike Kellie is sure that Keith recorded tracks that were never released, probably recorded at the Marquee club's studio, although the exact whereabouts of these tapes are unknown. Surprisingly, the EP was released in a picture bag with the band on the cover, sitting on a wall with Emerson just about recognizable. The standard of the playing is high and

The V.I.P.s were obviously a very good band. They also further stimulated Keith's eye for fashion by introducing to him the trendiest European garb.

As The V.I.P.s had never had a permanent keyboard player before, Emerson enjoyed a certain amount of freedom, adding his own lines to blues-based repertoire and helping to shape the way the music was presented. Yet this did not satisfy Emerson's developing musical vision – and he wasn't alone. As Mike Kellie observed, all of The V.I.P.s were searching for the same thing, "We were trying to be a concept band. We were evolving into something that had something to say, which is what some bands of the day were beginning to do... it was an evolutionary time." In the spring of 1967, Emerson left the The V.I.P.s amicably, in order to follow his own musical path. For their part, The V.I.P.s eventually realised their vision as the vastly underrated Spooky Tooth.

As Emerson criss-crossed back and forth between the UK and the continent, Lee Jackson had ended up kicking his heels in the house band at the Cromwellian Club, London throughout February and March 1967. They were called House Of Usher and the owner of the club liked them so much he paid for them to go into Regent Sound Studios in Denmark Street, London, to cut a couple of numbers. Although Lee has long since forgotten the name of the tunes, he does remember they were a bit poppy – a fact confirmed by the guitarist of the group later going on to join 1970s pop sensations The Rubettes.

During this time, Lee was re-acquainted with The Animals and some of the other bands he'd first met at the Club A Go Go in Newcastle. Chas Chandler, formerly of The Animals, had a reputation for exaggeration and one day he excitedly buttonholed Lee, telling him that he'd signed up the most amazing black guitarist. When he finally did hear Jimi Hendrix, the guitarist in question, Lee told him, "For once, Chas, you just might be right".

****

Hendrix wasn't the only American import to be causing a stir. P.P. Arnold (born Patricia Ann Cole) was a protégée of Immediate label boss, Andrew Loog Oldham. Hailing from the tough Watts district of Los Angeles, P.P. - or Pat as she was known - escaped a loveless marriage and dead-end jobs when she successfully auditioned as a backing vocalist with Ike and Tina Turner.

As an Ikette, she took part in the Phil Spector-produced classic 'River Deep Mountain High' and toured with the Turners for two and half years. After Charlie Watts and Bill Wyman caught Ike and Tina on stage at The Galaxy Club on Sunset Strip, the entourage were invited over to support the Rolling Stones in the UK in September 1966. Despite the gruelling 12 city tour in the UK - two shows per date, opening at the Royal Albert Hall on 23rd September and closing in Southampton on 10th October - Pat still found time to show Mick Jagger a few dance steps to incorporate into his flamboyant stage show. "He's still using them," laughs Pat at the memory.

Perhaps by way of returning the favour, it was Jagger who persuaded Loog Oldham to offer the singer a record deal. "I had already made my mind up to leave the group after the tour, when we got back to the States," recalls Arnold. "I wanted to go solo because I had seen a lot of the business in the two-and-a-half years and I thought I could make it. I looked at the English pop scene and I dug it. It's small and everybody's friends and together, so I decided to stay."

Pat and Jagger got on famously and she was groomed to follow in the footsteps of Chris Farlowe, who had secured a sizeable hit with the Jagger/Richards penned 'Out Of Time'. When it came to finding a suitable stage moniker, it was photographer Gered Mankowitz who coined the name P.P.

After signing for Immediate, she initially waited around at the office for things to happen but they took a long time to do so. P.P. Arnold's first single 'Everything Is Gonna Be Alright' flopped, but Oldham was convinced success wasn't far away and he turned to the up and coming singer-songwriter Cat Stevens, who came up with the goods with 'The First Cut Is The Deepest'.

Produced by Jagger, the track reached No.18 in the charts, requiring Arnold to go out on the road to cash in on her chart success. The problem was that her then current band, The Blue Jays, weren't up to the job. It was P.P. Arnold's driver, Mickey O, who suggested that Keith Emerson might be the person to become Arnold's musical director and pull a new band together. It didn't matter that Arnold hadn't even heard of Emerson – it was important that things happen - and fast. "I wasn't necessarily interested in just big names," Pat recalls. "The main thing was that the person had lots of talent. Keith clearly had that."

Emerson had some conditions before accepting this tempting offer, however. "I told her I didn't want to be a just a backing band, so she said I could have my own spot and my own name to split the show into two halves." The deal was a good one in which everyone emerged a winner. For Arnold, it meant that she now had a built-in opening act at no extra money. Emerson had managed to get a slot which enabled him to try out some of the musical ideas which were occupying much of his time outside of The V.I.P.s. There was no time to lose, "I was given about four days to get it all together," recalls Keith. Quitting The V.I.P.s, the search was on for the rest of the band.

Lee Jackson got the news at the Cromwellian club when an excited Keith came in and Keith related the details and offered him the job on the spot. The brief, as Lee understood, was that Keith was creating a 'kicking band' for her.

Emerson also found Ian Hague, a drummer who had played with Chris Farlowe and Don Spencer's XL5. Luther Grosvenor, guitarist of The V.I.P.s, was asked to join by Keith but turned it down. It was friendly music journalist, Chris Welch, who recommended that Emerson check out Davy O'List. Welch was the first to note the guitarist's potential. Writing in Melody Maker, he observed, "Another fine guitarist slowly emerging on the scene is David O'List of The Attack. Only 17, he is already developing a powerful blues guitar style." At that stage, O'List had been playing for just two and a half years.

****

Born in Chiswick, London, on December 13th 1948, David O'List was the youngest member of the group. He was brought up in an artistic environment. His parents were actors and his father played the guitar, so it was no surprise that the young O'List took to music. After studying at St Marks in Fulham, at twelve years old, David gained a scholarship at the Royal College of Music. Over a period of four years he studied trumpet, with piano as his second instrument. Interestingly enough, his exam piece for trumpet was a theme from Mussorgsky's 'Pictures At An Exhibition'. During his period at the College he performed with the London Schools Symphony Orchestra at the Royal Festival Hall.

However, classical music wasn't the only thing to command his attention. The Beatles were turning heads everywhere and O'List counted himself a fan of George Harrison. Yet, it was The Rolling Stones' first album which inspired him to take up the guitar in 1964. He loved the dirty R 'n' B sound of The Stones and soon formed his first band, My Little Candle, playing local house and garden parties. From here he joined an outfit called Little Boy Blue, who covered mostly Stones and Chuck Berry material in local pubs and youth clubs. Despite a favourable reaction to the group, conflict with his father forced O'List to quit the band and go back to the Royal College of Music for a final year.

THE ATTACK (FIRST LINE-UP – LEFT TO RIGHT): GERRY HENDERSON, RICHARD SHIRMAN, BOB HODGES, DAVY O'LIST AND ALAN WHITEHEAD (DECCA PUBLICITY SHOT)

After his exams, O'List joined the backing band of soul singer Richard Henry, while keeping his head above water by working weekends at the local supermarket. It was here he met another musician, Richard Shirman, from the R 'n' B group Soul System. Richard was shopping with his mother and, whilst queuing at the cold meats counter, he struck up a conversation with Davy about music.

Shirman described the outcome of the meeting as, "The beginning of a good and valuable friendship." But when legendary manager Don Arden took them on, they changed their name at his request because it was too 'airy fairy' and so they became The Attack. (Arden had made his name as an action man in the world of music; famed for his heavy tactics, he managed, among others, The Small Faces.)

At the invitation of Shirman, O'List turned up at rehearsal with his trumpet but, as things panned out, he ended up playing the guitar. When the guitarist Bob Taylor (later of Downliners Sect and Beggars Opera) left, Davy stepped in - although whether Taylor jumped or was pushed remains a mystery. The ambitious Shirman was anxious to succeed with the group and so wanted to raise the standard of musicianship – hence his keenness to recruit O'List.

The Attack recorded a cover version of The Standell's 'Try It' and although it earned some radio play, it quickly sank without trace. Thereafter, Don Arden suggested they try a demo which had landed on his desk by American songwriter, Scott English. Destined to become one of the signature tunes of the decade, it was called 'Hi-Ho Silver Lining'. In February 1967 at the IBA studio in Oxford Circus, The Attack laid down their version. Sadly for the band, ex-Yardbird Jeff Beck had beaten them to the punch and Beck's version went on to become a massive hit. It has been said, that Beck stole the tune from The Attack, but Beck had already recorded his version on January 19th and, furthermore, The Attack's rendition of the song is plodding and lifeless compared to Beck's effervescent classic.

It wasn't all bad news though. Radio DJ John Peel picked up on the flip side, 'Any More That I Do' and started giving it plenty of airplay. Written by Shirman, Henderson and O'List, the exposure the song received as Peel's signature tune - including O'List's guitar solo - impressed more than a few people. As O'List notes, "It was the biggest break I ever had." One person who heard it was John Mayall, who offered the guitarist a place in The Bluesbreakers following the departure of Peter Green and drummer Aynsley Dunbar.

Then, at the same time, Keith Emerson's offer came in. O'List had a choice to make. Although the Mayall spot was clearly the more prestigious of the two, O'List rejected Mayall in favour of the relatively unknown Emerson. "I realised that if I joined John Mayall, we would be playing his music," O'List reflects. "Whereas with Keith, I would be able to put more of myself into the music, which appealed far more."

By coincidence, Lee Jackson was an old friend of The Attack's Richard Shirman and was detailed to check up on O'List's credentials. Shirman classed Davy as 'brilliant'. With O'List on board, the line-up was now complete.

CHAPTER 3

HAPPY
FREUDS

"What that
band needed
was me!"

BRIAN DAVISON

THE REHEARSALS FOR THE NEW BAND began at The White Hart in Acton, London, in May 1967. Lee Jackson remembers, "We rehearsed only once with Pat and we saw her only one more time after this at rehearsals." The format of the show was Keith and friends would play an opening solo set, which consisted of material such as Ennio Morricone's 'Fistful Of Dollars', Bob Dylan's 'She Belongs To Me', Billy Preston's 'Billy's Bag' [Preston was the first non-jazz organist to impress Keith] and later on The Beatles' 'A Day In The Life'. They would then play the soul material that made up P.P. Arnold's set, requiring a complete stylistic switch to cover things like Aretha Franklin's 'Respect', Arthur Cronley's 'Sweet Soul Music' and, of course, Arnold's hit single 'The First Cut Is The Deepest'.

Just as Pat Arnold had to find a name, so did the band. It's still hotly disputed who actually thought of the name but is reckoned to have been coined when the band were on their way to their first gig. It was the only time that Pat travelled with the backing group in their van. Arnold was discussing the legendary iconoclast Lord Buckley and noting his slogan 'Here Comes The Naz' - a black slang term for Jesus, derived from his birthplace of Nazareth - she suggested The Nazz as the name. Due to Pat's accent, the entire crew assumed she had said 'The Nice'. It was only a few days later they discovered the mix up, but by then they had got used to 'The Nice' so they stuck with it.

Not everyone agrees with this version of events. In 1991, Davy O'List, in an interview with Terrascope magazine, gave an alternative account of the name's derivation, "P.P. Arnold came up with the name 'The Naz' for us; it's an American term for God and we liked the sound of it but were a bit uneasy about being called 'God', so The Nice was derived from that." However, in an open letter to the American ELP magazine Fanzine For The Common Man in 1992, O'List stated, "It was I who proposed the name 'The Nice', after P.P. Arnold suggested 'The Naz', on our way to the first gig." Still, in a recent television interview, P.P. Arnold claimed she thought of the name and Emerson agrees, confirming the story about the band's misunderstanding of her accent.

The exact location of The Nice's first gig has been lost in the mists of time but we know it was in May 1967. There have been three candidates for the venue put forward by the various members, including Bristol, The White Hart, Acton and the Isle Of Wight. Prior to the Isle Of Wight gig, the band played a trick on Pat by telling her she required her passport to visit the island – she allegedly sweated a bit over that one.

At an early gig at The Manor House, London, the advert for the evening proclaimed "She's groovy, she's lush, P.P. Arnold and her Nice." That gig was on July 1st and Melody Maker was there to see it. The headline read "P.P. Arnold, Soulful, Exciting at the Manor House." As befits a star, Arnold was always given a grandiose introduction prior to appearance on the stage, "And now all the way from the United States of America, Miss P.P. Arnold." Her set consisted of 'Sweet Soul Music', 'Lay This Burden Down', 'Respect', 'You Keep Me Hanging On', 'One Step At A Time' and 'The First Cut Is The Deepest'.

When they played Mojo's in Sheffield, they hit it off with the young owner, Peter Stringfellow. On July 23rd they played their biggest gig to date at the Blenheim Palace Festival, with Jeff Beck and Manfred Mann also on the bill.

As they criss-crossed the country P.P. and The Nice became part of that swinging sixties scene that enmeshed music, fashion and a large element of hedonism that most ordinary people had never known. It was a memorable summer for music. In June, The Beatles had released the epoch-making *'Sgt Pepper's Lonely Hearts Club Band'*. Davy bought the album just after it came out and, as he was the only one that owned a record player, they all piled around to his flat in Earls Court where they played it over and over again. Discussing it for the rest of the night, this seminal record was digested in a thousand ways. They were bowled over by the scope and depth of the music and excited by the potential it opened up! "Back then, people would experiment with lots of different blends. In fact, The Beatles experimented with ragas and Indian music, incorporating that into rock and roll" offers Emerson, looking back on The Beatles' influence, "So I thought, 'Why not do that with my band?'"

There was another album that was a very influential force on the band in the shape of a concept album called *'The Zodiac – Cosmic Sounds'*. Released on Elektra records in early 1967, the only credits on the sleeve are 'Original music composed, arranged and conducted by Mort Garson. Paul Beaver on electronic instruments and Cyrus Fayar on narration.' The music can only be described as wild, psychedelic and brilliant. Chris Welch explains there was one number in particular that Keith was into: "'Aries' was part of a musical portrait of the Zodiac, and pointed the way to play organ-based rock music, using lots of electronics and powerful drumming." 'Aries' was tailor-made for the kind of things the band were doing on stage and would do on record in the future, and the band would later record it for a 1968 BBC 'Top Gear' session.

Even though they were still playing second fiddle to P.P. Arnold's brand of soul, The Nice were beginning to build up quite a reputation. Keith outlines what this reputation was based on: "People were saying 'Hey what is this band playing? It's a mixture of jazz, a bit of rock there, there's a bit of blues'." What people were witnessing was the birth of a new genre of music, but at the time nobody knew what it was going to develop into. With The Nice segment of the show getting longer and the cheers getting louder, the group's days as a backing band were numbered.

A defining event in The Nice's history was just around the corner. Marquee club owner Harold Pendleton had organised the 7th National Jazz and Blues Festival, Windsor, for August 13th 1967. On the bill were Fleetwood Mac and The Yardbirds. However, as things turned out the big names weren't going to have all their own way. By dint of some good work by manager Andrew Oldham, The Nice were billed to appear separately from Pat. Shrewdly, Oldham wanted to see how the band would go down on their own. The results were startling.

"We didn't think we'd be doing our own spot," David O'List recalls, "But P.P. came up and said we could do this set in one of the side tents. We knew we'd have to come up with some way of pulling the audience away from the main tent." The situation was crying out for some good old fashioned one-upmanship and the timely intervention of some explosives. The Nice's roadie, Bazz Ward, had placed some joke shop smoke powder inside the Leslie cabinets - as the Leslies rotated, the smoke came billowing out. Some additional pyrotechnics were used: "I've no idea where they came from - probably Andrew Oldham," recalls Lee Jackson. "We let rockets off and more big thunder flashes. We used smoke powder and lit it in the back of the Hammond organ in the Leslie cabinets... We put this show on and all of a sudden the tent just filled. Pentangle - on the main

stage - were twiddling away and all of a sudden this third world war breaks out. Journalists came rushing in to see what it was all about." Appropriately, Jackson remembers that one of the numbers they played was 'Aries - The Fire Fighter'.

One journalist that didn't come rushing was Chris Welch - he was already in the tent with Davy O'List's sisters, Pauline and Suzie. Welch remembers that the people who came in were met by an amazing sight, "The crowd came in to see what was happening and found an extraordinary show, with Keith lashing a whip and guitars and drums blasting tunes like 'Flower King Of Flies'. The tent was packed in minutes and the crowd stayed. It was the first time

P.P. Arnold & The Nice,
National Jazz &
Blues Festival, Windsor
August 16th, 1967

This page, left-right:
Keith Emerson,
P.P. Arnold, Bazz Ward,
Lee Jackson

Opposite page, left-right:
Bazz Ward,
Sandy Sarjeant,
Ian Hague, P.P. Arnold,
Lee Jackson

I had seen a group actually in the act of winning its first following in quite such dramatic circumstances." In the following week's Melody Maker, Welch would praise The Nice for succeeding with some "very original and solid sounds."

Another person that was part of this spectacle was P.P. Arnold's dancer and friend, Sandy Sarjeant. Dressed in a body stocking with some strategically placed flowers covering her modesty, Sandy remembers the gig, "As I recall there was a good crowd there already. Pat Arnold wasn't involved with this gig. Eric Clapton was there and he asked me who I was dancing with. I was so nervous because the crowd were so close to the stage. It took me a while for me to pluck up the courage to go on." Sandy was one of the resident dancers on the popular television music program 'Ready Steady Go' (after winning a nightclub dance competition).

After this, the band trouped over to the main tent to take their positions behind P.P. Arnold. At the end of the show Pat freed two doves as a symbol of peace. Ironically, drummer Ian Hague was a little worse for wear and also had an altercation with a festival official, all of which caused consternation with the rest of the band. It was apparent Hague wasn't handling The Nice material as well as Pat's soul section. Looking back on this, Hague reveals, "I was not really interested in the direction they were taking. So I was not really committed. I remember Bazz saying to me 'This band is going places'. I remember thinking 'not with me they're not'." It didn't help that, according to Bazz, "Ian was partaking of plenty of chemical concoctions to get him through the gig." The problems with Hague grew and in time became a festering sore and his days were numbered. It was Keith who sacked Hague although, to this day, Jackson thinks that Hague was a very good drummer and thought the decision to oust him was a harsh one.

Of her erstwhile group, P.P. Arnold offers this perspective, "Keith was very serious, a genius and into his music. His mom and dad used to come to the gigs and provided a lot of support for him. Lee was the funny man. He was always cracking jokes and making everybody laugh. Davy was very shy and he was so young. Ian was a great drummer." Pat remembered that the band had a problem with Hague but she never had a problem with him personally, despite noting he had some depressive troughs. Even though they were a tight unit they didn't hang out together when off the road, because Pat would always be with her pals, The Small Faces and The Rolling Stones. That said there were times when the vocalist and group were close.

Lee Jackson remembers one hilarious night after a gig in Kidderminster. They had all piled into Pat's room to have some beer and sandwiches. O'List started rolling a joint and asked where the shit was. Pat replied "It's in my bag, Davy." After fumbling in the bag for a few minutes, O'List finished rolling the joint. To every ones dismay and then hilarity, they realised that Davy had crushed and added Maltesers instead of the cannabis!

If Hague was beginning to be a problem, another pressure for Emerson was in fulfilling the role of a backing band whilst trying to forge their own distinctive identity. If anybody asked the name of the band, he would comically reply: "B.B. Armpit and The Mice" and other self-deprecating responses.

The success of the Windsor Festival gig proved that the Nice were a viable group on their own. Andrew Loog Oldham turned up at a gig in Southampton in his Rolls Royce and informed the band that he wanted to see them in his London office in the morning. Lee Jackson was convinced they were going to get the sack, but he couldn't have been more mistaken. Oldham told them Pat was going on holiday and he wanted to sign them as a band in their own right.

In fact Arnold was returning to the United States because her work permit was running out and she had to fulfill a promise she had made. Prior to coming to England, Arnold had left her two children, Kevin and Debbie, with her mother. The deal was that after six months, if she was successful, she would return to the States and collect her children. The enforced separation was hard on Pat as her friend Sandy Sarjeant remembers, "Pat missed her kids terribly. She would phone them up and speak to them but then there would be a lot of crying. Pat was a very effervescent person but there were a lot of times when she was down." Following a happy reunion, when Pat did return from the States, she was surprised she had no backing group. As she recalls with her tongue in cheek, "Andrew stole my band." Asked when she became aware that The Nice were an entity of their own, she answered, "They always were an entity of their own!"

With Hague on the way out, The Nice were on the look out for a new drummer; as it turned out they didn't have to look far. Chris Welch was on hand to give them a tip. As Chris recalls, "Later on when their original drummer quit, he was in a bit of a state as I recall. I recommended my old friend Brian Davison who was out of a job following the demise of the Mark Leeman Five." In fact, Brian had already seen The Nice play. He'd gone along to the Speakeasy, London, to see a late night show with Chris. The gig was used as a try-out in preparation for P.P. Arnold's departure, although at that point she hadn't formally left. Brian was impressed, but he could see something was lacking. Recalling the gig, Davison concludes, "What that band needed was me."

Interestingly, Brian Davison had already missed an opportunity to play with the band earlier in the summer. Emerson had called him up and asked him to deputize for a gig in Brighton as Ian Hague was sick. Brian had to refuse because he already had a gig pencilled in for that day (the drum stool was eventually occupied for the one gig only by Billy Adamson, soon to join The Searchers). He remembers Keith saying, "Don't worry, we'll get back to you." Emerson remained true to his word. With Hague now sacked, he called Davison and asked him to audition at Bermondsey Boys Club. Lee Jackson was impressed when they heard him play 'Rondo', remarking in the broadest Geordie accent, "He'll do!" Bazz also remembers the day that Brian turned up for his audition, "There was a freaky looking guy with a mop of hair. But as soon he started playing I knew he was the boy for the job."

****

Brian Davison was born in Leicester on May 25th 1942, the second child to Bella and Jack. Like Keith Emerson, Brian was a war baby and Bella had been evacuated from London. His interest in drums was sparked by his Uncle George, a drummer in a jazz group playing standards. Uncle George quickly came to realize how much his young nephew wanted to be a drummer. He'd set him teasers like, "You can't be a drummer unless you can count four with your right foot and two with your left." So he practiced this exercise till he conquered it, at the cost of much pain in his shins. He soon realized that in order to get over this physical problem required even more practice to make the mind stronger.

On Friday nights his mother had a regular hairdressing appointment and this was Brian's cue to reach down an array of pots and pans, using ladles for drumsticks. Not long after that the family went along to a New Years Eve dance where his Uncle was playing. After 'Auld Lang Syne' and the chimes of midnight, George came and sat down with the family as the band had finished for the night. Out of the blue George turned to Brian and said, "If you get up and play to that record you can have that drum kit." Although it was a potentially nerve-wracking situation, Davison didn't give it a second thought. As soon as he sat down he knew exactly what to do.

Meanwhile, Brian's older sibling Terry, also a music nut, was busy building Brian's curiosity towards his instrument. In their regular record playing sessions he would say things like, "Listen to this and try to work out what Max Roach is doing." Never overbearing, he would point his younger brother in the direction of how to understand the subtleties behind a piece of music. Even today Brian fondly remembers how his brother was always encouraging. Brian's technique for tuition never really changed thereafter. He learnt to play the drums from listening to records, he only had one formal lesson. As he recalled many years later, "Art Blakey, Max Roach and many others taught me how to play the drums." His favorite records included things like the sessions from Norman Granz's epochal 'Jazz At The Philharmonic' gigs.

By the time he went to Secondary School, the instrument was a major part of his life. Not living far away meant he would never, like most boys, play football in his break. He would spend his dinner hour at home on his second set of drums. His parents had bought him a red glitter set for his birthday of which he was immensely proud. He was almost detached from school, as the only thing he liked - music - didn't really feature in the curriculum. The school assembly was the only place where he could listen to music in school hours. Consequently, he became frustrated, and tapping away on his desk got him into enough trouble to get the cane on more than one occasion.

When Brian was in his early teens, at the local youth club, he met a lad who had a trumpet, so they got together and the first song they played was 'When The Red Red Robin Comes Bob-Bob-Bobbin' Along'. Around about this time Skiffle was taking off and exponents like Lonnie Donegan were making a name for themselves. Brian, on the other hand, didn't identify with that music and lost touch with his peers. He met Terry Goldberg who played accordion at this stage but was gravitating towards the burgeoning pop scene. Brian still wasn't that interested in 'the new thing' but would cross paths with Goldberg again.

Brian left school and got a job on The London Evening Standard driving delivery vans. Even though it was hectic at press time, there were plenty of empty hours elsewhere to be filled, so he would take a drum and play it in the back of the van. Around this time his Uncle George offered him a gig as part of a jazz-based piano and sax trio. They played in pubs on a Sunday afternoon and evening which made him four times the amount he earned working on the vans. The young Brian had enough confidence to go straight into the gig without rehearsal. He can't really remember if he had any nerves, and is still grateful to his much older colleagues who gave him much encouragement.

A minor setback came his way early on that helped to firm his resolve. In those days, drum battles were a regular feature in dance halls and, brimming with confidence, Davison entered one such contest. Much to his surprise, he didn't win. Although Davison suspects that result was a fix, even to this day, the occasion did galvanise him to practice harder than ever before.

Shortly afterwards, Brian was reunited with Terry Goldberg who asked him to join a band called The Rocker Shakes. Although Brian wasn't too keen because he wanted to play jazz, Terry countered by offering that as the band already played blues, they'd give a little jazz a try. Duly persuaded, but lacking his own transport, Brian had to take his kit on the bus to the gigs. The band was playing the Jewish boy's club circuit in the East End of London, and before long they were making quite a name for themselves.

At one stage they had Mick Green, later of The Pirates, on guitar. It wasn't very long before the singer left, providing the catalyst for a new image. The new charismatic singer was named John Albert Ardrey and he was heavily into John Lee Hooker and jazz. It was at this time that their manager, Jeff Morrow, decided to create a name for the band. Thus, The Mark Leeman Five was born – named after lead singer John Ardrey's stage name. It was in this band that Brian acquired his nickname. One of the more astute members of the band noticed that Brian's playing bore a resemblance to that of the great jazz drummer Art Blakey. So someone remarked, "More like Art Blakey on the blink!" and so the name Blinky - which Brian now hates with a passion - stuck.

The Mark Leeman Five were going down well enough to play venues in Camberley and Henley and even the Twisted Wheel in Manchester. Occasionally they would play the popular 'all-nighters' though they were low down on the bill compared to such luminaries as Graham Bond, Georgie Fame and The Kinks. The band had a solid line-up, with Leeman/Ardrey and Brian augmented by Alan Roskams on guitar, Terry Goldberg on organ, and David Hyde on bass. They were heavily influenced by the Ray Charles Hammond Organ blues and Brother Jack Macduff.

By 1962 they had recorded a couple of demos, the second of which had indicated an impressive style that set their direction for the future. They recorded two tracks, 'Money' and 'Back Home' and this, coupled with constant gigging, was to provide an opportunity for a third set of demos the following year. They had got to know Jim Goff who was an employee of Pye. The studios at Marble Arch had just been refurbished and Goff needed to test out the facilities. Oddly enough, the demos were made in the middle of the night.

Brian turned down a lucrative offer of £50 a week from Joe Brown to join his Bruvvers Band as The Mark Leeman Five continued their rise, supporting Manfred Mann at

The Mark Leeman Five in 1965, Brian Davison in the foreground

the Putney Ballroom. The Manfreds then asked them to open for them at the prestigious Marquee club in London, which they did on many occasions. Furthermore, they gave Leeman the phone number of their manager, Ken Pitt (future David Bowie manager), and the subsequent phone call resulted in them being signed up.

From this point, it seemed that things could only get better. They appeared on 'Ready Steady Go' with The Kinks. Davison remembers a lot of hanging around and having to jostle for the gaze of the camera with all the gyrating punters who, it seems, anticipating Andy Warhol's famous statement concerning fifteen minutes of fame, spent the time mugging at the cameras for all they were worth. On another occasion, the group played at The Cromwellian and noted all four Beatles in attendance. Rave press notices accompanied this onslaught.

Signed to record under the Manfred's own production company, Manfredisc, the band's debut was 'Portland Town' c/w 'Gotta Get Myself Together' in January 1965. The single, produced by Paul Jones, features some great harmonica by Jones himself – Davison rates Paul as the greatest mouth harp player he ever saw. Unfortunately the single didn't chart, but things appeared to be continuing on the up.

The band travelled up to Blackpool to play a gig on the South Pier on 27th June 1965. They were billed below The Manfreds and The Spencer Davis Group. Backstage post gig, Mark chatted to their manager, Ken Pitt, looking forward to continuing the upward curve of their progress graph.

Unfortunately the graph was about to explode. In a break from routine, Mark declined to travel home in the group's van, preferring to remain in Blackburn where his long time friend, singer Julie Grant, was appearing. Grant's personal assistant offered to drive him to the venue. Back in London early next morning a bleary-eyed Brian Davison was awoken by guitarist Alan Roskams, who informed him that Leeman had been killed in a car crash. The girl survived.

The loss of Leeman was keenly felt by all those who worked with him. In the best show business tradition, the band decided to play on and drafted in singer Roger Peacock as front man. It was never the same again, however, and the band eventually folded on 29th July 1966, after a gig at the Flamenco, in Folkestone. [1]

Brian's involvement with his next band would see his first overseas trip in the late summer of 1966. On paper it was a marvellous opportunity but in reality it turned into a nightmare. Davison had joined a group called The Habits, who had a series of gigs booked up in France. Once there, they waited 12 hours at the station waiting for someone to take them to their lodgings. They then contacted the bemused promoter who had never heard of them. Manager Tom Keylock had blagged them into the country and then tried to fix them up with something 'on the hoof'. They weren't over the moon with their lodgings either. It turned out to be a brothel and the madam of the house would wait for them at the door demanding the rent. Luckily the owner of the club loved The Habits' improvisational blues-based numbers. In spite of this the band were stranded in France as the money they made from their shows went on the most basic living expenses and when the residency ended they found they had nothing with which to get home. It took them a month to save up their return fare or, as Brian puts it, "Organise an escape committee." As a fond farewell, the owner closed the club and the band played till dawn.

Surprisingly, The Habits kept faith in their manager and embarked on a Keylock-organised expedition to Belgium. This time things went well although their van broke down on the return trip just outside Liege. Another band offered them a tow and they managed to get near home.

TO WHOM IT MAY CONCERN

We, members of the Manfred Mann group, declare our opinion that the late Mark Leeman was an artist of considerable merit and that his talent so impressed us that we undertook to produce gramophone recordings of his work. We also arranged for him to make weekly appearances with us at The Marquee, Wardour Street, W.1, also to undertake a concert tour with us and to appear with us this summer on a series of thirteen Sunday concerts at the Rainbow Theatre, Blackpool.

His performance on the first concert of this series on June 27th convinced us that he was on the verge of a highly successful career in the entertainment profession.

The Mark Leeman Five group as it is now constituted is on the bill of our current tour and is enjoying considerable success.

Manfred Mann
Manfred Mann

Mike Hugg
Mike Hugg

Mike Vickers
was away

Paul Jones
Paul Jones

Tom McGuinness
Tom McGuinness

But when the rope broke by the Oval Cricket Ground in London, they abandoned the van and split up to complete the remaining part of the journey by bus. Brian neatly, and with some understatement, sums up The Habits experience, "It wasn't a rich group. We were living on bread, jam and wine. Half the time we had no money to get to the gigs so we just broke up."

After The Habits' split, Brian got a job painting floors but it wasn't long before he was out looking for auditions again. He saw an advert for the Mike Cotton Band, a soul outfit. He didn't want to play soul but needed the money. The audition was held in a pub but when he got there he saw about 15 drummers, all eager to get the job. Then, to his astonishment, Mike Cotton himself appeared and saw him in the queue. He greeted him by name, "Brian, what are you doing here?" Bemused - as he had never met Mike before - Brian told him he'd come for the gig. He whispered in his ear that he had got the job but he had to go through the motions of the audition. He wasn't in the band long but at least was back in business after the trauma of Mark Leeman's tragic death. However, the experience of chasing money left him with a sour taste in the mouth – "They were really nice people but I got completely frustrated sitting there like a machine. I decided not to play again until I could be part of a band with some freedom in their music."

Brian's next gig was the strangest of his career. Ironically, it was here that for the first time he was given artistic freedom by the bucketful with the unsung hero of the Hammond Organ, Don Shinn. Nick Jones of Melody Maker had a connection who got Don and Brian into Landsdowne Studio, at Holland Park, where they recorded, as Brian put it "Some really wild stuff." Then one day Shinn said, "I don't want to play anymore," and retired to Southampton. No more was heard of him or those recordings.

Brian got a tip-off from MM scribe and mate Chris Welch, who told him The Attack needed a drummer for a tour. It was here, in early 1967, that Brian came across Davy O'List. Brian enjoyed playing with Davy but he wasn't overly keen on the music. Front man, Richard Shirman, had been a big fan of The Mark Leeman Five and also admired Brian's playing. He remembers one particular gig with Brian, "We were playing at the Mojo Club in Sheffield, the original club run by the now legendary Peter Stringfellow. The set was going well and the packed club were appreciating us to the full. In those days it was the custom for drummers to take a solo. Brian was half way through his when a wag in the audience called out 'Ginger Baker the Second.' Brian stopped playing, put his sticks down, stood up and, to a rousing cheer, shouted 'No! Brian Davison the First!', sat down and finished an excellent drum solo. At its conclusion, the crowd cheered and stamped their approval."

The Attack was only to be short term and, before long, Brian would join O'List in The Nice.

NOTES

1 In 1991 *'The Mark Leeman Five Memorial Album'* was released. It includes the eleven tracks from the Pye Marble Arch, sessions. This album includes quite a wide spectrum of material and shows that the Five were a highly exciting blues band. One of the tracks is 'Get My Mojo Working' which Brian said they stretched out for 10 to 15 minutes on stage. One of Brian's lasting regrets is the recorded work doesn't get near what they were actually like in concert.

The Nice: Lee Jackson, Brian Davison, Davy O'List, Keith Emerson

CHAPTER 4

"THEIR INFLUENCES ARE MANY, BUT THEY ARE INDEBTED TO NO ONE"

"I've always hated copyists and I wanted a style of my own. With the organ that is extremely difficult."

KEITH EMERSON

THE INTRODUCTION OF the new line-up of The Nice didn't go as smoothly as everyone would have liked. Andrew Loog Oldham used The Nice to record the backing tracks for P.P. Arnold's first solo album. Complementing the group was the veteran session guitarist Caleb Quaye, who later played with Elton John, Madeline Bell and Dusty Springfield. Mick Jagger was set to produce and finish the album in a marathon session, starting at lunchtime on Saturday through till Monday. In fact, P.P. Arnold had taken Jagger to see The Nice in rehearsals some months before. Lee Jackson remembers this very well as it was on the occasion of Jagger's visit, that they decided to incorporate 'Rondo' into their regular act.

Jagger arrived at the session with Marianne Faithfull in tow. The pair had just travelled up from Bangor in North Wales, where The Beatles were with their newly adopted Indian guru, Yogi Maharishi Mahesh, where they had only just learned of the death of Beatles manager, Brian Epstein. The salacious, and apparently apocryphal, 'Mars Bar' story about Mick and Marianne had been circulating in the tabloid press at the time. Unfortunately, Lee Jackson got off on the wrong foot with the couple when he began to eat a Mars Bar as the pair first appeared in the studio. Faithfull scowled at the bass player, thinking it was a conscious wind-up.

Worse was to come. Brian Davison had a particularly bad time and had to be replaced by Jon Hiseman. Brian was devastated, as his professional pride had taken a dent. He remembers feeling pretty terrible as he left the studio. When the album came out, it was called 'The First Lady Of Immediate', and not one member of The Nice could recognise anything they had done.

Brian then had another nightmare to contend with - his only gig with P.P. Arnold at the Flamingo Club in London, 28th August 1967. He admitted that he couldn't 'get his head around' the soul material which comprised Arnold's half of the set. Bazz had to sit through the gig, behind the speakers, counting Brian through the numbers - although Bazz was a self confessed 'useless drummer' he had picked up enough of the act to be of assistance to Brian. Brian thought Pat a great and talented singer but there was no disguising his impatience to get on with the new dynamic material which The Nice were developing.

The first gig they played after Pat returned to the US was at the Big C club in Farnborough on September 1st 1967. As Bazz recalled, they were billed as

P.P. Arnold's backing band and consequently the punters expected some soul. What they got was 'Rondo', 'War & Peace' and 'Aries'. They went down very badly and the crowd got ugly. It didn't help when at the conclusion of their set the DJ said "Now let's put on some real music." It got worse, dangerous even, as there were a lot of angry mods milling around still smarting at having their evening ruined. Later the promoter was counting out the fee to Bazz in the corridor, while the disgruntled audience were streaming out. The promoter couldn't disguise his disgust, snorting "Do you think this band was worth £75?" Without looking up, Bazz meekly took the money and returned to the dressing room.

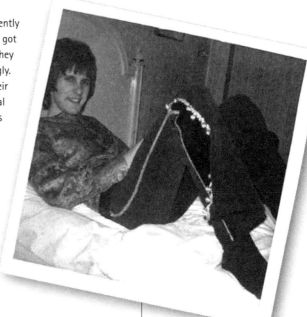

The Nice's schedule was becoming surreally hectic...

Above: Keith Emerson
Opposite: Davy O'List and Brian Davison

Yet despite such initial setbacks, the rave notices soon started to arrive. Under the headline "Hold On, Here Come The Nice!" Melody Maker proclaimed, "Once in a while there is an event on the group scene that fills the seeker of musical truth with feelings of great joy and happiness. Flashes of brilliance light up the usual drab and gloomy round, like the formation of Cream or the arrival of Jimi Hendrix. A new group has swum onto the horizon that isn't being hailed with great trumpetings or launched with deft publicity."

The article was written just a few days after P.P. Arnold left. The band were heavily into rehearsal as they honed their chops. Keith laid down some of the philosophy behind the band, "For want of a better word, I suppose you could call us a psychedelic group, but we'd rather you didn't. We are just trying to play the things we like and to be original. And it's not a weak or pretty sound. It's very hard-hitting and powerful."

One of the key elements of this 'hard-hitting' sound was Keith's Hammond Organ sound. He was searching for a particular sound that was, in his words a "Very percussive attacking sound." He heard it, as a lot of others did, in Brother Jack Macduff's 'Rock Candy'. As he recalled much later, "[Macduff's] organ sound was so growling, so angry. That's what I tried to imitate with The Nice. I didn't really like the Jimmy Smith sound, though I liked what he did."

In October the group recorded their first radio session for the BBC's 'Top Gear' – a show acknowledged by all artists to be essential for big and small bands. The session aired on 22nd October 1967 and was produced by Bernie Andrews. In some books, Ian Hague is down as drummer but he had departed many weeks before. The set comprised 'Flower King Of Flies', 'Sombrero Sam', 'Tantalising Maggie', 'Rondo' and 'The Thoughts Of Emerlist Davjack'. It was to be the first of many (ten in fact) such sessions and it wasn't long before DJs John Peel and Brian Matthew became big fans.

By the time Brian Davison joined, The Nice were already heavily into writing their own material – a process initiated and encouraged by Andrew Oldham. Additionally, they were busily preparing for the November tour with Hendrix. This was a star-studded, if inchoate and overloaded line-up. As well as Jimi there was Pink Floyd, The Move, Amen Corner, Outer Limits and Eire Apparent - who Hendrix later produced. It was a logistical nightmare but they eventually opened the tour on November 14th at the Royal Albert Hall. Because of the sheer numbers on the bill, The Nice only had ten minutes to perform. They only played two songs - 'The Thoughts Of Emerlist Davjack' and 'Rondo'. The limited time was a problem for everybody. Floyd's Roger Waters described their 17 minutes as a "Real nightmare."

Around this time, though, they made a crucial addition to the team, in the shape of lighting expert Eric Barratt. All the trimmings that surrounded the 'show' were now being taken into account Barratt had worked for Tony Stratton-Smith with The Koobas. His light show really enhanced what the band was doing on stage. But sadly, shortly after this tour, he would be poached by Chas Chandler to work with Hendrix.

Meanwhile, The Nice's schedule was becoming surreally hectic; after some of the gigs closer to London, they would come back to the studio in the small hours and record some more of what would become their debut album. Then they would have to rejoin the tour. Though this was hardly the ideal conditions in which to create music, at the time such a situation was fairly commonplace.

Rotating so many bands on one stage required logistical improvisation. This rebounded badly on Outer Limits. At the start of the tour it was decided that it wouldn't work out to have a drum kit for every band. So it was decided that they would use Brian's kit, but unfortunately their drummer was left handed and as a result the band didn't actually get to play much at all on the tour.

The whole entourage was schlepping so much gear between them that an extra vehicle had to be hired. It turned out to be a coach with all the seats taken out and Bazz had great difficulty getting the Hammond in through the fire escape door at the back. The crew had a new recruit for this tour in the shape of future rock star Ian Kilminster, aka Lemmy. Although in those days he didn't really have a defined skill they could use so he ended up as the roadie's 'gofer'. When Lemmy saw Keith sticking knives into the keyboard, he said to Emerson, "Here, if you're gonna use a knife, use a proper one." He promptly produced a Hitler Youth ceremonial dagger (Lemmy was a collector of Nazi memorabilia). The imbedded knives created a sustained sound, enabling Emerson to create sounds around the back of the Hammond.

Although Pink Floyd weren't technically great, the way they projected their music was impressive.

Lee Jackson remembers the soundcheck they did at the Albert Hall with all the lights. They did 'Set The Controls For The Heart Of The Sun' and Lee thought the music was like nothing he'd ever heard and the light show like nothing he'd ever seen! In fact the Floyd almost walked off the tour because they were told they couldn't use their light show. They had a cinema screen that they would project images onto and this was blocking the view of fans at the rear of the band. In the end, some of the fans had to settle for a restricted view.

The Floyd was still in possession of their mercurial inspiration, Syd Barrett. However, the tour did them no favours. Lee Jackson remembers an occasion when they were all waiting for Syd to turn up so the coach could leave. When he did arrive, Barrett had two girls with him - one on each arm. The coach driver told him that he couldn't take them on board, and so Barrett, unwilling to part company with the two girls, remained behind as the coach driver took off without him. As Davy recalls, "The Floyd were stuck for a guitarist. Incidentally, I watched them every night, and had picked up on what they were doing. They approached me about standing in for Syd, and I agreed to play, feeling most excited about the prospect of actually performing 'Interstellar Overdrive'... I walked on stage with Syd's hat on, and was greeted with loud screams of 'Syd - Syd - Syd'! I don't think to this day that people knew what was going on as they gradually realized I wasn't Syd. However, the number got underway and I stuck rigidly to the style that Syd had become famous for." It was an impressive performance.

The spotlight fell on O'List in another way. As Hendrix had asked for The Nice to come on the tour it was inevitable that he would watch their act and this understandably unnerved Davy. As he explains, "I was so daunted by it and shy, all the girls were screaming and I'd have to hold it together with the mind-blowing prospect of Hendrix watching me play!" The truth is that even though Davy was coping, he was still in his later teens and had relatively little stage experience.

Keith and Brian remember jamming with Hendrix on a few occasions. Hendrix thought The Nice were great, gushing "The Nice were my favourite group of the tour. Their sound is ridiculously good, original, free - more funky than West Coast." Keith was one of the few musicians on the tour who was technically in the same ball-park as Hendrix and they got on well. Looking back years later Keith recalled, "I did a tour with him. He had bought himself a home movie camera and, wherever we were playing, I'd see him looking between the amps, filming. He was always there. He loved the act. When he'd gotten his films developed there was hysterical laughter coming from his dressing room. I poked my head around the corner to see what the laughter was about, and they were running the film of me doing the bit with the organ! They were speeding up the film and running it backwards - it was completely stupid. Hendrix was great."

Melody Maker's Nick Logan lauded the performance by the top of the bill, Jimi Hendrix. The headline read "Hail Jimi!" The guitarist had saved the day because "The bill seemed it would never get off the ground." However, some of his most savage criticism was reserved for The Nice or, to be more accurate, Keith Emerson. Logan was obviously referring to 'Rondo' when he wrote "They worked hard through a lengthy instrumental during which Keith Emerson whipped and flayed the organ... it was all rather unnecessary, as this group obviously has the talent to make it without gimmickry." A fair point, but one which might have overlooked the theatrical element in headliner Jimi's own act.

The last gig of the tour was at the Glasgow Playhouse. It was here that all the roadies got together and decided they would play all sorts of tricks on the artists. Lee remembers two such incidents. The Amen Corner used to sing 'Gin House Blues', the last line being 'Give me more gin', at which point the roadies came on and put scores of empty bottles on to the stage. Keith was at the wrong end of one of these pranks. While Bazz turned his back they screwed down the Hammond with wooden panels - Keith got a shock when it came to the finale! But the jollity came to an end at the conclusion of the show when there was trouble in the crowd. The upshot was that the crews couldn't get the gear out of the building. Normally it wouldn't have mattered but, on this occasion, The Nice were booked for a short tour of Scandinavia – their first trip abroad. Bazz drove the van like a maniac to make it to Harwich on time but it was all in vain. They arrived to see the ferry sailing away. There was no alternative but to book in to a bed and breakfast for the night. They didn't have much money either as it had all been converted to travellers cheques.

Davy's mate, Johnny Plastic, painted some psychedelic designs on the back of Keith's Hammond and on Brian's drums (see photos above and opposite) – a sign of the times.

The Nice did not accompany Pat Arnold on the Immediate Records tour of Europe in the summer of 1967. Tour promoter Arne Jenson came up with only a few gigs, requiring the band, with some help from Arne's assistant, to start booking their own gigs in Sweden in order to make ends meet. As a consequence, the band ended up in a theatre in Gothenburg. Although their gear was set-up in the main theatre, the band was offered the opportunity to record a session for Swedish radio. The only problem was their gear was set up downstairs and the radio studio was upstairs. Unable to move their gear, The Nice had to make do with borrowed equipment. On the CD release of the session, Lee Jackson can be heard explaining the situation to the audience. They got home just in time for Christmas. It was an interesting way to end a triumphant year.

The late '60s saw the musical world at a crossroads and there was uncertainty in the minds

Above and left:

Gothenburg,
Sweden
December 1967

of some listeners as to what groups were doing and what direction they were moving in. Bands like The Nice were causing a lot of confusion at venues all around the country. A good illustration of this was at a Nice gig at a university early in their career. They were booked for a 'rave' - a shorthand term for a Saturday night drinking session that has little in common with the current coinage of the term. The subsequent university paper was full of feedback about the gig and a certain Christopher Thomas, of the Dept of English, vented his rage in the letters page. The enraged punter stated his complaint, "I have always been under the impression that one went to a dance to dance, i.e. to make a sequence of movements rather similar to an epileptic windmill. To fulfil this highly complicated and very exhausting pastime the music has got to be appropriate. Unfortunately, the music (rather questionable) of The Nice did not reach this basic requirement." Even though the writer thought the band would be good in a 'concert' setting. He ended his letter with, "For God's sake, don't get The Nice again."

Such complaints notwithstanding, a key aspect of the band's growing reputation was the standard of musicianship and the mutual respect that existed in the band. If people were going to stand and listen the music had to have more than a few chords. Even at this stage Keith was attracting a lot of the plaudits, but The Nice was far from being a one-man show. Davy was coming to the fore as well, as Brian Davison offered in an interview at the time, "I think Davy will definitely be one of the finest guitarists in the country if he keeps up his present rate of progress." Keith chipped in by saying that in one of the rare drum solos that Brian played - he only played them if the mood was right - he almost stopped playing to applaud when it ended. Lee was no slouch either having played with some of the biggest names in the British music scene.

The Nice's debut album was recorded at Olympic and Pye over a period of about three weeks. Originally, Andrew Oldham was keen to enlist Jagger as producer. However, as Lee Jackson recalls, "Mick Jagger was going to produce it but when they - The Rolling Stones - started doing the 'Satanic Majesties' album, he had to bow out and he said he didn't quite understand the music. It wasn't really him, he liked the power of it but we would probably understand it better so we would do it better on our own. So he suggested Glyn Johns engineer it." At that time, Johns was The Rolling Stones' engineer.

Andrew Oldham paid a lot of attention to the project. He was in the studio for most of the time and, according to Brian Davison, acted as a kind of 'part-producer' - making a number of suggestions but no more. It was controversial when Oldham claimed a producer credit. "We all thought we produced it," says Lee. "We had musical ideas but Johns provided the technical back up." One of these technical innovations was to provide themselves with a 16-track desk, before they even existed. The trick was achieved simply enough, by plugging two 8-track desks together. In this simple way they were able to have better facilities than any other band.

Recently Andrew Oldham was asked whether he had any shame about claiming producer credits. His answer actually confirms Brian's assessment of his role, "You are there to remind the artist of all the possibilities that are available to best serve the song and the performance. When recording a group the producer should also know when to leave the room, but he should always leave the tape running."

The most famous track on the album is a band arranged version of Dave Brubeck's 'Blue Rondo A La Turk'. The Nice called it 'Rondo' and it was to be forever associated with Keith Emerson. He'd been a fan of this piece for a while and, by this point, it was the centre-piece of the band's live show.

Copenhagen
May 1968

The day they recorded it was memorable. Brian recalls that the way the studio was set out, only he could see the control room, where Johns and Andrew Oldham were sat. The track was going well as they started to approach the five minute mark. As Brian glanced up to the booth he could see Andrew Oldham giving the 'cut' gesture. But Brian felt that the vibe was too magical to bottle out of. When they did eventually finish there was a great discussion about the length of the track. However, on this occasion the band stood their ground and they won. They argued that that was the amount of time they needed to develop the track properly - and 'Rondo' ended up lasting over eight minutes.

The whole thing develops from Lee's galloping bass (Greg Lake once asked Lee to show him how to do it, but never mastered it), an effect achieved by using the plectrum in a rapid up and down movement, a technique that Lee employed a lot. Davy's guitar perfectly complements the track as it spirals between Emerson's main riff and the rhythm section. And he isn't found wanting when he matches Emerson when wringing out the tortured notes. Listening to it today, it's no wonder the band wanted more than what Andrew Oldham had in mind. Out of all the tracks on the album, this was the one that signposted a possible direction for the future. Little wonder Emerson was on a high when he left the studio.

Keith used Jimi Hendrix as a benchmark for the perfection he aspired to. In 1995 he was asked about the first time he accomplished that level. "Without a shadow of doubt, 'Rondo'. I remember leaving the studio thinking, 'My God, where did that come from?' Just the solo on its own, is probably the only solo that would have been suitable for that cut, and it was totally improvised.

I always wanted to achieve an orchestral sound, even on the limited equipment I had then. If I wasn't hearing exactly what I wanted at that time, as there was nothing available to play it on, I adapted."

'Rondo' is a wonderful piece of work. However, the lack of a credit to Brubeck - not to mention the original composer of the theme, Mozart - is baffling. It was a habit that, surprisingly, Keith continued in ELP and eventually it got him into hot water. Oldham blustered his way around the thorny problem of how he managed to credit the song to the band. As far as the band was concerned it was called 'Blue Rondo A La Turk' by Brubeck, arranged by the band. It was only when the album came out they discovered that Oldham had credited the number to the band.

The album opens with 'Flower King Of Flies', another live staple. Starting with quirky percussion before Keith's piano gets into it's stride, the track has a classic '60s sound. However, by the time Lee starts to sing about 'letting the temple maidens sing' (he'd just read William Golding's 'Lord Of The Flies'), Davy weighs in with some heavy riffs while Emerson prepares his Hammond solo. It's an impressive opener and, with the title track to follow, a great start to the album.

'The Thoughts Of Emerlist Davjack' is really Davy's song with some additions by Keith. The drumming intro was Ian Hague's. Davy took the lead vocals on this track as he'd written the lyrics. Keith and Lee sing the backing 'ba, ba, ba', along with Immediate stable mate, Billy Nicholls. Recently Nicholls recalled the spirit that existed at the label in those days, "We were all helping each other out but like the other projects were never credited. None of us cared very much about that sort of thing anyway." The 'choir' was aided by some neat studio tricks. Lee remembers they were able to reach all the high and low notes by speeding or slowing the tape down. There was no surprise when this was chosen as the single, as along with 'Flower', it's the most accessible. The track wasn't given its title until a while after it was recorded. It was Davy's idea to use 'The Thoughts Of' after the 'Little Red Book', The Thoughts Of Chairman Mao. Keith remembers it was Lee who came up with the democratic concept of combining the band members' four surnames to come up with a name for the song's protagonist.

'Bonnie K' is the first indication of the band's rockier side. It's really a vehicle for some blistering riffing from Davy. The song was written by Lee and Davy so it's no surprise that Keith takes more of a back seat while Lee delivers some raunchy vocals. In those days, lyrics were often the subject of endless debate - Lee revealed that someone once wrote an article about his words, trying to find their meanings. He needn't have bothered. Lee wrote in a very abstract fashion - much the same way that Jon Anderson of Yes did later - and most of them didn't mean very much. Lee had a voracious appetite for reading all sorts of literature from Oscar Wilde to the above mentioned Chairman Mao, a thirst for self-education arising from his rigorous Catholic schooling. His reading enabled him to step outside and question what organized religion stood for. Oscar Wilde became one of his heroes, for he well knew that organized religion was in the vanguard of Wilde's persecution. Lee's childhood repression inspired him to come up with unconventional lyrics for the band.

Like most people at that time, Lee was listening to more than a little of Bob Dylan's recorded output, so he decided to try and create his own lyrical style by adding cryptic elements. 'Tantalising Maggie' has a strange structure and Lee sounds like he's singing through a megaphone. The desired effect was to mimic the voice of a Dalek – the metallic monsters from the then popular Sci-Fi TV programme, Doctor Who! The problems of recording vocals for the track were compounded with the addition of an impromptu choir of Bazz, Glyn Jones with a bogus Irish accent, as well as Davy's sisters giggling. At the line 'Maggie, Maggie keep yourself up straight, because if you don't it'll be too darn late', they kept breaking down in fits of hilarity and in doing so created the inspiration for the taped laughter inserted at the end. Musically, there's a lot going on and the piano flourish at the end - several descending arpeggios with two appended chords, from a piece by J. S. Bach's son Christoph - seems to appear from nowhere but fits beautifully.

'War & Peace' opens Side Two and was used as the show opener or closer, depending on the mood of the band. The tune was originally called 'Silver Meter' - the T-Bones recorded it but it was never released. However, between the time The Nice recorded the song and the test pressings coming out, Oldham had given it a new name and credited it to the band! One reviewer was mightily impressed, "My favourite five minutes of the whole album is 'War & Peace', though. Rarely were the group more together than on this instrumental, which seems to run like hell-bound train through war inflicted landscapes. The title couldn't be more apt, with O'List's snarling guitar snapping at Emerson's heels like a blood-hound, and constantly battling his omnipresent organ." Emerson and O'List certainly did provide a wonderful and challenging counterpoint to each other.

The next track, 'Dawn', is one of the most interesting things on the album. Lee wrote the lyrics but Keith suggested he whisper them instead of singing. He did try but his broad Geordie accent didn't lend itself to whispering, so Keith suggested "Let me have a go," which he did at Pye studios. Keith provides the intro which establishes a perfect ambience. Davy and Brian both contributed some musical ideas - it was Brian's idea to have the manic middle section. This rumination on human history provides many interesting lines. One of them would be modified and used later, 'Dawn is pregnant with promise and anticipation, but is murdered by the hand of the inevitable.'

The studio at Olympic turned out to be the harbinger of inspiration in more ways than one. Lee remembers it was used for a lot of orchestral work and, when they went in there to record, there were all sorts of instruments strewn all over the studio. It was an open invitation for them to try and find ways of using them. The harpsichord Keith used to provide the driving force in 'Dawn's middle section was found lying around in the studio from another session. Lee doesn't play on 'Dawn' but Keith adds a little bass on the Hammond's foot pedals. Jackson ended up producing the track.

The final cut is 'The Cry Of Eugene' and features trumpet and some great guitar by Davy. Written by Lee, Davy and Keith, it features some of Lee's trademark quixotic lyrics and is a great way to end the album. As a child, Lee had a Hans Christian Andersen illustrated book and for some reason, he recalled this when it came to the lyrics. Some critics thought the song was about the writer Eugene O'Neill.

During the sessions, The Nice recorded an extra track, 'Azrial (The Angel Of Death)', that wasn't used for the album but became the B-side of the single 'Emerlist Davjack'. Azrial appears as the Muslim 'angel of death' in Middle Eastern mythology. Strangely, this was the first track that Keith and Lee wrote together and would eventually be re-worked for the third album.

Beyond their own material, The Nice were actually offered Mike D'Abo's classic 'Handbags & Gladrags' to cover. "It just wasn't our style," says Lee. So it was recorded by Immediate stable mate Chris Farlowe.

The album came out to good reviews. Melody Maker emphasized their unique sound and there is an undercurrent that a new kind of genre of group is emerging, "Exciting, original and creative... Their strength is in their original material, lyrics, arrangements, improvising ability and sheer musical talent. There are interesting experiments with electronic and percussive effects, but the most important ingredient is sheer music, drawn from jazz, classical and pop inspirations, often raw, but always satisfying." American magazine Hullabaloo enthused, "We played the record to a frazzle. With the bass knob on our machine turned way up, we listened to 'War & Peace' at least a dozen times in a row... Take our advice. Get The Nice."

Praise was not universal, however. Queen Magazine panned the album. 'Dawn' was branded as an

"Keith did things with the Hammond that made our jaws drop."

"all-time bad record" and the main criticism was, surprisingly, a lack of variety. The reviewer was aware of Keith's standing as one the best organists around but argued that he wasn't used to the full. That's why the only track that received favorable comment was 'Rondo'. The Democrat would argue to the contrary that the group had 'the right type of original approach'.

The cover artwork shots of the band forcing their way through a plastic sheet were taken by Gered Mankowitz. "The Nice were very easy to work with and we always enjoyed working together," Mankowitz recalls. "The idea for the Emerlist Davjack cover came from the thought that the band were reinventing popular music and the image is supposed to represent rebirth! A lot of people found the image quite disturbing - I always preferred it in black and white and would have liked it used larger on the sleeve."

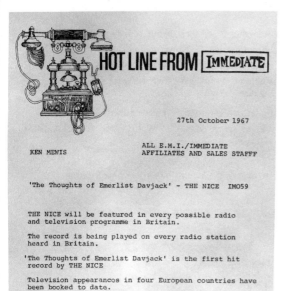

HOT LINE FROM IMMEDIATE

27th October 1967

KEN MEWIS

ALL E.M.I./IMMEDIATE
AFFILIATES AND SALES STAFFF

'The Thoughts of Emerlist Davjack' - THE NICE   IM059

THE NICE will be featured in every possible radio
and television programme in Britain.

The record is being played on every radio station
heard in Britain.

'The Thoughts of Emerlist Davjack' is the first hit
record by THE NICE

Television appearances in four European countries have
been booked to date.

They got DJ John Peel to narrate a sampler for the album which was distributed to radio stations. Peel's jaunty interjections told how the album's quality was no act. He was a massive fan of the band and pronounced that The Nice "will be here when all the others will be in Pantomime in Wolverhampton." Finally, Peel was to conclude, "Their influences are many but they are indebted to no one."

By the time the album came out, they were well and truly established at the Marquee, first headlining on November 6th. One fan remembers a gig from 1967 where Lee and Brian looked "quite ancient", Davy was described as a "beak nosed, cadaverous" individual, but the fan took note of the incredible sounds that emanated from his guitar. There was a high state of excitement about The Nice in those early days as people had rarely seen anything like them. But the focus of attention was Keith Emerson and his antics as the fan explains, "Keith did things with the Hammond organ that made our jaw drop. When he wasn't playing the thing, he would climb on it, leap over it, stick knives in it, whip it, lie underneath it, turn it off and on, flail his arms up and down the keys, crash the reverb spring, bash the insides with a drum stick, and generally behave like a lunatic." No wonder it wasn't long before they were one of the top bands at the Marquee. The question now was how to spread the word beyond.

CHAPTER 5

THE BIG APPLE

"New York scared
the pants off me.
Everything was
enormous."

BRIAN DAVISON

IN LATE DECEMBER 1967, the band signed up to a residency at The Marquee for the first four Mondays of the New Year - there was a fifth date on the contract but it was crossed out because the band were due to fly out to the States for their debut tour. However, there was a price to be paid for playing at the Marquee. The contract was restricting as they couldn't play within a radius of four miles for four weeks before the first concert, and four weeks after the last. They got 50% of the gross take at the door, less the cost of support. The opening band for the January 1st 1968, gig was Mabel Greer's Toyshop, later to evolve into Yes.

Their second session for BBC Radio 1 was taped on 17th January. They previewed a new track, 'Daddy Where Did I Come From?' - which would appear on the next album - and their radical reinterpretation of Dylan's 'She Belongs To Me', already a live favourite.

The night before, they had flown up - flying to a UK gig was a sure sign of success - to play the Newcastle Students Union. They had to get up at five in the morning to catch their flight back down to London. As they didn't get back to Lee's house until two o'clock, they decided that bed was not an option. Keith persuaded Lee's dad to play the violin. It was a magical moment for Lee as he had only seen him play it a handful of times before. It was then that Keith suggested he bow his bass. Lee had never considered it before but it was stored away in the memory bank. He would return to it later.

Hitherto, most of the British bands that went out to the States did so on the back of some kind of recorded success. The Nice didn't have anything like that - yet. But they did have Andrew Oldham and he knew Steve Paul in New York, owner of the prestigious Scene club, and was able pull some strings. Oldham had enjoyed American success with some of his artists and thought The Nice could cut the mustard. He therefore arranged an exchange with CBS Records for Blood Sweat & Tears to come over to the UK while The Nice would try their luck in the US. The Nice were the first UK name band to tour the US without a hit single. They were met at the airport by a CBS rep and provided with a stretch limousine - this was a different world indeed. They went to see Spirit at the Scene Club where they had been booked by Oldham for a two week stint.

Brian remembers the owner of the club had a shock, because he thought they were big time - probably another Oldham stunt - booked them into the City Squire hotel. Brian mused, "It was a top notch hotel with 24 hour room service. The doorman had riding boots and a red jacket." The bell boy who took their bags waited for a tip that wasn't forthcoming - he wanted $10 but the band was broke. Oldham was called at CBS studios and he grudgingly fixed them up with some cash, but they only lasted one night at Squires. They were switched to the lower market Presidents Hotel but that was still pretty good.

One incident during their time in the States illustrates why Bazz was appointed to take the cash from

Bazz Ward and
Keith Emerson,
The Marquee,
London

The two girls in
the front row
are Davy O'List's
sisters, Pauline
and Suzie

promoters. The Nice received two hundred dollars - to cover expenses - in two one-hundred dollar bills. Whilst in New York they hailed a cab and Keith gave the driver a one-hundred dollar bill thinking it was one dollar, and for good measure told him to keep the change. The fare was 88 cents not 88 dollars, and a NYC cabbie was 99 dollars, 12 cents up for the day.

New York had a profound effect on Brian. "It scared the pants off me. Everything was enormous. All the knowledge of the jazz clubs was in my head." Suddenly all the clubs he'd read about, like Birdland, were within walking distance. He was overawed.

There were, inevitably, a few problems on this tour. The first thing was a New York City garbage strike, which left the streets piled with rubbish and running with rats. Another problem was finding a reliable Hammond L100 organ. This was vital as Keith's act was based on having the more flexible model. All other types of Hammond had a generator while the L100 had an on/off switch. This was all part of the show in presenting the kaleidoscope of noises.

This had come about purely by accident. In a previous gig, their roadie Bazz had tripped over the wire and pulled the cable out. It made an incredible noise so Keith said 'leave it' because, as he observed, the Hammond had, in effect, become a huge pickup. Bazz put a call to Fred Romani of Hammond, New York, and pointed out the problem that the Scene club had only a B3. Eventually, after a lot of hard work by Bazz, the L100 was located.

They were given a great review from Fred Kirby of Billboard Magazine, in spite of the fact the fuses kept blowing all night. "A talented English hard rock group, The Nice, which opened its first American engagement at the Scene on Monday, 29th January 1968, displayed a high degree of musical ability and an organist, Keith Emerson, who could be one of the top rock musicians around... His music was intricate and intense." Keith's showmanship was appreciated but Kirby was keen to point out that the music always shone through. Lee, Brian and Davy were all praised for playing their part. However, as in England, their music caused a little bit of audience confusion and were not sure, at first, how to respond, "The young Scene crowd, which usually dances during the sets, as they did with One, an English-oriented American group also on the program, listened, watched and enthusiastically responded."

The Scene club was the 'in' place for a lot of celebrities. Lee remembers Andy Warhol took a shine to Keith and wasn't shy in making his feelings known to the keyboard player. He wasn't alone. One night Keith came up to Lee rather agitated, "This old bloke with a twiddly moustache is trying to jack me up." Lee had a smile on his face, "That's Salvador Dali." Keith's answer was succinct, "I don't care what his name is - he's not getting up my arse!"

The Scene was an enjoyable gig, although Brian recalled recently that the band didn't go down particularly well. He remembers they 'died a bit of a death' there - Lee and Bazz remember it as being the very opposite and that they 'went down a storm'. Davy remembers a great time too, "That was incredible, like being in a film or something. I have so many vivid memories of it - every second was exciting. We played the Scene club in New York and Andy Warhol and the Velvet Underground turned up to watch us." Keith acquired Judy Garland's black hat. She left it on his Hammond so Keith purloined it. He wore it many times after that. It became a bit of a trademark.

Cleo Odzer, a young beauty obsessed with fame - usually the fame associated with music and musicians - was a Scene club regular. "The [Scene Club] musicians were gorgeous and talented, with long hair and velvet clothes," she recalled. "I had a new boyfriend every two weeks when the bands changed." When she was eighteen she met someone who really enraptured her. "He'd just arrived from England to play at the Scene. Famous in England," Cleo reflected, "He wasn't really appreciated in the States." The person she was talking about was Keith Emerson. They got engaged and she even went to visit him in England. It all ended after a Time magazine piece on groupies, with a quote from 'Super Groupie Cleo'. When Keith saw it he hit the roof and broke off the engagement. Odzer denied it all and said it was someone else called Cleo. She subsequently made a documentary called The Groupies. As she later admitted in a rapacious style, "I hadn't been raised to be poor or to work for a living."

With the two week residency up, they found out that Andrew Oldham had booked them into the Whiskey A Go Go in LA. They had another shock as they were all kitted out for winter and when they arrived the temperatures were sweltering. Checking out the club, they introduced themselves to the manager who had never heard of them! Suspecting that this was some kind of stunt pulled by Oldham, they all looked at each other, "Shit!" It was Bazz who saved the day by announcing "We are guests of Andrew Oldham and Mick Jagger." They were given a table at the front of the club and watched UK group The Hollies on stage. O'List quickly got talking to someone else who was watching the group, David Crosby. Oldham, who had by now shown up, turned to Lee and said, "He shouldn't hang around with him, he's a known spiker." It happened, Davy was spiked, and it affected him very badly. It was noted by the rest of the band that this was the time when Davy's personality problems started to emerge.

Once again, the Whiskey dates saw the band supplied with a B3. Bazz had to contact the company who supplied them, Modern Music Rentals, and sort out an L100. They played with Grand Funk Railroad who had a novel way of protecting their gear by chaining it together, which made it tricky for Bazz to get the Nice's equipment on stage. The problems mounted when Lee had a bout of tonsillitis and there wasn't really a replacement in the band. Keith couldn't sing and Davy was too shy, and in the end the hapless Jackson had no choice but to soldier on.

When the Whiskey gigs were over, The Nice had to drive to San Francisco for a set of gigs. Bazz thought, "400 miles, we'll do that in a day," and the band all agreed. However, they insisted on taking the 'scenic route'. The journey was an interesting one as Brian and Davy dropped a couple of tabs of acid but, whilst on the mist-shrouded Pacific Coast Highway, Bazz had to stop the car because Brian and Davy were hallucinating and claiming they were seeing things in the murk.

Whilst all the public attention is fixed upon the musicians upon the stage, it is often easy to forget the critical role played by people like Bazz. The term roadie doesn't really describe the many functions which Bazz would cover in the course of a working day. For example, the band didn't understand tax but they had to get to grips with it. Bazz had to laboriously explain to them the details of State tax and City tax, and halfway through Keith interjected, "Where did you learn all of this?" Exasperated, Bazz replied "On the fucking plane on the way over. It was in a brochure called 'Going to America'."

It was in San Francisco that The Nice first came into contact with the legendary Bill Graham. All concerned were somewhat intimidated by Graham's fabled unpredictability, but there was no doubting the man's charisma. Lee also noticed how sophisticated the local audiences

were. As Graham had put on a lot of the shows in the area, the audiences were used to different types of act, but they always showed appreciation of a good band. It didn't matter if they were rock followed by a country or even jazz. The Nice played the original Fillmore West, third on the bill to The Who, Cannonball Adderley and The Vagrants, who would later become Mountain. Once again, Emerson was unable to get a Hammond L100 and so had to be content with a Hammond C3. It meant he couldn't use the gamut of 'sounds' he had available on the smaller model.

The American tour illustrates the importance of Andrew Oldham. While other bigger name bands were still waiting for opportunities, Oldham went out and created one by hustling The Nice into the US. It was a gamble because the band didn't have a 'name', but even though the tour wasn't a great financial success, it meant that they would be prepared for future travails in America. Back in London they made a triumphant return to The Marquee where above their billing for February 26th 1968 said 'Welcome Back From The US.' They had only made it back home earlier that same morning.

In early March a Chris Welch article appeared in Melody Maker headed 'Groups In Need Of A Break'. The Nice were featured alongside Family, Timebox and Eyes Of Blue - a group that included future Gentle Giant drummer, John Weathers. The whereabouts of two of the groups is unknown but it's a timely reminder just how thin the difference between success and failure. Even though nothing much happened for The Nice in the next few months, save for recording a new single, it would take another publicity stunt from Andrew Oldham to propel the band into the limelight. In fact, it was the single that would give Oldham the chance to sniff out another opportunity.

Burbank, California
February, 1968

For all this, The Nice were looking for a change in how they were managed. They realised there was a conflict of interest in having a manager who was also effectively their record company and publisher; the dual role also stretched Oldham's resources a little thin. "We wanted a management independent from the record company," Lee explained. In April 1968 they decided to replace Andrew Oldham with Tony Stratton-Smith as their manager.

Tony Stratton-Smith had been a sports journalist for the Daily Express in the early '60s, very quickly establishing himself as a freelance writer. He had plans to write books, actually writing one on Pele but it was never published. He went to the 1962 football World Cup in Chile, after which he ended up in Brazil where he met composer Antonio Carlos Jobim who suggested that he try his luck in the music business. Trying management, his first band was Paddy, Klaus and Gibson. Klaus was none other than Klaus Voorman, who later became famous for designing the sleeve for The Beatles' 'Revolver' album and playing in Manfred Mann's band. By the time The Nice met Stratton-Smith (or 'Strat' as he was known) he was still involved in a yearly football annual which brought in a decent amount of money.

He managed a succession of artists but couldn't make the breakthrough for any of them. At that time he was thinking about quitting the business as he really couldn't afford to lose much more money. Ironically, he ended up taking on a band that was already in debt to the tune of £5,000 - The Nice.

Lee phoned Stratton-Smith after a recommendation from Strat's PA, Gail Coulson, asking him to be their manager. Strat was working out of ex-Who producer Shel Talmy's office and wasn't initially too keen, as he explained, "I didn't want to manage them at first, because I was then seriously thinking of quitting. When they called I was on the point of going abroad, but nevertheless I agreed to consider their offer. When I eventually returned from Switzerland they were still there on the phone! So I decided to see them play live at the Marquee. Once I saw them in action I knew I had fallen for it again."

"I spent an afternoon with Tony at Shel Talmy's office going over all the things Oldham was or was not doing," Bazz explains. "Strat had enough evidence to prove mismanagement and so was able to break the management contract with Oldham."

Strat paid the £5,000 debt the band had racked up with Oldham for retainers and recording costs. The band were free to go. Strat was confident that he had a band that was going places. To him it was only a matter of time. He was surprised that they hadn't already made it big and was pretty sure of the reason why, "With respect to Andrew Oldham, I don't think he ever really had any faith in them. He didn't try to help the band, or even hang on to them. I think he totally underestimated what The Nice was about. That's why they brought me in. They wanted somebody who would pick up their career by the scruff of the neck and slam them into the concert halls." Oldham, understandably, was not over the moon about the coup. At the Speakeasy they had a blazing row over the lack of support Oldham had given the band.

Stratton-Smith brought his own style to the scene - one which paid no deference to anything other than being himself, as one admirer put it recently, "We live in a time when record company executives seem to be getting greyer with each passing day. Managing a label is increasingly perceived as no different to, say, managing a vacuum cleaner company. It is a situation that Tony Stratton-Smith would have certainly decried before returning to consider his racing form over a glass of wine. Or twelve."

In short, Stratton-Smith knew where he was going. He set about creating one of the first dedicated, independent progressive record labels, Charisma, which went on to become a huge success.

As expected, the tour of the United States had a profound effect on the band. So much so they decided to go into the studio to record a new single which was based on Leonard Bernstein's number 'America' from 'West Side Story'. As Keith explained at the time, "We noticed, particularly in New York, how much violence there is in America. It's the older people though, and the younger people are trying to do something about it. The close atmosphere in New York has something to do with it." The inspiration this episode provided was convenient because they were looking for a show-stopper to take the place of 'Rondo'. Consequently, Bernstein's 'America' came to mind. Keith had already used a snippet of 'America' in 'Rondo' during the show.

However, The Nice hit a block when they tried the piece, as Lee explains, "When we actually started to try and work it out, the song just didn't fit together somehow, so after a lot of work we left it. A while later Keith was in a record shop, looking through the classical stuff, when he saw the cover of Dvorak's 'New World Symphony' with skyscrapers and so on." When they got into rehearsal they tried the piece and found and it was a perfect combination. Dvorak's piece depicted the calmer side, whilst Bernstein's 'America' depicted the uglier side of society. They

HIT SINGLES MAKE HIT ALBU

P. P. ARNOLD "ANGEL OF THE MORNING" IMO67
THE NICE "AMERICA 2nd AMMENDMENT" IMO68
SMALL FACES "THE UNIVERSAL" IMO69

IMMEDIATE happy to be a part of the industry of human happiness

added their own section called '2nd Amendment'. The combination was a personal success for the band who, contrary to reports, didn't dislike America but were fascinated by the mixed emotions the place invoked in them.

However, this love/hate relationship with America created all sorts of different tensions. Lee remembers that by the time the track was released, both Robert Kennedy and Black Civil Rights leader Martin Luther King had been assassinated, and the band had wanted to make a point about how the 'progressive' leaders of that country were seemingly all being murdered. They had already decided this was urgent enough even before Robert was killed, but now it was positively red hot. Lee remembers that they specifically wanted to concentrate on the gun laws and avoid moving into overt politics – which explains why the '2nd Amendment' tagged onto the end of Bernstein's theme was such an aggressive piece of music. The title comes from the 2nd Amendment to the US Constitution, which stated that 'A well regulated Militia being necessary to the security of a free State, the right of the people to keep and bear Arms, shall not be infringed.' These two lines still had massive ramifications for American society, providing the pro-gun lobby with a constitutional justification.

As the band were recording the track, two ideas emerged. The first came from Lee who suggested transposing the killer line of 'Dawn' and using it at the end of the song. This time it would be 'America is pregnant with promise and anticipation, but is murdered by the hand of the inevitable.' The original context was effective but this added another dimension. This was the time of a great anti-US feeling in the UK, fuelled by the Vietnam War, a sentiment shared by most of the rest of the world. However, whilst some observers thought The Nice might be making a musical comment on the escalating war in

Vietnam, the truth is the band knew very little about the conflict in South East Asia.

The other addition to 'America' was to use P.P. Arnold's son, Kevin, to utter the amended words. Pat had popped in to see her old friends and carefully coached Kevin who delivered the lines with

When In Rome...

Above and opposite: At the time of the Rome Pop Festival, May 5th 1968

aplomb. As well as this, they used shrieks (Andrew Oldham provided the manic laughter) and a starting pistol to convey an atmosphere of violence which Davy's slashing guitar added to immensely.

Emphasizing the utterances of Pat's son, the publicity poster for the single showed the band with Kevin and Brian Davison's nephew, having their faces covered by a photo of Martin Luther King, John Kennedy and Robert Kennedy. It was a controversial and provocative move. Though the band tried to distance themselves from any overtly, political direct action, it wasn't long before some eminent revolutionary socialists were knocking on the door of Immediate Records, asking them to become involved in anti-American marches.

Just after the band recorded 'America' they flew out to the Rome Pop Festival which was held on May 5th. The old T-Bones manager, Giorgio Gomelsky, was the compère to top names such as Ten Years After, Pink Floyd, The Move, Brian Auger and a superb American harmony group called The Association. But in spite of the 'big guns' present, it was a financial disaster with only 4,000 people turning up.

The Nice were filmed and somewhere there exists the precious evidence, mouldering in some vault. It has yet to surface. It was here that the Italian police ran amok and baton charged the tiny crowd. From Rome, The Nice flew to Scandinavia for a short tour with Ten Years After, Fleetwood Mac and The Fugs.

'America' was released in June and quickly acquired the tag of the longest single yet released. It clocked in at over six minutes which, for those days, was little short of incredible. Amazingly, the single made it to No.21 in the UK charts, a genuine hit. In the June 29th edition of Melody Maker the headline was 'Nice Marathon'. They gave it a great review, with Chris Welch paying special attention to Brian who "underpins the group with his battling drums."

The B-side is a little gem too. 'The Diamond Hard Blue Apples Of The Moon' - a song about Brian and Davy, the title a reference to the unattainable - features Davy on trumpet and Keith provides some Hammond feedback mimicking a steam train. It's undoubtedly a catchy little tune but all attention was naturally focused on the A-side.

Soon the storm clouds were gathering as a quote from the record company attempted to dampen down the perceived anti-American angle. They assured readers it was a 'comment, not a protest on the current American scene'. Their assurances were to be all in vain.

Their new manager was working on all fronts for his protégés but he was powerless to prevent Andrew Oldham pulling one last stunt from under his nose. It was to prove an escapade of reckless abandon, all for the return of some short-term gain.

CHAPTER **6**

ROAD MAPS,
A STARTING PISTOL
& SPRAY PAINT

"It was purely
a symbolic
thing really."

TONY STRATTON-SMITH

THE SUMMER OF 1968 saw The Nice put on a defining performance at London's Royal Albert Hall. Oldham had somehow managed to secure The Nice a place on an anti-apartheid event, 'Come Back Africa'. Held on June 26th 1968, it had been organised in aid of the 'International Defence and Aid Fund to commemorate Human Rights Year and South Africa Freedom Day'. The fund had been set up in the 1950s and had paid defence costs of trials held in South Africa against the disenfranchised black majority. The Albert Hall show was organised by Canon John Collins who at that stage was creating awareness of Nelson Mandela's imprisonment. The United Nations Special Committee on Apartheid was also in attendance. As such, the event attracted many of the more progressive-minded artists.

It was a black tie event. Artists like Marlon Brando, Sammy Davis Junior (a late addition to the bill) and John Dankworth and Cleo Laine were there. Contemporary acts on the bill included Brian Auger, but The Nice were the only real 'rock' band appearing that night. Even though they had only a small part to play it would turn out to be the 'hit' of the event.

Around this time, the band was using many kinds of theatrical devices during the performance of their hit single. A starting pistol had been acquired and a road map of LA from their first tour was taped to the microphone stand. Prior to playing 'America', Lee fired three 'shots' into the map, representing President Kennedy, his brother Bobby and MLK. This kind of symbolic display went down a storm with the crowd, so much so that Jack Barrie - manager of the La Chasse club - suggested they could make more of it. At other gigs they tried out variations on the theme and at one Marquee gig, Jackson burned a draft card of a visiting American to tumultuous applause. Emerson had also burned paper replicas of the Stars and Stripes at previous gigs.

It was well known that such activities were part of The Nice's act, so Royal Albert Hall manager Frank Munday sought assurances from the producer, Ted Kotcheff, and the band, that this kind of thing would not take place. On the night of the concert, Munday had his assurances.

UK character actor, Warren Mitchell, hosted the evening. At the time Mitchell was enjoying huge popularity playing a racist, bigot, Alf Garnet in the TV sitcom, 'Till Death Us Do Part'. Sitting in a chair on the corner of the stage, he introduced the band by telling the audience, "And now I'm going to tell you a Nice story."

The Nice played several numbers as part of the show - it was obvious which would be the climax. Keith went up and played the Albert Hall's huge pipe organ to start 'America'. This made a big impression on the audience but, as he explained in the '70s, it didn't last long, "While we were performing 'America', during the guitar solo the drummer would be hammering away, the bass rocking away there. All the people would see behind the organ was this big sheet of canvas and I went up there and I had spray paint and I sprayed up the Stars and Stripes, you know?" So as Davy played his solo, Keith started his aerosol work, the 'flag' was attached to two microphone stands. When he finished he moved it close to where the audience was sitting. It was then that Lee unplugged his bass guitar, calmly walked over and put it through the 'flag', leaving a gaping hole.

The Stars were actually cut out and placed on a second sheet and placed on the main sheet - Keith only sprayed the red horizontal lines. He sprayed the red paint very liberally so that it would run, giving the impression of spilt blood. This would also make it easier to burn. But there was a problem - as he went to apply the dolorous stroke he realised he had no matches on him. He

hadn't left them in the dressing room, he'd dropped them on the floor, as photos later revealed. Socialist Warren Mitchell came to the rescue and in full view of everybody he passed his lighter to Keith. "While I'm doing this spraying up thing," Keith explained, "He's sitting on the side of the stage going, 'Go on, boy, yeah, that's great.'"

Royal Albert Hall
26th June, 1968

Keith Emerson before setting alight the American 'flag', and wearing a hat once owned by Judy Garland!

When they finished the number there was no applause. Photographs of the gig captured the negative reaction of the audience. As soon as they came off stage the balloon went up and the story broke in the following day's national press where it was announced 'Albert Hall Bans Pop Group'. Frank Munday had taken drastic action. As Munday explained, the main reason for the ban was for safety reasons, "I have banned Mr Kotcheff and The Nice from ever setting foot inside the Albert Hall again. Apart from the fire hazard, it was a calculated insult to the flag of a friendly nation - Mr Kotcheff gave me an undertaking that it would not happen and I accepted his word." The hapless Kotcheff was understandably miffed and

felt more than a little let down by the band, "I gave an undertaking to the Albert Hall, but I do not accept responsibility for what happened. I asked the group not to burn or deface the flag, but I could not go on stage and stop them during the act."

The Nice were not the only ones to have been banned from the Albert Hall. The exclusion list includes Frank Zappa, James Brown and Funkadelic. Hall manager Frank Munday argued that it was to do with the damage and the general demeanour of the fans. Munday told Melody Maker that, "It's the general deterioration of public behaviour that's gone on over the last few years." This was a blow to groups as the venue was, and still is, regarded as a prestigious place to play. But Munday was keen to point out that they would still book pop acts like The New Seekers and, of course, the Hall would continue to host the grand flag-waving - as opposed to flag-burning - exercise known as The Proms.

The Marquee
4th July, 1968

Left-right:
Keith Emerson,
Brian Davison,
Lee Jackson,
Davy O'List

Stratton-Smith realised it could have been worse, "It wasn't an American flag as such. If it had been, we may not got off as lightly as we did with the American Embassy when subsequently we wanted to go to the States. However, the whole purpose of the episode was to convey the band's concern at the assassination of Robert Kennedy... they wanted to make this gesture that the country was crumbling under violence. It was purely a symbolic thing really." However, Strat revealed there was some debate prior to the show, with good reason, "I did warn the band before their show that I thought it was going to be misunderstood, but Andrew Oldham who was still their record boss persuaded them otherwise."

On July 4th 1968, American Independence Day, The Nice tried to counter the negative feedback by playing a rousing set at the Marquee decked out in American garb. This was Strat's way of presenting a positive image of the United States and undertaking a little damage limitation after the Albert Hall incident. Davy and Brian were dressed as Puritans to signify the Pilgrim Fathers who sailed from Plymouth to America. They'd gone down to Bermans (the famous theatrical suppliers, who provided The Beatles' *'Sgt. Pepper'* uniforms) together to get their costumes. Lee dressed as his American Civil War commander namesake, General Lee, while Keith was dressed as Uncle Sam with a garish Stars and Stripes waistcoat. The concert was filmed by French television but has never surfaced.

Late July saw the band hitting overdrive as a headline in Melody Maker proudly proclaimed 'Last Thursday The Nice smashed all box office records at The Marquee Club... previously held by The Rolling Stones, The Who, Manfred Mann, Spencer Davis, The Cream and Jimi Hendrix.' Lee remembers the queue snaked back to his flat in Old Compton Street. He didn't know it was for the Marquee until he saw Jon Gee was counting them. When Gee reached the number that was required to break the record he closed the doors. Brian remembers the intensity of the night's performance left himself and Keith totally drained. It was so hot they couldn't breathe because of inadequate ventilation in the dressing rooms. Club manager, Jon Gee weighed in saying "Give them some air!" and desperately trying to get people away from them.

On July 27th they played a free concert in Hyde Park, London, with Traffic and The Pretty Things. The Nice had a gig in Norwich on the evening, but they never made it. They went down well, as Disc confirmed, "The Nice, who are the best group in the country to see live on stage - and in the open too are quite staggering." The New Musical Express observed it wasn't all power, though, "'Rondo' was its usual brilliant display of power, improvisation and Keith Emerson acrobatics. 'Little Arabella' was next, providing a few minutes of relief and showing that the band can perform the slower numbers as well as its more renowned faster ones." In fact, one night at Klook's Kleek, London, 'Little Arabella' didn't provide Lee with much light relief, although the audience had plenty. Lee used to do a little shuffle as he sang this number and on that night he had a spectacular fall, much to the hilarity of everyone.

On August 10th, Melody Maker reported that composer Leonard Bernstein had successfully blocked 'America' being released Stateside. Record Mirror reported that 'Bernstein is peeved.' It got worse. They'd had offers of a five-week USA tour for the autumn of 1968, a tour that offered a great chance to make their stateside breakthrough, but it was now in jeopardy due to the negative reaction to the Royal Albert Hall performance. Suddenly the flag-burning seemed a gross act of folly. It was time for the management to eat humble pie. Tony Stratton-Smith and Lee Jackson went to the American Embassy a couple of times to virtually give an undertaking that they would not 'create revolution' in the USA.

Keith told Record Mirror, "It's tremendously exciting. We've already made one trip to America, but a lot of things went wrong - for part of the trip Lee Jackson lost his voice through tonsillitis, on other occasions we had really serious equipment problems. But we learned a lot. This time everything will be done so that our thing can be seen to best advantage." In the final analysis they couldn't save the tour, but it was rescheduled for the spring of 1969. This was a massive blow as the album was going well and 'Rondo' was receiving much airplay. So much so that Immediate considered it as the single in place of 'America'.

marquee artists

1 0 AUG 1968

Artists representation & management

Marquee Artists Agency Limited
16 Carlisle Street, Soho Square,
London, W1
Telephones: GERrard 6601/2/3

Directors:

D.C.Barber
H. Pendleton

Licensed annually by the Westminster City Council.

C O M M I S S I O N   N O T E

Artiste's Name .... The Nice, ...

Date .... 5th July 1968. ....

In consideration of your procuring for me the undermentioned engagement(s) which
I hereby agree to accept through your Agency

with .... National Jazz Festivals Limited. ....

at .... Kempton Park, Sunbury on Thames. ....

on .... Saturday 10th August 1968. ....

.... £125.0.0. ....

at a Salary of ....

I agree to pay MARQUEE ARTISTS AGENCY LTD, a commission of .ten.% of the gross salary.
*Equally divisable with Ellis Wright agency.
I also agree to pay a like commission on further engagements with the same Management

Even with the US dates postponed, the band maintained a relentless touring schedule. They flew to Switzerland to record a television show which was planned as Swiss TV's first colour transmission. The band fell out with the producer of the show. They had bought some beer with them and were cracking open a few bottles when the producer asked if he could have some as well. The request was responded to with enthusiasm but Roger the roadie (Bazz's assistant), was unaware of this. Seeing the producer drinking the band's beer, he hit him in the mouth and floored him. The producer was on the floor holding his mouth while Strat pleaded with Bazz, "You've got to get rid of him."

Big events were coming thick and fast. On August 10th they made their second appearance at the 8th National Jazz and Blues Festival, this time held at Kempton Park (they were paid £125). It was in fact, as Jack Barrie related recently, "The Marquee's Annual Rock Festival!" The bill was highly eclectic featuring bands like Marmalade, Tyrannosaurus Rex, Jerry Lee Lewis, Ronnie Scott (The Nice watched his act from the wings) and Ten Years After. The Nice were introduced on stage by Jon Gee, who had to cope with more than his fair share of aggravation. Some rockers got overexcited during Jerry Lee Lewis's set, trying to mount the stage - this led to a few flying bottles and several people were hurt. But by the time The Nice went on, all was calm. Opening with 'Rondo' they had the crowd eating out of their hands. 'Little Arabella' went down particularly well, now destined for their second album. Roy Harper joined them on stage for a number. The headline in Melody Maker was 'Music triumphs, despite rain, accidents and rockers.' Chris Welch gave the band a fine review.

In the light of recent shenanigans the band showed they had learnt some lessons, as Record Mirror pointed out, "There was an incredible reception for their final number 'America', which has been a hit despite so few radio plays. The atmosphere built up throughout, driven by Brian Davison's dynamic drumming and staggering light effects to the impressive ending in which Keith threw knives into the organ, then set light to it. Wax on a sheet of fabric on the back caused the fire to form the word Nice. When the back of the organ had burnt away, an American flag was produced from within but despite encouragement from the audience, it was taken away unsinged." At the conclusion of the gig Keith waved the American flag above his head.

There seemed no way the band could avoid the Bernstein feud. In late August they made their first television appearance on the BBC's 'How It Is', playing their single 'America'. The preamble to their appearance was a commentary on the recent controversy. And it gave Bernstein a chance to get his own back, "It was reported recently that Bernstein has banned the version of his song 'America' as performed by The Nice. He is reported to have said 'they have turned it into an anti-American dirge'." The truth is that Bernstein never held any grudges against Keith, he later visited Emerson, Lake & Palmer when they were recording in Paris in the '70s. Keith claimed recently that Bernstein even had a crush on him and tried to pick him up!

The fact that 'America' was one of the longest singles yet recorded served to bring to the boil an issue that had been festering for some time. In late 1967 an article appeared in Melody Maker that, for many, brought the singles/albums debate into the open, 'Cream declares war on singles' was the headline. Eric Clapton announced that Cream had no desire to release singles any more. The problem lay in the fact that serious musicians felt restricted by this formulaic approach. Clapton's stand was brave, "The whole music scene in Britain is ruled by the chart and people are brainwashed into thinking that the No.1 represents the best music available. It's horribly immature and it's got to go."

The music scene was fragmenting and a number of groups were breaking into the mainstream with a music that necessitated a longer framework than three minutes of vinyl permitted. The perception that progressive bands hadn't much to offer other than their latest hit single was holding these bands back. For if these bands were to develop fully, then sooner or later there had to be an audience willing to go with them and, as Brian Davison remarked when The Nice went solo, "Yes, they are starting to listen." Bands that catered for people to sit and listen and take in the music were gaining ground. The Nice were at the forefront of this new musical movement.

The 8th National Jazz & Blues Festival, Kempton Park on the 10th August, 1968

During 'America' an American flag was produced but, despite encouragement from the audience, was taken away unsinged. Note Bazz with spliff.

By the summer of 1968 the band started to think about a follow up to *'The Thoughts of Emerlist Davjack'*. The press were in a state of huge anticipation, in particular Melody Maker who noted how they were creating their own sound, "The Nice are now one of Britain's top groups, ranking with Cream and Jimi Hendrix. Their music is unlike anything being played by a modern pop group in Britain or America. It is violent, often neurotic, yet rich in chords, harmonies and melodies. They have the drive of a blues band, without playing blues. They improvise as spontaneously as a jazz group... they are free as a psychedelic group, but with vastly superior instrumental ability."

The praise was pretty much universal and the prestigious gigs were coming thick and fast. It was a good job too because, as Bazz recalls, "We weren't getting any money off the record company." The pressure was on them to gig constantly as it was the only way the band and their entourage could earn money.

As the band grew in popularity and success, the band's crew was increased to include two other roadies, Alan Smith and John Robson, to help Bazz with his duties. Alan Smith, originally recruited simply as an equipment roadie, came from the band Creation, with whom Strat had had some involvement. When the band demanded they have their own car (they were sick of travelling in the van), he became the band's personal driver. Consequently, he took over a lot of Bazz's jobs, such as booking hotels and collecting the gig money. He later worked with Brian Davison's Every Which Way before moving on to The Who. John Robson, meanwhile, was a computer programmer by trade. He started out driving the band but was transferred to the equipment van when Alan Smith took over. It was mooted that Bazz drive the band but it could never work because Keith didn't trust anyone else with his Hammonds.

Ever since the formation of the band there had been no major calamities. However, a gig on September 29th at the Fairfield Hall, Croydon, brought forth a festering crisis within the band.

The band were due to appear with The Rolling Stones in a BBC2 television colour spectacular in aid of the British Olympic Appeal for the upcoming Mexico games. They played a new piece, 'Ars Longa Vita Brevis', which was started by Brian blowing a whistle. Keith got up to his usual showmanship on 'America'. The climax of which was when he went behind the Hammond and started hitting the reverb tray with a stick, whilst waving the American flag over his head.

Halfway through a number, Brian had a problem with his bass drum. Bazz ran onto the stage but, on exiting when he'd fixed it, Davy smacked him in the mouth. It was astonishing that Bazz, who was a take-no-crap bruiser, didn't decorate the wall with him. But as he explained recently there were two reasons why he didn't, "I was taken by surprise and I refused to hit a member of the

BBC

BRITISH BROADCASTING CORPORATI

KENSINGTON HOUSE RICHMOND WAY LONDON W

TELEPHONE 01-743 1272 TELEGRAMS BROADCASTS LONDON T

CABLES BROADCASTS LONDON-W1 TELEX 2

23rd August, 1968.

The Nice,
c/o John Martin,
1 Wardour Street,
London, W. 1.

Dear Lee, David, Brian, Keith,

Thanks a lot for Thursday. The number was great and I'm only sorry you won't be able to see it next Friday.

Hope we will see you again on the programme

Yours sincerely,

Tony Palmer

Tony Palmer

band!" Afterwards the reason advanced by Davy was that Bazz and Brian had been conspiring against him. Sadly, by this late period, Davy reacted like this whenever he saw conversations going on that didn't involve him. He developed a serious persecution complex. As a result, he was quite detached from the band and in Brian's words, "Davy became like Syd [Barrett], a shadowy figure."

The truth is that Davy had lost his bearings a while before Croydon. Lee, Brian and Bazz are all in agreement that the problem started to get out of hand after his drink was spiked by David Crosby, at the Whiskey A Go Go in February of that year. The guitarist became increasingly unreliable and he had acquired the nickname Davy O'Late. They had a few problems at the Marquee. After the soundcheck (rehearsal) Davy had gone home but hadn't turned up as the gig approached. Bazz decided to phone him.

"Davy, would you like to come down to the Marquee, there's a good band on?"

"Who?" replied O'List.

"Us, you prat!"

This happened on several occasions and within a short period they had played many of the numbers as a three-piece. On another occasion, the band had to carry on without O'List. "He started to thrash the strings," recalls Lee, which resulted in him just snapping them. One of the most famous manifestations of Davy's unreliable behaviour has been well documented by Keith who complained he was cranking his guitar up too much and drowning him out.

Another instance was when they were again playing the soon to be recorded 'Ars Longa Vita Brevis' suite on stage. Brian takes up the story, "As I was preparing for my drum solo, Davy would go straight into the guitar intro in the 'Second Movement'." The band had no alternative but to omit Brian's solo. Furthermore, Brian remembered he started playing out of key at various times and at one time during rehearsal he couldn't understand a point Keith was trying to get across to him, regarding a chord structure. Brian recalled it as being something that Davy had done many times before and was well within his capabilities. Yet, O'List broke out into a sweat and couldn't do it.

Lee remembers they had a some problems during 'America'. Davy would play his solo in a certain key, and then at the end he would come back, then Keith would play his solo in another key and the band would move up to that key. But there were times when Davy would just stand there after his solo and do nothing. Suddenly he would come crashing in, playing yet another different key, totally ruining Keith's solo. The anxious glances between the remaining three told everything.

Another story illustrates Davy's confused state. The band came into a £1,000 windfall by dint of changing booking agents. They had started with Barry Dickens and then moved onto the Ellis-Wright Agency. John Martin came along and was confident that he could do a lot more with the band than Ellis-Wright. So he offered them £1,000 pounds to sign with him – a lot of money in 1968. It was decided that each member of the band would get £200, with the remaining £200 equally shared out to Strat (he was on 10% as manager) and Bazz. Keith bought a new Leslie Cabinet with his but Davy, as Bazz recalled recently, "Went out and bought a Les Paul Junior and decided to paint it white. The only problem was he left all the fittings on and used a can of paint he bought at Woolworths. It was a fucking disaster!"

Stratton-Smith scrutinised the chemistry of the band and Davy's increasingly errant behaviour attracted his attention. O'List would later recall, "He (Stratton-Smith) started following me around the clubs pretending to be friendly but as it turned out he was trying to elbow me out of the band. He'd seen us play quite a lot and saw the attention Keith was getting with his on-stage antics, and mistakenly thought that Keith was the centre of the band. What he didn't understand was that a lot of the theatrical ideas came from me. I was the one whose parents were from a theatrical background. I suggested right at the start that Keith shouldn't sit down at the keyboards but stay standing. Stratton-Smith started accusing me of taking drugs all the time which was ludicrous - I wasn't taking LSD, I'd never seen cocaine and I didn't know what heroin was - honestly, I was really green about it all. He was still trying to pull that one on me though. Two or three times he took me out to dinner and started needling me, 'we don't like what you're doing on stage, we don't like how you behave. Don't you think you should see a psychiatrist and perhaps leave the band?' Who was this bastard? For two years I'd put my whole life into this band, invested everything."

Lee Jackson saw things differently, "Strat actually wanted to keep Davy in the band and initially made efforts to keep him in. Davy's behaviour changed and if it wasn't illicit substances that were responsible for his erratic behaviour then he must have been in urgent need of psychiatric help! Davy's trousers used to be pock marked by the ash that dropped off his joints. He never bothered to brush them off - he was too stoned. The idea Davy was really naive about drugs is rubbish."

Strat could see that O'List was now a lost cause but the rest of the band that had ran out of patience. The day after the Croydon gig, Keith phoned up Lee and Brian, asking them to come over for a band meeting. The general consensus at that meeting was that Davy had to go. A couple of days later they had a gig at the Ritz, on Bournemouth's esplanade. It was Davy's last appearance. After the gig Davy was sacked in the dressing room. Strat wanted to tell Davy in private but the band wanted it done in their presence as a way of confirming their solidarity with their manager. Lee remembers Davy didn't say anything as Strat told him. Indeed, Davy sat in the back of the gear van all the way back to London and never said a word. Sometime into the journey they were stopped by the police. The police were always stopping vans that looked like a pop group transport in the hope of finding some drugs. The policeman saw Davy and said, "What's wrong with him? He looks a bit rough." After a short delay they continued their journey into the night.

Looking back on O'List's departure from the band, journalist Chris Welch offered this view, "He had been 'spiked' during a trip to the States and he became both mentally and musically confused. He took the flower power and hippie scene too seriously, and while everyone experimented with dope and acid, he got caught up in the madness and was damaged to the point where he had to be dropped from the group - which incidentally caused him great grief and anguish from which he has never really recovered." In the same interview, Chris confirmed that Davy was influenced personally by Syd Barrett.

At the time, the reasons for Davy's departure were shrouded in mystery. An announcement in the 12th October edition of the Melody Maker stated the 'parting was amicable'. The paper revealed Gordon Langstaff (his name was actually Malcolm Langstaff) as the replacement. Furthermore, in subsequent interviews, Keith muddied the waters and created the impression the whole rupture had been a case of warring egos, by complaining that the guitarist got all the chicks, etc. Keith also claimed that Davy was frustrated by his inability to copy Larry Coryell. It is perhaps worth remembering that Davy had only just turned twenty when he left the band but had achieved a lot. His work on the debut album wasn't just promising in patches, it was brilliant. The sadness was compounded by the presence of Davy's sisters, Suzie and Pauline, at post-Davy gigs. They had followed the band since its very inception and were naturally upset at their brother's sacking. However, they would remain loyal to the group right up until its end.

In 1991 Davy talked to Terrascope magazine about his split with The Nice. "I was worn out from continuous travelling, gigging, promotions and suffering from volume fatigue," he explained. "A friend of Lee wanted to get into the 'big time' pop business. With favours and money he assumed management of The Nice, although I did not care for him. Lee influenced Keith to adopt him. I wanted to form The Nice label and management, so that the band could have complete financial control, which it deserved. However, this man, Tony Stratton-Smith, began to push me out, for he secretly wanted control. Charisma was in fact a brain child of myself. A conspiracy grew against me in the band, a fight over fame fortune, limelight and future wealth." Even now Davy still thinks that Stratton-Smith had a personal grudge against him and that was the reason why he was sacked. "I was too upset to go to Keith and ask him if this nonsense was for real," he told Terrascope, "So that was it, I left the band and waited for Keith to get in contact. I shouldn't have, I should have gone straight to Keith, but I didn't." Remarkably, in spite of this resentment that had built up over the years, he attended Stratton-Smith's memorial service in 1987. "Nobody thought in terms of over touring and volume fatigue in those days," Lee Jackson comments. "That was the lifestyle - it was never questioned, you just got on with it."

Davy has also made some extravagant claims concerning his role in the genesis of The Nice. "The classical-rock-jazz fusion was completely my idea," he insisted, "And I introduced Keith to the idea, thinking he may be suitable as an organist... I introduced my music to Keith, knowing his background, and knowing that he had never been exposed to such genius music. Keith could not be bothered one way or another. If he had never met me and I had stayed with The Attack or taken the offer to replace Clapton [it was actually Peter Green] in John Mayall's Bluesbreakers, Keith would never have made it and there would definitely not have been an ELP. King Crimson needed The Nice to feed off, as did Genesis, Yes, Asia, Jethro Tull and numerous groups all over the world." Davy obviously had problems, but he was such a talented guitarist and it is sad that he never really did anything after his departure from The Nice.

When *'The Thoughts Of Emerlist Davjack'* was re-released in a 20th Anniversary celebratory edition in 1997, it was credited to 'The Nice Featuring Davy O'List'. The liner notes were written by O'List under the pen name, The Big Seal. The notes are interesting for the absence of any extravagant claims made for their author's contribution to the band, other than having his name 'featured' over Keith Emerson's. In fact, no claims of this nature can be found until the '90s.

In the small print of the sleeve notes it states, "The only legal release of The Nice paying full royalties to The Nice." One thing for certain is that the band never received any royalties from Oldham's Immediate label, although Davy is convinced that they did. For years he has accused the band of denying him his share of these monies. However, neither Lee, Keith nor Brian received anything from O'List's 20th Anniversary release either. It's clear that the wounds that were opened up in the ousting of Davy will never be healed. Of O'List, Lee Jackson believes that, "In the beginning he was great. He had loads of potential. But it all went wrong."

Davy O'List can be seen as another victim of the 1960s drug culture. There were many casualties from the period; some died, while many survived in different degrees of health. However, one can't help but have sympathy for Davy and we can only imagine what it was like for him to watch The Nice go on to consolidate their success in his wake.

THE SCHOOL MOTTO

"I heard music that,
in some ways,
I later heard in Yes."

STEVE HOWE

CONTRARY TO POPULAR MYTH, O'List's departure from The Nice was followed by a determined effort to acquire another guitarist. The band never considered, at that stage, that they would be anything other than a four-piece. However, in subsequent interviews Keith has implied an alternative explanation for why Davy had to go, "It was really because the guitar players were out there pulling the girls, and as the keyboard player you'd sit there in the background unnoticed... I felt I had a lot to say and I was fed up with being drowned out by some bloody guitar player who fancied himself as another Pete Townshend, so I began making so much noise on my own there wasn't any point in having a guitarist in there any more."

No wonder there were whispers of betrayal from O'List supporters and no surprise that articles cropped up, proffering what has become the standard interpretation of events, i.e. it was a fight for musical supremacy between Keith and Davy. O'List's argument that he was the dominant creative force in The Nice, rather than Emerson, is roundly rejected by Lee Jackson, "Keith will always be the centre of any musical environment he is in. His overall knowledge of music is phenomenal. His record speaks for itself."

The rift between Emerson and O'List continued to be the subject of much rumour and speculation. A typical response is the following passage from a '70s press piece,

"Most probably the reason for getting rid of Davy was that Emerson was rapidly taking over the group's musical direction, which became totally dominated by his on-stage antics." But, as the same article acknowledged, The Nice did enact an earnest search for a replacement.

The band considered several guitarists but the one that caught their attention was a young man from a group called Bodast. His name was Steve Howe. He was invited to come down and audition for the band. At that stage Steve was not really well known, so it was a good opportunity for him. The Nice were keen to secure him, as were Jethro Tull, who were looking for a replacement for Mick Abrahams (coincidently O'List had also auditioned for Tull, rehearsing with them for a couple of weeks, but nothing came of it).

Steve Howe remembers the time well, "I went down and played, and Keith and I really hit it off. We played a bit and talked a bit. Then we went down to the bar and met their manager. I was going to join." He got as far as envisaging the headline in Melody Maker - 'Steve Howe

Joins The Nice!' It might even have worked out but Howe decided to reject the offer, as he explains, "Overnight, I changed my mind for reasons that quite soon afterwards I thought were wrong. But be that as it may, it gave me a little bit more hanging-around time before I met Yes." However, it was only after he joined Yes that he realised just what a ground-breaking band The Nice were, "I heard music that, in some ways, I later heard in Yes."

Having failed to secure their man, The Nice continued as a three piece. Lee remembers that Keith was determined to incorporate some guitar into the act. Keith asked Lee to go through the fretboard with him. The idea was for Keith to play the guitar part in the 'Second Movement' of 'Ars Longa Vita Brevis'. Keith was confident he could translate the knowledge of keyboard into the guitar but he couldn't move his fingers with the required speed. Keith tried it out at a gig in Wales and it was a disaster. Lee told him, "Keith, there no one to touch you on the keyboard but you'll never be a guitarist!" Consequently, Keith gave up trying to learn the guitar for the second time - forever as far as we know.

The first gig without Davy was at The Toby Jug, Tolworth. Gradually the depleted band seemed to gel as a trio, as Lee recalls, "We were reading all the body signals from Keith. He would crouch down and that would signal a change in tempo." This gave reign to lots of improvisational sections whenever the mood took Keith. Furthermore, he had two musicians who loved to stretch out. They were always a great live act but now it was going to another level.

At this time their set included 'Little Arabella', 'Rondo', 'America', 'Daddy Where Did I Come From?', 'Brandenburger' and a cover version that was turning into the barnstormer in the act. Writing in the New Musical Express, Richard Green, enthused about a recent gig in Holland, "At the Sunday afternoon gig, Dylan's 'She Belongs To Me' took on a new shape when The Nice played it and this must have been one of their best sets ever." Green confirmed the chemistry the band had on stage, "Lee watches Keith's every move and puts his bass to every use and possibly some more. Brian stares towards Keith and doesn't so much - as many drummers do - just lay the foundation, but constructs and helps erect a total that becomes one of pop's unscaleable heights." They received a standing ovation and came back to do 'War & Peace'.

On this trip to Holland, Brian had been strip-searched for the umpteenth time. As Tony Stratton-Smith remarked, "One in a hundred people get searched and it's always a pop group [sic]." However, on one occasion Brian was obliged to eat an offending substance in order to avoid detection. During the flight the NME's Richard Green purloined the unattended microphone, "Ladies & Gentlemen this plane is flying at 20,000 feet, with the exception of Brian Davison who is flying at 37,000 feet!" On the first day in Holland, Brian was so hyper he got Green out of bed at five o'clock in the morning to go with him for a walk along the beach.

Above and left:

Lee Jackson,
Wessex Studios,
London

As soon as they got home it was straight back into the studio to put the finishing touches to their second album. 'Ars Longa Vita Brevis' was actually Lee's art school motto and it meant 'Life is short, art is long.' Recorded between Pye and Wessex studios, the whole album has an intellectual feel to it. Keith's sleeve notes refer to Isaac Newton's law of motion and ruminates on this in relation to the fertile music scene. He ends by giving his own spin on the school motto, "Tomorrow is yesterday's history and art will still be there, even if life terminates." So it was strange, not to say brave, that they decided to open with 'Daddy Where Did I Come From.'

The song's subject matter, sex, generated plenty of press interest. As Lee remarked, it was a disappointing approach to take, "They're all interested in that song, but the other side is one number with a symphony orchestra." Keith Emerson takes the lead vocal on this track. Lee's lyrics are far from abstract here. They represent an attack on the prudish morality that still existed despite the 'swinging sixties' climate. Tony Stratton-Smith plays the embarrassed father as he nervously fends off questions about the 'birds and bees' and where babies actually come from. Tony really felt embarrassed by the part (perhaps because he was gay) and only agreed to do it under last minute pressure from the band. The song is quite funny and at one stage the flustered father-figure mixes up the word 'fornicate' with 'pollinate'. The child's voice is Brian's nephew who happened to be in the studio. Lee remembers they recorded a better version with Davy on guitar, during the sessions for the first album, on which "Davy played brilliantly!"

'Little Arabella' had already been established as a concert favourite by the time they recorded it. Lee wrote this about a personal friend at the time but won't reveal the identity of his inspiration. Keith didn't like the first set of words that Lee wrote, so he went away and had to come up with some more. There's some great work from Keith here, his Hammond is both restrained and soulful. Keith's playing in this period exhibited real feeling and was a feature of his playing in the later period of the band. The trumpet was added by a session musician.

'Happy Freuds' is the next track - it was the only one that wasn't road tested on stage - and completes the opening trio of short 'knockabout', less serious tracks. Keith handles some of the vocals again - thankfully it was the last time he ever did with the band. At this stage it appeared that the album was going to be close in content to their debut. However, the remainder of the album would show that they were going in a new direction.

The songwriter/performer Roy Harper was a friend of the band and he suggested they do an adaptation of the theme tune to the television news program This Week, the 'Intermezzo From The Karelia Suite' composed by Jean Sibelius. He reckoned it would go down a storm as the show was very popular. By this time Keith had been working on it for a while, they'd been playing it live since mid-1968. The track gave the band the opportunity to display two unusual aspects of their act on vinyl. The first was that Keith indulged in some Hammond feedback, this was exactly how it appeared in the show. The second was Lee playing his bass with a violin bow. This presented a problem because the fretboard of a bass guitar is flat, so it was impossible to play separate strings. A viola and cello is cambered so any string can be played separately. Lee's solution was to play the top string (in the later period of the band he used the bottom string). Another problem was that the bow had rosin on it - standard for a violin bow - so it would grip better as it passed over the string. But after Lee had finished playing, the rosin had to be wiped off the string with cotton wool soaked with lighter fluid. Bazz would do this on stage, requiring a few seconds delay before Lee could carry on playing.

The last track on Side One is 'Don Edito El Gruva' or 'Don edits the grooves'. It is a homage to their engineer, Don Brewer, who was producer-turned-engineer for the album, an inspired choice of Tony Stratton-Smith.

By this time Keith and Lee had a tried and tested method of writing, "I usually start with one phrase which I work on until I've got a melody," Keith explained. "I tape this and hand it over to Lee." Sometimes Keith would 'la, la' the melody on the tape. Lee would then write the words. This was the method they used throughout their career together.

In contrast to Keith and Lee's writing methods, Lee explains that the main piece on the second album was provided by their departed guitarist, "It started with a riff Davy brought along. Keith fancied developing it, so we got into that. I came up with the name 'Ars Longa Vita Brevis' and the lyrics, and whatever I felt like writing about was what they got, and we developed various pieces and turned it into a suite." The suite is in four parts. All of the orchestra parts were recorded at Wessex Studios – a converted church – mostly in one hit.

The opener is 'Prelude' which has some great interplay between the strings and the Hammond. The next part is the '1st Movement - Awakening' which is rather strange, not least because it features a fine drum solo and Brian was well known to dislike drum solos on stage. Apparently Brian had just done an equipment deal with Paiste and wanted to showcase the gongs he'd received. It was also a chance for him to get a song-writing credit. Some additional effects during the solo are provided by Keith whacking the reverb on the Hammond.

The '2nd Movement - Realisation' is next. This was the number that Keith developed. Davy's guitar part is played by Malcolm Langstaff (who had been named as O'List's full time replacement in the band by Melody Maker) and this theme reoccurs later in the suite. Lee had come across Langstaff in his native Newcastle. He was in a band called The Kylastrons (his nickname was Kylastron) and they had quite an original act. Lee recalled recently, "They played a frightening version of 'In The Hall Of The Mountain King'." So, on Lee's advice they got him in.

Lee provided lyrics and they are as inscrutable as his early works, for example: 'Life is too short to paint a kiss / So sing a picture, paint a song / Take it home and bang your gong / Life is an ill-cast comedy for fools'. Keith's contribution is heard at the end of the section with some funky piano that has a Latin American feel to it. Davy claimed that he played on the album, but Lee revealed recently that Langstaff learned the part by listening to Davy on a BBC session which featured an early arrangement of the piece.

The '3rd Movement' is probably the most beautiful piece of music The Nice ever recorded. Keith decided to adapt Bach's 'Brandenburg Concerto No.3' and he sticks very close to it. They called it 'Acceptance - Brandenburger'. Whilst in the Keith Emerson Trio, he had experimented with fusing different types of music. He noticed the similarity of Bach and Charlie Parker and set about improvising something based on the two. He was a great admirer of the work of French jazz pianist, Jacques Louissier, who was also doing similar work. Brian Davison remembers the recording session very well. The orchestra's string section came into the studio with a jaded attitude: 'let's get this out of the way, then we can go home'. However, by the time they started recording, they'd got into it so much so that in Brian's words, they were "really cooking!" They really got into the spirit and even stayed for the mixing too! If there was one track that epitomises the successful combination of rock and the classics, this is it. Keith contributes some stunning Hammond and harpsichord here too. The strings end the piece by brilliantly, and movingly, segueing into the next movement.

'4th Movement - Denial' effectively ends the suite, save for a little section at the end. After some spunky Hammond, the piece returns briefly to Davy's riff from the '2nd Movement'. There were some that thought Davy might have got a credit here. That he didn't left a sour taste in the mouth of some parties. Bazz remembers a conversation with Stratton-Smith and both men thought that Davy had been sold a little short on this point.

'Brandenburger' was decided upon as the single to herald the album's release. It would have made more commercial sense to have released one of the shorter cuts on Side One, but it was heartening that the band were sticking to their guns and releasing what they felt comfortable with. 'Daddy Where Did I Come From?' might have generated more press coverage, but 'Brandenburger' was released in late November 1968 to very good reviews. Melody Maker's Chris Welch was as enthusiastic as ever, "It's a cheeky, entertaining and brilliantly executed combination of modern group style performance with a Bach theme." Disc was equally impressed, "All in all very interesting, strangely, very good to dance to and I like it."

The visual impact of The Beatles' *Sgt. Pepper* album had elevated the humble record cover to the point where it was regarded as a work of art in its own right. The Nice were especially keen to be part of this growing trend, coming up with an idea for a circular album sleeve. Brian Davison made a cardboard mock-up to show how it might be done. Oldham rejected the idea for The Nice but gave it to the premier band on the Immediate label, The Small Faces, for their *'Ogden's Nut Gone Flake'* album. Undaunted, The Nice returned with a suggestion of a triangular shaped sleeve. This too was turned down.

It wasn't long before the band came up with another concept. The idea was to have x-rays of each member of the band. Whereas the first album showed the birth of a group, this one would be looking inside the band. Gered Mankowitz was brought in, again, to photograph the x-rays as a montage. As he recalls there were lots of technical problems, "The *'Ars Longa Vita Brevis'* cover shoot was very interesting and a tremendous challenge. I can't remember who came up with the idea for the skeletons - it might of been as a result of a brainstorming evening with Andrew Oldham! We would all get stoned and these silly ideas would pop out! Anyway, I discovered that I wouldn't be allowed to x-ray the band, which was the original idea, because of health and safety issues. So I brought a job lot of old x-rays from a private clinic in Knightsbridge. "I built a life size light box in my studio and proceeded to create this jigsaw human skeleton from the x-rays that I had purchased. I then cut out various organs from sheets of coloured plastic and placed them within the jigsaw. I did a triple exposure on an 8"x10" camera, and one of the sheets of film became the album cover! I was under tremendous pressure from Immediate Records because the cover image was very late, and I found it very tricky technically, so I had to work through the night! We put out a cover story that we had injected the band with coloured dyes and had them x-rayed against doctor's orders to create the image! The cover won an award for Best Album Cover - I believe from the NME - and I went on TV to receive it from Eamonn Andrews! I shot a straight, very close-up portrait of each of the guys on the same 8"x10" camera to go with the cover, but I don't think they were ever used." Oldham, of course, fed the press stories that the band had booked into a clinic for the x-ray cover.

The album was released to mixed reviews. According to Melody Maker, the album was a vast improvement on the debut. Furthermore, sensing the winds of change, it concentrated on the ground-breaking aspect of the project and the way they used the orchestra. It was hailed as "A major breakthrough in pop group experimentation. In fact, the phrase 'pop group' becomes obsolete in view of their bold and imaginative cross breeding of classical, jazz and rock and roll music." Paying tribute to the many musical influences, the paper declared it a major success. Record Mirror likewise endorsed it, though the RM reviewer wasn't quite convinced about the orchestral presence, "The addition of strings and things is perhaps not really necessary except that it makes the whole production just that bit more polished and complete." In some respects *'Ars Longa Vita Brevis'* is The Nice's worst album - the short tracks do pale in comparison to the suite - but, most importantly, it marked out where the band's future direction lay.

In November 1968 the band embarked on their first Irish tour. The most prestigious gig was when they played at the Belfast annual music festival, at the Whitia Hall at the invitation of Michael Emmerson of Queens University. They opened the festival and impressed everyone, especially Emmerson. "I knew they were good from their records, but I didn't realise they were that good." After the gig they were enjoying a hand-rolled cigarette, which was being passed around, when they had a shock. Chris Welch takes up the story, "Suddenly a voice bellowed:

'Gentlemen - the Prime Minister!' In came the haggard looking leader, Captain Terence O'Neill, who was asked to stand and pose with the group, who hastily concealed the still smouldering joint behind their backs."

The last major gig of the year was playing to 3,500 ecstatic fans at the Second Prague Beat Festival held at Wenceslas Square in Prague, Czeckoslovakia, on December 22nd. The Nice played the gig without the services of the redoubtable Bazz. Overwork and drink had led him to the brink of a nervous breakdown and on Strat's instructions took a sabbatical.

The gig itself though was a triumph. The opener 'Rondo' was greeted by one of the mightiest roars Keith had ever heard: "I thought someone had turned something on somewhere. I just couldn't believe for a moment or two that it was the crowd." It was

heartening that the 'Ars Longa Vita Brevis' suite went down almost as well as 'Rondo'. It seemed a long way to go to just for one gig, in those days anyway. Tony Stratton-Smith was upbeat, "I'm glad we've come here. Glad we've made contact. It's a good thing to do."

CHAPTER **8**

THE ENGLISH
INVASION

"That's it,
I'm finished,
I'm off."

LEE JACKSON

THE START OF 1969 saw the Nice making preparations for a forthcoming tour of the United States. In the meantime, in February, the band took part in a concert at London's Institute Of Contemporary Arts. Being the sixties, it was a multi-media show where various art forms were combined to forge new associations and directions. It was The Nice's first foray into this kind of area and indicated the sort of development which was taking place in the rock and art worlds. Keith played an excerpt from Eduardo Lalo's 'Symphonie Espagnole' (Lee later added lyrics and it became 'Diary Of An Empty Day') with violinist John Mayer. [1] Brian collaborated with Mike Hugg from Manfred Mann, who played keyboards, and Lee read some poetry. In a spirit of openness and with a desire to break down barriers between audiences and performers, The Nice asked if the audience had any questions. They very quickly wished they hadn't as many questions pointedly dealt with Davy's departure. The band blatantly side-stepped such queries with the oft-used 'party line' about amicable splits and such like.

Above and right:
Boston Tea Party,
March, 1969

Ever since the band's previous US tour plans had been scuppered by the Albert Hall debacle, Strat had worked tirelessly in presenting a positive image of the band with regard to the USA. In a November 1968 interview with Go Magazine, he outlined his perspective, "We received far more publicity in America over the controversial Dr. Martin Luther King poster and the American flag incident than we imagined. They were both widely misunderstood, but it seems that some factions took them seriously and still resent what they believe to be the implications." It was clear that Stratton-Smith still expected a little bit more trouble on the tour.

One of the major problems The Nice had encountered during their first US dates was the use of inadequate hired equipment. However, this time round, they would ship out some of their own gear and ensure that a recuperated Bazz and Hammond technical boffin, Bill Hough, were sent out a week ahead to bed down any technical difficulties. Hough's great achievement was to get more sound from the Hammond. One of the major technical problems was that the Hammond Organs had to cope with American voltages, which were different from the UK. Hammond Organs operate by way of a generator motor, so the voltage and cycles of mains power was crucial. In the UK, it was 240 volts at 50 cycles, whilst in the USA it was 117 volts at 60 cycles. Without the correct voltage and cycles Hammond Organs will not work. So to avoid a repeat of previous problems, the band decided to buy two Hammonds while actually in the US. Strat bought a L100 and Leslie, with American voltage settings, from the Terry Reid Band. Keith decided he wanted yet more sound, so Strat bought the latest Hammond model, the A105 soon after he arrived. They brought over with them the Marshall amps, PA, guitars, drums, gongs and Leslies. The Leslies were converted to the American voltage settings. The 'dartboard' was also brought over. This was Keith's original custom-made Leslie-type cabinet. At that stage it was just a speaker cab used for his knife throwing routine. The knife throwing would sometimes go wrong, usually when Emerson forgot to sharpen them. As a result they would bounce out of the 'dartboard'. On one occasion it grazed Brian's arm and, on another occasion, one of the knives landed in between the legs of a girl sitting in the audience!

In the middle of this technological minefield, Strat pulled off a major coup by securing a unique deal with equipment manufacturer Ampeg. They agreed to supply the amps and cabinets for Keith and Lee and it wasn't long after that the band started appearing in adverts publicising the Ampeg gear. Today it would be called sponsorship - in 1969 this kind of endorsement had hardly been heard of.

Although many of the technical problems had been anticipated and pre-empted, the logistics of the tour fell far short of satisfactory. They were still playing one-off gigs and without a proper tour itinerary in place. Although some gigs were pre-arranged, the Boston Tea Party and the Fillmore East for instance, Stratton-Smith spent a lot of time talking to bookers, Premier Talent, to get information about the next few shows. This caused horrendous practical problems, and sometimes confusion reigned. On one occasion the crew drove to Pittsburgh only to find out they were in the wrong town. Bazz recalls one night when they finished at one o'clock in the morning in New York and had to be in Chicago the very same evening for another gig. Bazz and Alan Smith had to keep the supply of pills coming in order for them to drive through the night and make the show.

They were due to rendezvous with the band at the Holiday Inn, which was located in Lakeshore Drive. Bazz found the hotel but he couldn't see a way of getting to it. Exasperated, he asked a policeman who showed him the way. However, he was so exhausted and angry, he drove right into the hotel's entrance awning. There was a loud, extended banging and tearing sounds. At that very moment, the band was sitting in the bar with Strat who, in his affected upper class English accent announced "Ah, I take it Bazz has arrived!"

They were going down well at most gigs. But this wasn't England, as a gig in not far from Chicago was to illustrate. They played the gig to a very small crowd. At the end of the show Bazz went to collect the money. The promoter refused to pay the $1,000 as had been agreed. The promoter, still smarting from the poor turn-out told him, "No way!" When Bazz pressed the point, the promoter produced a gun. Bazz quickly retreated to the sanctuary of the dressing room. Strat, forgetting where he was, said, "I'll talk to him." "Tony, he's got a gun," was Bazz's worried reply. In the end the band settled for $300 and high-tailed it out of the place, chalking up the other $700 dollars to experience.

On the 9th and 10th April 1969, The Nice played the highlight of the tour at the Fillmore East, New York. They were due to appear with Ten Years After and Family. Bill Graham had booked

them in for two shows a day, one at 8pm and the other at midnight. A man of conviction, Graham had booked Ten Years After the previous year on the strength of hearing one single. It wouldn't be long before they would be one of the big hits at the upcoming Woodstock Festival. The publicity posters billed it as 'The English Invasion'. Before the opening show, Ten Years After keyboard player Chic Churchill goaded Keith, saying "So you don't use the American flag anymore?"

Fillmore East, New York, April 1969

As they approached the second show Keith called Bazz over to him, "When you put the Hammond on you'll notice a flag behind the reverb tray." Bazz's blood froze and his response was succinct, "Fucking hell!" "I really thought someone would kill him if he carried out (the threat)," Bazz recalls. In the end, Keith didn't get the matches out but did make full use of the flag. "I got into a bit of trouble in the States with the double organ," Keith later explained. "I split the audience right down the middle when I took the American flag and spread it out over the tipped organ which I left playing while going full blast on the other. Those who liked it, however, really dug it and even threw flowers." But many didn't like it. As Bazz pointed out, the American flag was everywhere in the States and they didn't take too kindly to foreigners messing around with it. Some shouted, "Go home, limey." Bill Graham didn't like it either but forgave them.

Lee Jackson, mindful of the trouble such stunts could get them into at this volatile time, was furious with Keith and gave him a verbal dressing down, "That's it, I'm finished, I'm off!" To Lee things were getting out of hand and Keith had put them in a really dangerous situation with his cavalier behaviour. Plus of course he was angry about the lack of consultation. Brian recalled it differently, insisting it wasn't a dangerous situation at all, but, as he put it philosophically, "Let's just say we were finding our edge!"

Strat pulled off a coup just before the first gig. He noticed that engineer Eddie Kramer was set up for recording. So he did a deal with Bill Graham to record The Nice. All four shows were recorded with startling results. Billboard magazine reviewed the gigs on the last day, with The Nice receiving a terrific endorsement from Ed Ochs, "The Nice, whose nowhere name belies the darkly subversive organ attack at the hands of the dedicated and demonic Keith Emerson, are at their best, as instrumentally mesmerising as any rock heavy in the highly respected profession of terrorising the senses." However, as he pointed out, it wasn't a one man show by any means, "Brian Davison on drums and Lee Jackson on bass assisted brilliantly in the mind-destruction, recorded for the discriminating head heavies on the Columbia-distributed Immediate label."

Interestingly enough Ochs described their most controversial hit 'America' as 'black comedy'. He described the band's music as 'symphonic fury'. It was a good shot too, after all the term 'progressive rock' was still some way from formulation. The following day they went to Detroit for three gigs with The Velvet Underground.

The tour went on for three months and got as far South as Miami, Florida. In fact Miami was

where CBS chose to trial release 'America' as a single, in spite of Bernstein. Lee thought that strange considering that in those days Miami was a millionaires' playground and so the audiences were hardly likely to be representative of most states. Surprisingly 'America' did well, selling 25,000 copies. Thence it was North to Toronto, Canada, where they played a gig with Brian Auger and Julie Driscoll. That gig went down well but there was a bit of trouble too. There were a few youth gangs, one of Scottish immigrant stock. Although not naturally disposed to violence, they were most certainly disposed to drinking a lot and after the show they were determined to have the autograph of Miss Driscoll. Keith takes up the story, "She signed them all 'Jools' as she usually does, but when they got outside, they figured she'd written 'Fools'. She had to explain it to them. A few of them came into our room and deliberately started provoking us, but we put them off as nicely as possible."

By the time the US tour came to an end the band were well and truly drained. No wonder, if the interview with Circus magazine is anything to go by. It seems that Jonathan Kundra was determined to dig up some juicy stories almost to the exclusion of the music. One exchange between Brian and Keith, however, illustrates that the band weren't always in accord with each other. Keith opined that groupies are doing the right thing by throwing themselves at musicians, especially foreign ones, "I think some of them have got the right idea. They like to make you happy because you're away from home. It's a nice kind of service, you know?" Brian's reply was, "You condescending bastard!"

As the tour finished sometime in May 1969, Emerson stayed on to play some sessions at the Record Plant in New York. Earle Doud was producing an album that was a 'who's who' of the music scene at the time. Included in the line-up were the likes of Eric Clapton, Jeff Beck, Mitch Mitchell and musicians from bands like Canned Heat, Traffic and Janis Joplin's band. Keith played on three tracks, Floyd Cramers 'On The Rebound', 'Mother Nature's Son' by The Beatles and 'Freedom Jazz Dance' by Don Ellis. Of course with that kind of line-up, there were many contractual wrangles (for example, Jeff Beck appeared as A.N. Other) which delayed the release of the album until 1973, when it appeared under the title of 'Music From Free Creek'. Beck claims that he was tricked and misled as to what the project was about, dubbing the album 'Music From Ripoffsville'.

Back in the UK and feeling refreshed, The Nice recorded a Top Gear session on June 2nd. It was notable for Roy Harper writing some impromptu lyrics for the Sonny Rollins number 'St Thomas'. Shortly after, they were booked to play at the Lyceum, London, with US band Steppenwolf and ended with them recording the biggest-ever attendance at the venue for a rock concert. They even had to make room for the press by constructing a special box for them as there was such a mass of fans around the stage. Another novel event at this gig, Brian remembers vividly, was when they opened up a section of the roof because it was so hot. The Nice performed with a choir and took the crowd by storm.

On June 21st 1969, the group were in Antwerp with Colosseum and Yes. Lee had a novel idea for the show based on Bernstein's 'West Side Story', "There was a stage at either end of the hall. My idea was as Yes finished their set with 'Something's Coming' we would start our set immediately at the other end with 'America'. Nobody else thought it was a good idea so it didn't happen."

By now Keith's musical vision was becoming ever more ambitious. At the 1969 Bath Festival of Blues, Emerson unveiled a Scottish Pipe Band. Keith decided to use Bob Sargeant - who later arranged the strings on the

The Nice and Yes prepare for the Antwerp Pop Festival, Belgium June 21st, 1969

Bath Festival
28th June, 1969

Left-right:
Tony Stratton-Smith,
Brian Davison,
Keith Emerson,
Lee Jackson

'Five Bridges' album - to do the sound. The problem however, as everyone acknowledged bar Keith, was he didn't know anything about sound; he was first and foremost an arranger. He turned round to Bazz and forlornly said, "I don't know what I'm down here for." Bazz had the perfect solution. He told Bob to stand at the mixing desk, which was on the side of the stage, with some headphones on, "And when Keith looks over just smile and he'll think you're doing the sound. When, in fact, it'll be me."

As The Nice were headlining they were able to effect an impressive, if not overblown, entrance for the Pipe band. They were caught in the spotlight as they marched around the perimeter of the crowd to the strains of the 'Karelia Suite'. Richard Green of the NME was impressed by the spectacle, although not quite sure of the success of this marriage, "The sound of The Nice and the pipes blended strangely and it was heartening to see a group experimenting with music in this way." They opened with 'America' and played two Dylan songs, the evergreen 'She Belongs To Me' and 'Country Pie', which Lee delivered in a 'shouting whispering voice'. In the end the pipe band played only a few numbers with The Nice. It was obvious that Keith was going to come up with more and more grandiose concepts. As time went on Keith could see the musical possibilities opening up before him and he was prepared to go in any direction. He brought to mind Orson Welles famous comment regarding a Hollywood studio, "It's the greatest electric train set a boy ever had!"

The fact that they were one of the top live acts was evidence enough of the extent they were gelling as a unit. However, unlike many contemporary acts, The Nice were not in line with the consensus that dictated that musical influences must be American. "The basic policy of the group is that we are a European group, so we are improvising on European structures," Lee explained. "Improvisation can be around any form of music - most of the early Led Zeppelin material was conceived by Jimmy Page while improvising... in a blues format, so we're taking European work. We're not black Americans, so we can't really improvise and feel the way they can." This aspect of policy was the main construct in the achievement of The Nice's unique sound, as Keith outlines, "I get most of my ideas through improvisations which occur during an evening. I find that you play your best if you're in a relaxed frame of mind."

Things did go wrong from time to time, however. Keith recalled the night they did a magical improvisation on 'She Belongs To Me', and the next night he took the song along the same lines and only to find that it didn't work. They played the same song in a completely different way and there was a problem, as Keith laughingly remembers, "We knew we had to get back out of it, but we didn't know how to. We were just standing there smiling at each other, but somehow we got back." As Brian had stated, it was all about finding your edge.

With the third Nice album due for imminent release, the band embarked on one of the biggest disasters of their career. Their second Irish tour was set up by Tony Stratton-Smith in order to promote two of the bands he managed. As well as The Nice there was The Bonzo Dog Doo Dah Band, fronted by the inimitable Vivian Stanshall. The Bonzos were memorably eccentric and their remarkable act shocked and delighted audiences. Even though they tended to create the impression of musical inadequacy, they were good players. Roy Flynn was a friend of Strat's, from the old days, and was now manager of Yes and got them on the tour as well. The idea was that they would trail blaze across a fledgling market by covering both Northern Ireland and the Republic of Ireland. Chris Welch compared the trip to something more akin to The Beatles' 'Magical Mystery Tour'. The spirits were high when they set off. Even Don Joy, the band's accountant came along as he sensed the prospect of an interesting trip.

BATH FESTIVAL OF BLUES
RECREATION GROUND

THIS SATURDAY
UNE 28th   FEATURING:

FLEETWOOD MAC
JOHN MAYALL • TEN YEARS AFTER
LED ZEPPELIN • NICE

CHICKEN SHACK • JON HISEMAN'S COLOSSEUM
MICK ABRAHAMS' BLODWYN PIG • KEEF HARTLEY
GROUP THERAPY • LIVERPOOL SCENE • TASTE
SAVOY BROWN'S BLUES BAND • CHAMPION JACK DUPREE
CLOUDS • BABYLON • PRINCIPAL EDWARD'S
MAGIC THEATRE • DEEP BLUES BAND • JUST BEFORE DAWN

D.J. **JOHN PEEL**

FRESHMENTS & HOT SNACKS WILL BE VAILABLE ALL DAY	In case of bad weather there will be a substantial amount of undercover accommodation	**IN ADVANCE** All day 18/6, Eve. only 14/6 **ON DAY** All day 22/6 Eve. only 16/6

TICKETS OBTAINABLE FROM BATH FESTIVAL BOX OFFICE,
ABBEY CHAMBERS, ABBEY CHURCHYARD, BATH, SOMERSET

On Friday, July 18th, they flew from London airport to Belfast, Northern Ireland. In the taxi on the way to the Hotel Europa (which later had the dubious honour of being the most bombed hotel in Europe), the driver asked Stanshall what he thought of the place. He didn't have his diplomatic hat on, "We've only been here five minutes - and so far it's been pretty awful." The gig that evening was scheduled for the Ulster Hall. A fleet of taxis were organised to take all the bands to the hall because - a bad omen - the coach they ordered failed to materialise. The afternoon was spent setting up the gear and jamming. Lee remembers being glared at by the Reverend Ian Paisley - this was his Sunday residency. The touring party were really quite ignorant of the political and cultural situation in Ireland and this was to get them in a little trouble - not least because of their dress. This was at a time when it was not uncommon to see people dressed in outlandish colours or combinations (early on in the band's life, Lee would wear a full set of Tibetan monk's robes and bells around his neck). Back home they were used to a few guffaws but all they extracted here was a lot of staring.

Chris Welch remembers the concert went down very well with the underdogs Yes getting the most applause. Chris wasn't disguising his love for the Bonzos (he recently wrote a book on Stanshall). "The Bonzos were brilliant throughout. How else? As a fan from their earliest days, it cheered me to find them as funny as ever, while having made their act supremely professional." It was quite a feat for a band that always seemed in the middle of chaos. They played rock and roll and they had their satirical numbers. It's doubtful whether they were completely understood - that goes for anywhere, not just Ireland. However, it's fair to say that the Bonzos act was not something the Irish had seen the likes of. Chris also observed that The Nice had dropped some of their gimmickry and concentrated more on the music rather than the visuals for this tour.

The situation in Northern Ireland was coming to a head between the Protestants and Catholics. Civil Rights wasn't just a prize to be gained in parts of America. Throughout the province, tensions were running high and there were many marches and counter-demonstrations from both sides of the political divide. The Catholics argued that the Protestants held all the positions of power and were using that power to discriminate against them in the field of jobs and housing. Chris Welch, writing many years later, owned up to the ignorance of mainlanders, "We saw strange rumblings of discontent, long before they were reported back in England; we noted the curious reaction when the Bonzos saxophonist innocently played 'Rule Britannia' in the street outside the Ulster Hall (warnings were growled from passers-by) and the bizarre practice in the villages we drove through, where every manhole, gutter pipe and telephone pole was painted red, white and blue. We assumed they were having a village fete." In Republican areas of Northern Ireland the chosen colours were green, white and orange (the 'tricolour' of the Republic of Ireland). The Belfast gig was the only one in Northern Ireland. The remaining two gigs were in the Republic of Ireland, Dublin and Cork on Saturday and Sunday.

The entourage headed south. There were three Transit vans, one for each of the band's gear, and a coach to carry the band members. They made their way through the picturesque lanes for a matinee concert in a boxing stadium in Dublin. The DJ for the trip was B.P. Fallon, who was travelling in the Nice's transit van with his girlfriend. The concert was attended by 1,000 fans, the best turnout of the whole tour. What they didn't realise was that in Ireland, generally, the populace hadn't quite caught up with rock music in the way that it had taken hold in the UK. Fashion lagged behind too. Only Yes had played the afternoon concert because the ticket sales were so bad, and once again they went down a storm, as the Irish crowds continually found their music more accessible than the other two acts.

Early on Sunday, 20th July 1969 they left Dublin to make their way to Cork. The entourage knew little about the venue but there were rumours of it being a football stadium. As with everything else on this tour they would have to wait and see. But when they got to Cork they realised that the stadium was actually some way out of the town. So with everybody thinking the journey was never going to end they finally found the stadium but then they couldn't find a way of getting in. Bazz recalled recently, "Spinal Tap has nothing on this gig." Through the gates they could see the stage set up opposite the main stand. The Bonzos driver, Fred Munt, drove down a ramp to find the entrance, but had no joy. When they did get in (they prudently removed some pillars to facilitate entry) they could see all was not well. On close inspection the stage could only be described as makeshift and there was a conspicuous lack of people, neither fans nor officials. Lee later found out that one of the reasons for the lack of fans was that an Irish show band had pasted their posters on top of the ones advertising the 'British hordes' gig.

Worse was to come when they followed a cable that came from the stage across the field. The crews started to set up the lights but a few of the lads started receiving electric shocks. The wire across the pitch was a succession of electric kettle leads that led to the changing room. They found to their horror it was connected to the light bulb socket - in other words, the wire was not earthed. Bazz quickly came to the conclusion that they couldn't possibly do the gig and informed Strat.

Ulster Hall, Belfast
18th July, 1969

Opposite: with
Chris Squire and
Bill Bruford

Chris Welch recalls what happened next, "The troupe of travelling musicians sat down on the pitch in their satin gear and cried with laughter." Just when it was thought things couldn't get worse, they did. This hot sunny afternoon had brought forward a terrible stench. In the next field was the Cork Pork Abattoir, and the air was rife! With spirits at an all-time low, Strat and the accountant hove into view. The troupe had found their scapegoat and there was rebellion in the air. Vivian Stanshall lit the torch of revolution as he cried, "Debag the rotters!"

Chris remembers the scene vividly, "The portly manager and his equally portly accountant were chased across the pitch by a yelling mob of musos intent on removing their trousers. Nobody had ever seen Strat run before - and he put on a surprising burst of speed." But they were saved by a unwitting diversion created by Bonzos sax player, Roger Spear, who chose that moment to let off a cherry bomb, one of the many used as a stage prop for the band.

By this time a few fans had turned up but were disappointed to be told the show was off. Meanwhile, the troupe of travelling musicians - and Strat - had already set off down a country lane to find the nearest pub. They decamped to the 'Silver Key' where Stanshall greeted the landlord with his effected upper class voice, "Landlord, 30 pints of your best Guinness." It wasn't long before the piano in the corner was utilised by Keith. He tore into 'Honky Tonk Train Blues',

'Nutrocker' and finally John Lennon's 'Give Peace A Chance', which was quickly adapted to 'Give Booze A Chance'. The locals loved what Chris called 'the craziest concert ever'. Things got out slightly out of hand when one of the locals accidentally smashed a glass on the piano - he had only been using it to beat time. For the musicians,
it was time to go home.

As the coach sped off to the airport, Chris was somehow left behind. He accepted a lift off one of the locals and they made their way to Shannon Airport. By the time he got on board everyone else was onboard and awaiting to go. He remembered Stanshall ranting and raving, "We are all nudists and we want our freedom." However, everyone remained fully clothed. Chris never did like flying and Viv fed off this fear and, turning to the stalwart MM journalist, said, "Chris, if we crash, we'll be fucking legends."

The Irish tour was a financial and artistic disaster, and Strat lost a great deal of money. However, such trips were the future; the world was opening up, communications and fast travel would facilitate this. It wasn't long before major-league bands would make foreign travel the mainstay and home gigs would be few and far between. This was a shrinking world, as Chris summed up, reflecting on the Irish jaunt, "Did we really watch Neil Armstrong make his lunar landing from the safety of London on the same day we got into a punch up in an Irish pub?" There was no doubt the world was getting smaller.

NOTES

1 John Mayer was born in India in 1943. He showed an aptitude in music from an early age and won a scholarship in Bombay. It was from this that he came to England to study at the Royal Academy of Music. He soon secured a position as violinist with the London Philharmonic Orchestra. He had ideas of fusing Indian and Western music as early as the 1950's, an ambition he was to realise in collaboration with Joe Harriott's jazz quintet. It was future manager, Don Norman, who came up with the name of the Harriot – Meyer outfit, Indo-Jazz Fusions. They were a great success but there was no doubt that Mayer was the leader of the band. Sadly Joe Harriott died in 1973 but John Mayer is still making music with his new Indo-Jazz fusions, which includes his son, Jonathon. John Mayer later worked with Keith Emerson on his 'Piano Concerto No.1' from ELP's *'Works Volume 1'.*

CHAPTER 9

EVERYTHING AS NICE AS STRAT MAKES IT

"That's not our
Keith up there,
it can't be!"

PETE RIMELL
(Keith's second cousin)

THE RELEASE OF THEIR THIRD ALBUM, simply called *'Nice'*, would be the litmus test of whether the group could at last translate their on-stage success to record sales. It would also confirm the wisdom of taking on Strat as their manager.

Even though the album had a mundane UK title, its American counterpart is anything but - it was released, intriguingly, as *'Everything As Nice As Mother Makes It'*. The half-studio and half-live format created the possibility of the best of the both worlds and, when it came out, that was precisely how it was received. 'Mother' actually refers to Tony Stratton-Smith, the name was coined by New Musical Express journalist and friend, Richard 'The Beast' Green, who remarked how Strat looked after the band like a 'mother hen'. He was always there to ensure things went smoothly for them. Consequently, they all came to love and trust him implicitly.

The studio side was mostly recorded at Trident studios in London. The opening cut is 'Azrael Revisited' and it is a good opener. Originally, the track had been recorded with Davy O'List and released as the B-side to 'The Thoughts Of Emerlist DavJack'. Keith uses a quote from Rachmaninov's 'Prelude in C Sharp Minor'. Rachmaninov had composed the piece after reading Edgar Allan Poe's vision of a man being buried alive and coming back to life. This was the reason Keith decided to de-tune the piano slightly - with drawing pins - to lend a slightly 'distressed' veneer to the sound. There's also some great percussion by Brian towards the climax. Keith described in the sleeve notes that he didn't endear himself to Amen Corner for the damage wrought to the piano - unable to tune the piano back to normal they were left with a 'Winifred-Atwell's-other-piano sound', as Keith jokingly called it. Lee remembers nothing about Amen Corner being there, but he remembers that they used Atwell's piano and they recorded 'Azrael' in between her sessions.

The next track is Tim Hardin's 'Hang On To A Dream'. Lee first met Hardin on their first visit to the States in 1968 and loved his work, especially this song, mostly for its sheer simplicity. The band ran through the melody on piano as they did with most things and they soon came to the conclusion that this was the instrument to use. However, this track gave Brian more than a few problems. He tried to construct a rhythm for it starting with hi-hat and adding bass drum and tambourine once the song got moving but, try as he might, it didn't work and in the end he settled for just the tambourine. Duncan Browne conducted the choir to immense effect.

When they played at the Sheffield City Hall, the idea was for Brian to hit a triangle on a string and then swing it in the air to achieve the shimmering effect every time Lee sang the lyric 'dream'. When Lee did just that he noticed an immediate audience reaction. What had happened was that just as Brian hit the triangle the string had snapped and as a result the triangle had been catapulted across the stage. Lee remembers asking the audience, "Has anybody got any string?" They tried it again but to no avail as everybody cracked up.

'Diary Of An Empty Day' had been previously performed at a 1969 gig in London with John Mayer, shortly after Davy left. Lee wrote this in the middle of a 'writer's block', hence the words 'I can't think what to say. My mind's a blank today'. In an interview with IT/SS magazine he gave an insight into his method, "I can't sit and write words in a crowd or jot things down on envelopes... I like to be completely on my own and just sit or lay on my bed with a cassette and a bit of paper scribbling." Lee was inspired, or otherwise, to write these words on a very dull journey from Newcastle to Birmingham. It was then they gave it a more apt title. Melody Maker paid particular attention to Lee's playing on this "complex progression that involves an entire octave. Lee Jackson's bass is particularly good here." The acoustic guitar at the end is played by Lee, who just managed to get by with his limited knowledge of the six-string.

At the time of recording, Keith was heavily into jazz and the last studio track illustrates this beautifully. 'For Example' is a tour de force, although Lee thought it was all getting too complicated at this stage. The opening actually came from a rehearsal warm up; party recorded in London and partly in New York, the joins certainly don't show. The first set of horns are provided by the London connection, Alan Skidmore, Joe Harriott, Chris Pine and Kenny Wheeler. To say it swings is an understatement and there's a wonderfully Gothic middle section played by Keith. The piano drives the last part of the cut and Brian adds some funky vibraphone. The second set of horns were recorded in New York and were played by Joe Newman, Pepper Adams and John Surman. There's some top grade playing here and they even manage to insert cheeky references to 'Norwegian Wood' and 'America'. It's a great side of music but it does strike one that Keith was having a touch of writing block too, with three of the four songs being non-originals.

The second half of the album is culled from the famous Fillmore East gigs of April 1969. The original intention had been to record a live album. It was something they had talked about for a while. But for some reason they weren't happy with all the material - hence the studio side. The opener is 'Rondo (69)' (now renamed) and is considerably faster than the versions played in '67/'68. This was something that was to be more and more of a feature in Keith's playing. It's simply the best version of the song ever recorded. The fact that it contained Keith's Hammond-wrestling antics led to a crisis in the clothing department, as he kept splitting his trousers, something which is referred to humorously on the album sleeve with the 'urgent telegram' back to England for 'more trousers'.

The final track is the live staple 'She Belongs To Me' by Bob Dylan. Chris Squire once said recalling the early days of Yes, "We wanted the big sound of The Nice but with more melodies." This is the big sound that Yes admired so much. It's Keith's best work on the Hammond bar none, caught just before speed of execution began to obsess him, his playing exhibiting great variety. It's not hard to understand why this band was often judged the best act on the planet. Towards the end of the track when Lee sings the line 'You're just a walking antique...' it ushers in a most dynamic instrumental section which captures the magic of a great band in full flow. At one point even

Bazz Ward with
the 'Fire Engine'
The Nice's tour
van, in1969

Keith is upstaged by this fantastic rhythm section. There are so many great runs it's difficult to keep tabs on it all. Lon Goddard of Melody Maker described the climax as "The finale to a monumental performance, it is the epitome of their musical character and stands magnificently alone in music today."

This track illustrates how musicians sometime are not the best judges of how a gig has gone. "I felt completely off form," explained Keith. "When we got on stage I forgot it was being recorded, but when we came off I thought it must have sounded really bad. Then a guy burst into our dressing room and said 'Come and listen to this'. I couldn't believe the sound they had got. We were all really knocked out." All four shows were recorded and in the second part of this song there is a little bit of trickery, for it combines the tapes of two performances for one of the numbers. For some reason they decided to use 'She Belongs To Me' in two parts. No matter, it doesn't detract from their finest hour. The strange studio/live format of this album would, in fact, be repeated again for the last two albums.

In an NME article by Richard Green, he began his piece by stressing the uniqueness of the band, "Musical competence and showmanship rarely go hand-in-hand." In the interview Keith declared himself happy with the album in both sound and quality but wasn't too happy with Immediate and the album cover. The original idea was to include photos from a London shoot. However, it's obvious from Keith that Immediate were fending off the band with regard to the photos, "We went to Hamburg and Immediate said they were still being used. When we got back, we phoned and were told that the proofs weren't ready, so we went to the printers and had a look at the proofs ourselves... I nearly cried, they were so poor." Lee explained recently what had happened, "Keith had included his own snaps of places we'd been to like Kennedy Airport, Rome and even Weston-Super-Mare, to save the hassle of getting them developed himself. Andrew Oldham saw them and preferred Keith's 'home snaps'." In spite of having an agreement about passing proofs the band were completely circumvented. Furthermore, 25,000 sleeves had already been printed.

9TH NAT
JAZZ·POP
BLUES F
Previously at Wind

An NJF/MARQU

Artistes Appearir
(in alphabetical orc

AFFINITY
AYNSLEY DUNBAR
BABYLON
BLOSSOM TOES
BONZO DOG BAND
BREAKTHRU'
CHICKEN SHACK
CHRIS BARBER
CIRCUS
CUBY'S BLUES BAN
DRY ICE
EAST OF EDEN
ECLECTION
FAT MATTRESS
GROUNDHOGS
HARD MEAT
JIGSAW
JO-ANN KELLY
JUNIORS EYES
KEEF HARTLEY

Such problems aside, the album was an immediate hit and reached No.3 in the UK charts. Ironically, the very success of the album led inevitably to a big row between the band and Immediate Records. The lack of royalty payments, the sleeve debacle and the general inertia speeded up the severance of the Immediate Records connection. Strat was on the verge of finalising the creation of his own record company, Charisma Records. It was a label, which in time would boast The Nice as the first major signings on its roster of bands.

On the 10th August, The Nice appeared at the 9th National Jazz and Blues festival at Plumpton, Sussex - their third consecutive appearance there. Whereas two years ago they appeared on the main stage as a backing band to Pat Arnold, this time they were appearing with a 40-piece orchestra conducted by Joseph Eger, and the Scottish pipe band that had accompanied them for the Bath Festival a few weeks earlier. Keith first heard of Eger on their last tour of the States and it was a concept that appealed to him immediately, as he explains from an interview with Tops Pops, "I heard he had been experimenting with mixed-media concerts. The New York Symphony did a concert using the Joshua Light Show from the Fillmore East. I went to see him and played an arrangement of 'Ars Longa Vita Brevis' to see if he would be interested in doing something with us. He liked the idea and agreed to come over."

The Nice headlined on Saturday. The orchestra started off with 'Brandenburger'. "Keith's organ ranged over the orchestra and violins linked movements of the piece," Melody Maker reported. "Much like a classical music concept, it twisted between jazz and chamber ensemble influences." As in Bath, the pipers entered the gig with the 'Karelia Suite', and they marched around the stage to tremendous applause. It was at this point that Keith unleashed his spectacular offering, as Melody Maker dramatically portrayed it, "Emerson tipped his organ on its side, threw every switch in the keyboard, hauled it around in a circle as he played and pounced on it, slamming it back into the immense musical production." There is no doubt audiences were seeing something totally unprecedented. And they were lapping it up.

8·9·10 AUGUST
1969

PLUMPTON

RACE COURSE
near LEWES, SUSSEX

KEITH TIPPETT JAZZ GROUP
KING CRIMSON
LONG JOHN BALDRY
LONDON CAST OF 'HAIR'
MAGNA CARTA
MICK ABRAHAMS' BLODWYN PIG
NOEL MURPHY
PETER HAMMILL
RON GEESIN
ROY HARPER
SOFT MACHINE
THE FAMILY
THE JAZZ SOUND OF JOHN SURMAN
THE NICE
THE PENTANGLE
THE PINK FLOYD
THE SPIRIT OF JOHN MORGAN
THE STRAWBS
THE VILLAGE
THE WALLACE COLLECTION
THE WHO
YES !

The band managed to get in a solo 'She Belongs To Me'. The crowd stood, jumped and cheered the band to the echo as they put ever more pressure on the stage barriers. 'Rondo' was imaginatively interwoven with the 'Troika' movement from Prokofiev's suite 'Lieutenant Kije' and made a spectacular combination with its application of the deft and the raunchy (Keith had realised the two pieces shared a common time signature).

After the gig, Richard Green asked Lee, "What was there left to do?" Lee's reply was enthusiastic and flippant, "This is just the embryo. It's a question of where we can do it, not what we can do. If we could do it at Carnegie Hall with a full orchestra - that's between 90 and 120 - we would. We did this tonight for the giggle of doing it for the entertainment of the crowd." The headline in Melody Maker was 'Who and Nice steal Plumpton Festival'. All agreed it was brilliant! This is Lee's favourite gig with an orchestra because the chemistry was right that night. He came off stage so high he downed four quadruple brandy-and-cokes in 20 minutes!

At this time Keith's reputation as a showman was sky-high. This was rather strange considering Keith's normal quiet demeanour offstage. Keith's second cousin Pete Rimell remembers vividly the first time he saw Keith in The Nice. It was an all night gig at the Birmingham Bingley Hall (where now the International Convention Centre complex stands). During the performance he was transfixed and confused, "That's not our Keith up there, it can't be." How was it that his on-stage persona could be so different? Keith explained at the time, sometimes paradoxically, "It's a natural instinct for me to perform in this way on stage. The music is very important, but the music can take you to certain heights... You have to go one stage further, and my complete climax comes through violence. It's through exercising this violence on stage that I can be subdued off stage." Straight after the gig Pete went backstage and was reunited with the Keith he knew.

There was a feeling that with all of the mixed-media projects that by now were coming in torrents, Keith was beginning to eclipse Lee and Brian, and this brought into question the idea of The Nice being a band of equals. Even with an orchestra Keith was always the star because his was now the lead instrument. This is not to denigrate Lee and Brian's contribution; as a trio The Nice were rated as one of the best live acts in the country.

One of the key factors behind the live success was the band's ability to project their sound. In fact, prior to Davy's exit they had never really bothered with sound that much because it was never an issue. However, Davy's exit sharpened the debate about sound. Bazz remembers that, in the early rehearsals as a three-piece, the band asked him to itemise the differences in the sound made by the new configuration to that made by the quartet. It was a result of Bazz's assessment that they realised that Davy's sound had to be replaced. Consequently, the means to boost that level of sound quickly became the number one priority, but it wasn't going to be easy.

They were so successful in this it even created an unforeseen edge in the band. A great deal of competition developed in the band in this area. It started with what was known in the band as Emerson's 'Berlin Wall Of Sound'. Bill Hough had made major strides in beefing up the levels that Leslie cabinets could take from the Hammonds. By mid 1969 Keith still had his dual-Hammond attack, the L100 and the A105. Each Hammond had a Leslie 122 Cabinet with an extra Horn Section (custom-built by Bill Dunne). He also had 2 Marshall 4x12" Speaker Cabinet Systems driven by a Marshall 100 Watt PA amp and his custom built Leslie (this was also known as the 'dartboard' because Keith threw his knives at it), also powered by a Marshall PA amp.

This extra horn section was the upper part of a Leslie which gave the sound a lot more 'top', due to the fact of what remained of the Leslie was shorn of its bass section. This was an idea that Bill Dunne had developed after seeing The Band on the second US tour. They were on the same bill as The Nice and had used an upper part of a Leslie as a salvage job after their van crashed.

Bill Hough later built a mixer unit that was plugged in to both Hammonds because Keith wanted the sound of the Hammonds to come out of all the Leslies at the same time. Bazz explained recently what happened, "The L100 goes into the mixer unit and then to the Leslie and the Rotor Leslie nearest to it and the same with the A105. Both Hammonds are connected to the 'dartboard'

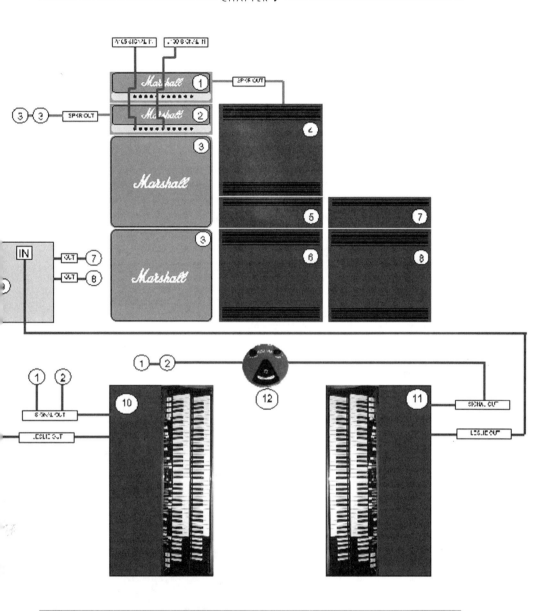

KEITH EMERSON'S STAGE RIG

1	Marshall 100W head	**7**	Leslie 122 Roto Top (L100)
2	Marshall 100W head	**8**	Leslie 122 (L100)
3	Marshall 4x12" Speaker Cab	**9**	Ampeg Combo / Mixer Unit
4	'Dartboard' Leslie (100W)	**10**	Hammond A105 Organ
5	Leslie 122 Roto Top (A105)	**11**	Hammond L100 Organ
6	Leslie 122 (A105)	**12**	Dallas Arbiter Fuzz Face

Wiring by Bazz, Artwork by Phil

Leslie and Marshall cabinets by way of Marshall amplifiers. The mixer unit then sends the signal from each organ to all the Leslie cabinets." By using Marshall amps in the set-up there was yet another interesting facet. As Bazz explains, "This enabled Keith to use the 'Fuzz Face distortion unit' for the sound on the 'Karelia Suite'. The feedback was created by switching the L100 off but it was still connected to the Marshall amps. Which, in fact, became a giant pick-up."

The only drawback to the system was that the tremelo/chorale switches would only work on the pair of Leslies connected to each Hammond. So Bazz would have to be on hand to switch off the tremelo/chorale if Keith went to a different Hammond. The mixer unit utilised an Ampeg combo amp as the power supply and so Bazz could boost the signal and add reverb if required. This was an important innovation and was developed over a long time and a lot of trial and error. Bazz would not elaborate on the 'inner workings' as, although he had helped in their development, "They're Keith's sound and that means they belong to him. You can duplicate the equipment but not the sound. Let's face it, Ludwig could build a similar drum kit to the one used by Led Zeppelin, but only John Bonham could reproduce the same sound. It also took Keith's unique talent to make the Hammond sound the way it did."

As a result Keith finally nailed down the Brother Jack Macduff 'Rock Candy' sound he had been looking for since he first took up the instrument. As he explains, "You use a Marshall amplifier with the presence and treble turned full up – it exaggerates the contact sound."

Over the years, there's been a lot of talk about the Hammonds that Keith was using in his time with The Nice. Strangely even Keith himself has forgotten, judging by some interviews he's given. Bazz puts the record straight, "Apart from the odd time when we had the B3 and C3 as spares, Keith only used the L100 and A105 during his time with the band. And I should know because I helped to fix them and heave them around half the world!"

The Hammond organ had existed since the early 1930s and had hitherto coped because musical environments had not yet stretched the instrument to beyond it's design capabilities, with regard to sound requirements. In the mid '60s a swath of new musicians - Brian Auger, Graham Bond[1], Steve Winwood - were all using the instrument to marvellous effect. Keith had highlighted this problem in 1965 when he wrote to the Hammond Organ Company. Even though he was rebuffed, it was only a matter of time before the onslaught of electric music via the vehicle of rock and roll would illustrate that necessity is the mother of invention, and it was Keith's Hammond techies, Bill Hough and Bill Dunne, who were inventing ways of modifying the instrument (Hough had worked for Georgie Fame before The Nice).

WINTER GARDENS, MALVERN

FRIDAY, JULY 4th, 1969

•

THE NICE

+

TEA & SYMPHONY

•

8.30 — 11.30 p.m.   Licensed Bar   Admission 12/6

Lee was using a Vox Wyman bass guitar and it wasn't long before he started to acquire his own 'wall of sound'. Initially he used 4 Marshall 1x18" Cabinets with two Marshall Amps, but after a meeting with Newcastle Amp Maker, Greg Burman, it was beefed up even more, although it made moving the thing incredibly difficult. After Burman weaved his magic, Lee had 2 Special Cabinets each containing 4x12" speakers and 4x15" speakers. They stood 6' high x 4'6" wide x 18" deep. Lee had wanted four separate cabinets but Burman had given him two sets of two cabinets joined together, making shifting them a nightmare for the roadies.

Brian always had a pretty basic kit, he played George Hayman drums, his main indulgence being a set of Paiste Chinese gongs that were given to him by the company.

Around the release of the third album, Emerson recorded with singer Rod Stewart. The chaotic nature of the session stuck in Keith's mind, "I remember members of The Faces being in the studio at the time. The session itself wasn't very organised, it was more like everyone jamming as a band... It was a track that was created in the studio. Rod Stewart didn't have his own ideas or particular way of working, and he didn't seem to want to tell people what to do either." The track was called 'I Wouldn't Ever Change A Thing' and appeared on his album *'An Old Raincoat Will Never Let You Down'*. Anyway it was an easy £50 for Keith. Also around this time The Nice appeared on a track for Roy Harper's album *'Flat Baroque and Berserk'*. The track, 'Hells Angels', was recorded at Abbey Road. Old T-Bones drummer Brian Walkley drove Keith to the session.

On August 22nd 1969, they played at the all-night Humberside Festival, in a place called Sproatley, taking the place of Thunderclap Newman at the last minute. Chicken Shack, Pretty Things and Third Ear Band were also on the bill. This was small beer compared to the Isle Of Wight Festival they played six days later. The Nice topped the bill on Friday and went down a storm - making a rare festival appearance as a trio - opening with a relatively new addition to the repertoire, Tchaikovsky's 'Pathetique'.

"The performance of the evening!" was how Brian Hinton described the Nice's set in a history of the festival entitled 'Message To Love'. "It seemed incredible in those more innocent times that a three-man group could produce such sounds. They concluded with their electric treatment of the 'Intermezzo From The Karelia Suite', booming over the creek in the first hour of Saturday morning. Each instrument, despite the tremendous volume of noise, was clear, and they served up a straight set of hard playing... Drummer Brian Davison was (still) compared by many to Ginger Baker, while bassist Lee Jackson added hoarse vocals to the overall mix."

Most of the pre-publicity of the Festival had focussed on the appearance of Bob Dylan the day after but this was something of a disappointment for many, as the singer was kept waiting for hours. When he got to play, he performed for just over an hour. The Nice were determined to see Dylan, cancelling a gig in order to do so. Others were just as determined. There were hundreds of celebrities in attendance and Lee remembers the queue for the loo was particularly long for the women. The sight of people like Yoko Ono and Marianne Faithfull queuing up amused him.

The schedule for the following month could only be described as lunacy. October 9th saw them play the first of five consecutive gigs, scattered all over Europe. They played at the end of a pier in Oslo, Norway. It was a nightmare as Keith recalled in an interview in 1996 with Impressions Magazine, "Everybody was smoking weed and you only had to get on stage and you would get a high yourself. During 'Rondo' this lady jumped up on stage and took all her clothes off and danced around!" Heady days indeed.

<u>Equipment used by the Nice.</u>

<u>KEITH EMERSON.</u>

One Hammond L 100 Organ and One Hammond A 105 Organ.
Two Leslie 122 Organ Tone Cabinets (one for each organ)
On the Leslie for the L 100, there is a special Tweeter Unit as well.
Both organs are then fed into two extra cabinets, one a Marshall 4 x 12
speaker cabinet, and one a special "custom" built Leslie cabinet, which Keith
had made to his own specifications. These are powered by two 100 watt
Marshall PA Amplifiers, one set on Treble, and one set on Bass. In addition
the direct feed from the L 100 goes through a Dallas Arbitor Fuzz Face, which
is used mainly on the Karelia Suite. All repairs to these organs, by the way,
are carried out by Bill Hough, of Compton Organ Co. (Who went with us to USA),
and is at present designing an organ for Keith.

<u>LEE JACKSON.</u>

One Vox Wyman Bass, Grey Model Herco Plectrums, and for strings,
Lee uses Rotosound Flat wound on 4,3, and 2nd string
and Rotosound Round wound on 1st, as this is best for bowing. The Boys are
made by Paul Veigt of London.

Amplification consists of one Marshall 100 watt Bass Amp, and one Marshall
100 watt Multi purpose amp. These are connected to four Marshall 1 x 18"
Bass Cabinets, two set on treble and two set on Bass, and connected by a
"split" guitar lead.

<u>BRIAN DAVIDSON</u>

Brian uses a George Hayman Drum Kit comprising of
One 18"x18" Bass Drum
One 14"x14" Floor Tom Tom
One 12"x12" Tom Tom
One 14"x5" Snare Drum
The fittings are a mixture or Premier (Hi-Hat) Rose Morris (Stands) and
Ludwig (High speed Foot Pedal)
Brian also has a standard Slingerland Kit which he keeps at home for
practice.
Cymbals are
Pair 16" Avedis Zyldjan Hi Hat Cymbals
One 18"   "   "   Fast Ride Cymbal
One 20"   "   "   Crash Cymbal
One 22"   "   "   Crash Cymbal

Brian also has a set of Paiste Chinese Gongs, which were given to him when
the Nice played in Switzerland.
For sticks, he uses Slingerland Dave Bailey, while awaiting some made for
him by Rose Morriss.

NOTES

1 The Graham Bond Organisation played a gig with The Nice in 1968 at Exeter University. Lee remembers the toilet was too crowded, so they decided to relieve themselves into pint jars. Bond came in, noticed the glasses with light coloured liquid in them and said, putting one to his lips, "Ah, scrumpy cider." He spat it out very quickly.

THE FIVE MIGHTY BRIDGES

"The object is to break
down the barriers.
There shouldn't be any
restrictions."

BRIAN DAVISON

IN THE SUMMER OF 1969, The Nice were commissioned to write a piece of music for the Newcastle Arts Festival, Lee's hometown. Michael Emmerson, who had promoted a gig on their first Northern Ireland tour, was on the Festival team. Keith wrote the piece which would become the 'Five Bridges' suite in the strangest place, as he recalled in the early '80s, "I was on a plane with these turboprop engines, and when I leaned my head against the window I could feel their rhythm and hear all the pitches coming out through the undertones. I drew out some bar lines on an sick bag and wrote the theme to the suite right there in the air."

The plan was to fully orchestrate the piece for a recording, but the band didn't have the orchestra for the premier and played it as a three piece at the Arts Festival. They went on the stage of Newcastle's City Hall at midnight to a tumultuous roar from the fans. Lee's lyrics beautifully capture the spirit of Newcastle. St James Park is the home of Newcastle United, and Lee describes the Saturday afternoon ritual of the football match, the drinking afterwards, etc. It's too often the case that the music overshadows the lyrics but Lee's words are a fitting homage to his home town.

Richard Williams of Melody Maker remembered the crowd wouldn't let the band go. The acoustics were just right - Keith would remember that and come back and record 'Pictures At An Exhibition' at the same venue with ELP - Brian's performance was described as 'free and swinging'.

The following day The Nice set off to the First German Blues Festival in Essen, West Germany. They had to drive down to London Airport, where there was some doubt as to whether they could get their gear on the plane due to an industrial dispute. It was Bazz who saved the day, goading the desk clerk with "I'll bet you £25 you can't fit all our gear on the plane." Although they were a few quid lighter, the gear did wing its way to Essen on time.

Over the three days a host of big names performed, including Fleetwood Mac, Muddy Waters, Pink Floyd, Deep Purple and Alexis Korner. Events would conspire to make this a festival to remember. The problem started when about 2,000 fans arrived without tickets. When they were told that the venue was sold out, a number of them fought their way past security guards and gained entrance to the hall. The police arrived with tear gas and truncheons rained down on the fans. Outside , bluesman Alexis Korner and the rhythm section of Taste pacified the crowds that couldn't get in. The Nice performance was hindered by a lack of beef to the sound. Richard Williams recalled that they sounded a little 'tinny' in the vast auditorium, and he felt Deep Purple took the honours that night.

The punishing schedule continued as they made their way to Amsterdam the following day, at the famous Concertgebouw hall. The final gig of the five-day madness was Dunstable, England, and there were terrible problems getting some of Emerson's gear back from Amsterdam. One of the Hammonds hadn't got a cover and so the airport wouldn't load it. They said it had to go on the next freight plane. In the ensuing argument the band finally got an assurance it would go with the other gear on the passenger plane. However, after take-off an official came to them and told them the Hammond hadn't been loaded and would follow on the next freight plane. Keith was horrified and told Bazz to go and get it. "Keith, we're 20,000 feet up, what do you want me to do, dive out and swim back to Holland?" came Bazz's quick reply.

In the end, the instrument was returned but was slightly damaged, to the extent that Bill Hough and Bazz were working on it when the band came on stage for the Dunstable show. Bazz had picked up a lot of quick remedies over the years when it came to repairing the Hammond. In order to repair keys broken by Emerson's knives, a couple of coke bottles would be used to raise one keyboard section, to enable work on the lower section.

The next big gig presented a different set of technical problems. They were appearing at the Fairfield Hall in Croydon, London, to perform with the Sinfonia Orchestra. Although the band were without a current deal, it was understood that this gig would be recorded and released as 'Five Bridges'. For all his experience on the road with The Nice, Bazz had never had to mike up a symphony orchestra. Also, the 17-foot concert grand piano Keith insisted on using was too big to fit on the stage with the orchestra and the other gear. In the end the band had to get special permission to leave the lift doors open, leaving the piano partly in the lift for the duration of the gig.

Anticipating the difficulties of balancing the sound of the rock band and orchestra, Bazz had prudently put a call out for some help to the roadie fraternity. Even Charlie Watkins (owner of WEM - Watkins Electrical Music) came down to help. For such a high profile and well trailed concert as this, there was an awful lot of improvising behind

'Five Bridges' Concert at Fairfield Hall, Croydon 17th October, 1969

the scenes. In the end, Bazz decided to bluff it. He realised they couldn't mic every part of the orchestra and get it in synch with the band. Bazz's solution, born more of desperation than of expertise, was to use three large microphones strategically placed to provide optimum coverage - they can be seen on the album cover.

King Crimson were supporting, the running order dictating that they went on at 7.45 but had to be off stage by 8.30. Greg Lake doesn't remember much about this gig but does recall seeing Keith furiously pacing round during rehearsals trying to get the sound right, looking rather worried. He had good reason to be alarmed as The Nice had only had a few hours rehearsal together with the orchestra. There was a lot at stake - the orchestra cost two and a half times what the band were paid for this gig, and then there was the cost of bringing conductor Joseph Eger over from the States.

The printed running order for the show suggested that they were trying to create an ambience more associated with the 'classical' rather than the 'rock'. The orchestra opened with 'Symphonie Fantastique' by Berlioz, which received strong applause. The band then joined the orchestra for the 'Karelia Suite'. The horn players - Alan Skidmore, Joe Harriott, Chris Pine and Kenny Wheeler, appearing ostensibly for the 'Five Bridges' suite were liberally employed throughout the concert, most notably on 'For Example'. They saved 'Five Bridges' until almost the end. The sight of Keith moving from piano to organ was an inspiring sight and went down well with the crowd.

The show ended with the orchestra playing Prokofiev's 'Troika' followed by the band playing 'Rondo', both combined into a continuous ten minute showstopper. They left the stage to an impressive five minute ovation. They returned to encore with 'Rondo' and 'She Belongs To Me' without the orchestra but joined by Alan Skidmore.

Ironically, the band that had helped take rock music away from being an accompaniment to dancing had come full circle. The set saw fans dancing in the aisles for much of the gig. As 'Rondo' kicked in these dancing fans surged to the foot of the stage and were soon joined by a many others. No doubt to get a closer view of Keith's antics with the Hammond.

The after-show relief was tangible and Keith in particular was 'buzzing'. Everyone was so glad it was over and that it had gone so well. There had been a degree of tension in the build-up to this gig. It had only been a few days earlier that Keith had told Brian that the orchestra would be doing the whole gig, Brian having thought the orchestra would only play on 'Five Bridges'. Even though he was initially angry at not being consulted, Brian soon got behind Emerson's vision.

However, playing with the orchestra led Lee to a devastating conclusion. "I got a terrible awakening when I discovered that symphony musicians couldn't swing," he told Par Lindh in September 1994. "They had no concept of playing in time and rhythm." Asked if that meant they were stiff, he replied, "Very stiff, wooden. String players now aren't. Young players have grown up in the era of rock. These were people who didn't know anything about rock." Even though Lee acknowledges certain members of the orchestra did exhibit a certain amount of disdain towards rock, many of them were intrigued with what they were trying to do. Lee even managed to discern an instrument-driven division, "A lot of the horn players were jazz men at one time or another - the strings and the oboe were the main dissenters." There was a comical moment when a member of the orchestra asked Lee a question about the band's approach, "How do know when to come in without a score?" "When he [Keith] gives me a nod," Lee replied deadpan. "Well, how do you know when to get back?" the classical musician retorted. "When he gives me another nod."

With that in mind there is no doubt that Keith and Joseph Eger were pioneers. Keith's admiration for Eger is obvious from the sleeve notes to the album. The bridges of the title of the piece was also a reference to the musical bridges that two men felt were being built by collaborations of this kind. "Since that first meeting we have on various occasions been catalysts in combining the music from our different backgrounds forming sometimes a fusion," Keith explained, "And other times a healthy conflict between the orchestra, representing possibly the establishment, and the trio representing the non-establishment; ourselves having complete trust in a rebellious spirit and highly developed, broad minded, music brain whose reformed ideas have been frowned upon, almost spat upon by some so-called music critics. That being Joseph Eger, the fighter."

It must be stated that there were other pioneers on the scene. In 1967 The Moody Blues had recorded the concept album 'Days Of Future Passed' with the London Philharmonic Orchestra. One month before The Nice recorded 'Five Bridges', Jon Lord of Deep Purple had premiered his 'Concerto For Group And Orchestra' at the Royal Albert Hall, conducted by Malcolm Arnold.

Keith and Jon Lord had been in contact for quite a while - Lord wanted Keith to perform at his concert but it never came off - and they wished each other the best of luck before embarking on their own genre-busting projects. Both bands attended the other's concert to provide mutual support.

Lord was just as open-minded as Keith as to the benefits of these mixed-media projects: "I'm more interested in the pop but there's a tremendous amount of enjoyable and emotional release in classical music. A lot of my generation don't believe this, but it's as exciting as the pop world. It's not stuffy." Lord also fended off claims he was being pretentious. It was something that Strat was also aware of, "There's something in Keith's ideas, but he knows it's still in the novelty phase. But it's a matter of logic that if you can harmonise orchestral texture with the primitive line-up of a group you can hopefully expect something new and good will come out of it. Keith just does not feel he's quite got there yet." For Lord though, his 'Concerto for Group And Orchestra' was a one-off event. Keith wanted to take this experiment much further and so did the rest of the band.

After the recent Plumpton festival, Brian had been more forthcoming about the philosophy behind the mixed-media projects, "The object is to break down the barriers of music. It is to try to make people realise that music is music and cannot be categorised. We'd never say we would stick to just three people, we can play with one orchestra, two orchestras or just have four people playing other instruments depending on what sort of sound we want to create at that moment. There shouldn't be any restrictions." Obviously there was a creative element in coming up with their own pieces but there was also a dynamic which led them to use other people's music.

As Keith stated just after the Croydon gig, "Basically we feel that there are elements of music which are dying out in the sense they're becoming less popular - jazz and classical music in some forms are in danger of dying out because they don't relate to things of today. We're taking these elements, adapting them to our own style and joining them to make a new kind of music." The evidence that they took up the challenge is incontrovertible. On the *'Five Bridges'* album they had their own original concerto, they fused Bob Dylan and J.S. Bach, and they used pieces by Tchaikovsky and Sibelius, combining them with the band and orchestra as well as liberal amounts of jazz licks from Keith's Hammond. All in all, it was quite a blend.

After the heady acclaim of their mixed-media projects, it was soon back to bread-and-butter touring for the band. On the 29th October 1969, The Nice opened a tour of Europe with a gig in Basle, Switzerland. In the aftermath of the gig they adjourned to party at the hotel. Keith located a piano and played a well-received impromptu set. However, while Keith was still playing, a man in a very smart suit and short hair walked over to the piano and asked if he could trade licks. Everyone was aghast. Did this man know who he was talking to... the greatest rock keyboard player around? Lee remembers they sat back and knowingly nodded to each other in anticipation of a really good laugh. The young man in the suit then proceeded to blow everyone away with a brilliant display of musicianship. How good it was can be gauged by Chris Welch's comment many years later, "Mr Emerson was not best pleased at these incursions into his territory." The name of the mystery piano player was Patrick Moraz.

The European tour ended on Bonn, West Germany, on 7th November and just two days later they were once again taking part in a mixed-media extravaganza at the London Lyceum with John Mayer and The City Of London Ensemble. They were supported by the highly rated Rare Bird, who were signed to Strat's Charisma label. The show took a similar format to the Croydon gig and they played 'Five Bridges' again. The set also included Dylan's 'Country Pie' and Hardin's 'Hang On To A Dream' and opened up with 'She Belongs To Me'.

It was an evening of mixed high entertainment. Keith asked John

Mayer to play something exciting and he came up with a piece of Hungarian Gypsy dance music, 'Gypsy Carnival', ably backed by The Nice. The audience were treated to a rare drum solo from Brian and Lee was in good vocal form too. Added novelty in between numbers was provided by compère Vivian Stanshall who provided a witty counterpoint to the seriousness of the occasion. His recently cropped hair also turned a few heads. He cheekily came on after some of the songs with a board held above his head with a mark out of ten on. His act went down a storm and he even duetted with Lee as the band reprised 'Give Booze A Chance' from the pub in Ireland a few months before. No wonder the crowd stamped their feet at the show's conclusion.

Straight after the set, the band flew to the USA to begin another ill-fated tour. Yet, for all the group's star seemed to be in the ascendant, there were some signs of dissatisfaction with the current regime. In an interview with Melody Maker in March, Keith had commented, "Vocals are our weakest point and always have been. We don't claim to have good voices but we think Lee does a very good job. It's a question of getting more confidence." When asked whether they ever considered a separate singer, Brian offered support to Lee, "I don't think it would work out. The music is the most important thing for us." Eight months after giving the interview, Emerson showed signs that he wasn't so sure.

Below the surface Keith was growing more dissatisfied with the band and was thinking of making changes. By the time of the US tour he was thinking about a new band and had tried already to recruit Jack Bruce and Chris Squire for this secret future project. Squire was keen, but didn't have faith in himself as a lead singer, "Yeah, I'd love to do it," he told Keith, "But I couldn't handle a lead vocal. I only feel confident doing harmonies."

The tour started at Ungano's club in New York where The Nice shared the bill with Fleetwood Mac. Jimi Hendrix was in the audience and jammed with both bands at the end of the show. Meanwhile, Greg Lake's band, King Crimson, were also in town to play at the Fillmore. The KC entourage also turned up at Ungano's to watch The Nice perform.

Stratton-Smith did not want Keith to split up The Nice, but was beginning to accept the inevitable. Hoping to manage Keith's next project, Strat suggested Keith recruit Greg Lake (and quite possibly it was Strat himself who had initially approached him). Keith was impressed by Greg and, having got nowhere with Squire and Bruce, was aware that singing bass players were in short supply. However, when it was put to Greg, King Crimson were on the up, with an enormously well-received debut album under their belt and, though Greg liked the idea of working with Keith, having finally achieved the success he'd worked so hard for, was dismissive about quitting Crimson for the new venture.

In spite of Keith's disillusionment, The Nice went down well wherever they played and got two standing ovations in Detroit, where they were on the bill with Buffy Saint-Marie. Detroit made quite an impact on Keith, "I've never seen so many people lying in the streets," he told a reporter. "You don't know whether they're dead or drunk and nobody takes any notice... There is a frightening atmosphere. In Detroit you see white police glaring at the coloured people and you wonder what's going on."

The next big gig was with The Allman Brothers Band, at the Boston Tea Party on the 4th, 5th and 6th of December. Lee was the only one who liked them. The Allmans passed the time in their dressing room firing blanks from their replica Colt 45s. The Allmans were keen for The Nice to play 'America' so they could burst on stage firing their guns, but unsurprisingly the band declined the offer.

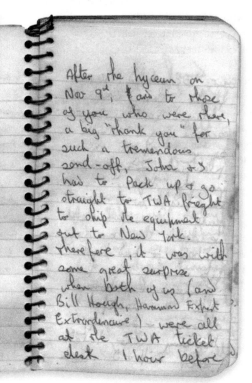

In the middle of the tour, while the crew were making the long drive from Buffalo to San Francisco, Strat and Keith flew to New York, apparently to fix one of the Leslies. There were rumours, however, that the two men hadn't taken such a long detour just to oversee the repair of a bit of kit (the Leslie was never fixed). It now appears Strat and Keith went for some unspecified purpose related to Keith's clandestine future plans, and in fact an entry in Bazz's diary indicates that Keith and Strat did fly back to New York on a few occasions during that tour. By now Keith had decided, rather bluntly, that, "The Nice had outlived its usefulness."

Bazz Ward's diary detailing The Nice's 3rd US tour, late 1969

From this point on, Keith's behaviour started to deteriorate. He didn't seem happy with anything and started to blame the equipment which led to a blazing row with Bazz who, as a result, left the band for a short time though Strat persuaded him to come back.

If Keith was still keen to recruit Greg Lake, he was about to get another chance as The Nice's San Francisco dates involved sharing a bill with King Crimson at Bill Graham's Fillmore

West, from the 11th to the 14th December. Who was headlining had yet to be decided. EG Management put pressure on promoter Bill Graham to put Crimson on before The Nice. Graham's reply was that he didn't care whether Crimson were bigger than The Nice in England – which wasn't true anyway – this was San Francisco and that was that. Each band would play two shows but King Crimson ended up with the least desirable slots. It was decided that Crimson would open and close the show with The Nice playing a one and a half-hour set in the middle.

Though King Crimson's tour had been extremely well received, by the time they arrived on the West Coast there was some dissent in the band camp. Multi-instrumentalist Ian McDonald and drummer Michael Giles were unhappy with the direction in which the band was going and a split appeared imminent. Suddenly staying with King Crimson didn't seem such an attractive prospect for Greg Lake, and he decided to reconsider Keith's offer. "It was like a secret Iron Curtain deal," Greg later explained. "Tony Stratton-Smith made the initial move while he was still handling The Nice but meanwhile I instructed my people - EG Management - to approach Keith. Keith and I spent two months talking, and we didn't play a note for that period."

Keith and Greg later told the NME's Nick Logan how "Suggestions in New York turned into decisions in San Francisco."

Ironically, during this time Lee Jackson became friendly with Greg Lake, and the two musicians would often have a drink together during the Fillmore residency. Though apparently, in spite of what has been claimed, Greg had still not definitely made up his mind to join Keith by the time both bands made their way home. He just needed another push. "[Greg] spent Christmas thinking about it and then decided to stay with King Crimson," insisted Crimson guitarist Robert Fripp. "But increasingly it became obvious there would be differences in direction if Greg remained, and he still really wanted to work with Keith. So I put him in a situation where he would have to leave by stipulating that unless I had the final say with the music, I wouldn't continue Crimson." So Fripp effectively forced Greg's hand.

This unlikely gig was cancelled due to illness within the Isleys

MADISON SQUARE GARDEN PRODUCTIONS
IN ASSOCIATION WITH ANDAR FIVE PRESENT

SAT. NOV. 15, AT 8 P.M. & 11 P.M.
THEIR ONLY NEW YORK APPEARANCE

THE ISLEY BROS.
THE NICE
DAVE "BABY" CORTEZ
SOUND BY HANLEY

MAIL ORDERS FILLED PROMPTLY

PRICES: $6.50, 5.50, 4.50, 3.50
FOR INFO. CALL 564-4400

For mail orders make check or money order payable to Madison Square Garden. Enclose self-addressed stamped envelope and add 15¢ per order for handling. Never mail cash.

the felt forum MADISON SQUARE GARDEN CENTER
8th AVE. BET. 31st & 33rd STS.

After the San Francisco dates, The Nice returned to New York where they finished with two days at the Fillmore East, supporting The Byrds. As with the earlier 'English Invasion' gigs, the shows were recorded for future use. The band then returned to the UK for a few weeks rest before they started their final tour.

Early morning after a gig in Weymouth, 1969

Left-right: Tony Stratton-Smith with roadies,
John Robson and Bazz Ward

CHAPTER 11

SWITCHED-ON EMERSON

"Have a listen to this!"

KEITH EMERSON
to **LEE JACKSON**

ON JANUARY 24TH 1970, The Nice flew to Paris to appear at the Olympia, accompanied by Keith's wife Elinor (who he had recently married, around about the time The Nice recorded 'Five Bridges' at the Fairfield Hall). The gig was filmed in front of a sell out crowd of 2,000 fans. Joseph Eger arrived from Israel, where he was conducting charity concerts, just in time to catch the show. The following day they recorded a TV show and played a couple of numbers. One of them was one they'd written especially for the show and was a tribute to their friend, NME scribe Richard Green. They called it 'Along Came The Beast'.

The British leg of the tour opened at the Colston Hall, Bristol, on January 27th 1970. Tour promoter Derek Block got 15% of the gross take at the door. Block booked the halls but the band paid for them. Fortunately by this time the group had discovered the lucrative potential of merchandise. Posters and programmes were printed and hauled around in the gear van. The posters paid for the hall and the programmes paid for the hotel. That left the band with about £2,000 - quite a haul considering the average weekly wage in Britain then was about £30 (the band split the gig money equally three ways). The tour took in most of the big cities, including Manchester, Liverpool, Sheffield and The Royal Festival Hall in London.

Bazz noticed a change in Keith's demeanour during this tour, "For some reason just before they would go on stage, Keith would go for a piss or something. The result of which was that when he came back he would be behind the other two. So he would always enter the stage last. I thought that was strange. It was only later on that it all made sense. Coupled with the garish silver suit he started to wear later on."

It was at the Festival Hall shows (they played two gigs on the same day, Saturday, 7th February) that Keith first used the Moog Synthesiser. For a number of years Keith had been experimenting with different sounds that the Hammond could provide so it seemed logical that he was attracted by the Moog. As he explained in an interview given around about that time, he was always looking for something new. He had worked with different combinations of speakers and amplifiers which sometimes produced freak harmonies. While Keith was happy with the incredible sounds he could get from the Hammond, some of these sounds were only available on an ad hoc basis. There appeared little chance of predicting to a fine extent when and where all these sounds could be extracted. But what if something came along that would offer the potential to do all of that and more? Certainly there was nothing available in the market at that time. However, something was already at an experimental stage that would set Keith's creative juices flowing.

Legend has it that Keith first heard about the Moog Synthesiser in his local record shop, when the man behind the counter suggested he listen to the 1968 Walter Carlos album *'Switched On Bach'*. Keith actually got to hear it on the in-flight headphones while *en route* to New York for their 2nd American tour and Lee remembers vividly how excited he was when he heard it. "Have a listen to this!" he excitedly exclaimed, passing the headphones to his bandmate. Keith bought the record as soon as he got to the 'Big Apple'. Walter - soon to become Wendy Carlos after a sex-change operation - Carlos's actual contribution to the development of the Moog Synthesiser has often been understated.

Keith and Lee in rehearsal at the Lyceum

It was here, at a later date, where Keith informed Lee of his intention to split up the band

While studying for a doctorate in Physics at Cornell University in 1963, Robert Moog earned some spare cash by selling Theremins – the eerie wailing instrument featured to great effect on The Beach Boys 'Good Vibrations'. Moog met Herbert Deutsch at New York State School Music Association, where he was demonstrating the Theremin. It wasn't long before Moog and Deutsch started to discuss electronics. They decided that the world needed a more solid electronic invention. Within a short time they came up with the basis of what would be the first modular Moog system.

The Moog was a huge machine that resembled nothing so much as an ancient telephone exchange, but while there were plugs and wires all over the place, the contraption also had a keyboard. It represented a major breakthrough. A demonstration at the University of Toronto music studio was to change everything. The head of the studio, Myron Schaffer, was so impressed it led to them getting an exhibit area at the forthcoming Audio Engineering Society. From this show they received enough orders to keep the project going.

Walter Carlos was the first serious musician that Moog worked with. Hitherto, Moog had mainly worked with technicians. A student at the Columbia-Princeton Centre, Carlos also worked for an engineer at Gorham Recording. After Carlos called Moog to order various bits of equipment, Moog realised the student was extremely knowledgeable about the technical side of music, and Moog also knew he had done a couple of experimental Bach pieces on a crude system. Not long after this, Carlos saved up the substantial sum required to buy the first Moog modular system. Working with producer Rachel Elkind-Tourre, the result was the ground breaking *'Switched On Bach'* album.

Winter Gardens,
Bournemouth
6th February, 1970

As Moog himself acknowledges, the preview of the album to a selected audience was devastating. He was giving a lecture at the prestigious Audio Engineering Society when he decided to preview some of the album to the assembled technicians. "It was the last movement of 'Brandenburg No.3'," Moog explained. "I walked off the stage and went back into the auditorium while people were listening, I could feel it in the air. They were jumping out of their skins. These technical people were involved in so much flim-flam, so much shoddy, opportunist stuff, and here was something that was just impeccably done and had obvious musical content and was totally innovative. The tape got a standing ovation." This was the breakthrough Moog had waited for. Carlos was, in actual fact, Dr Robert Moog's first test pilot. However, somebody else was needed to take over the next stage of development. That someone was Keith Emerson.

In spite of Keith's initial burst of enthusiasm, he wasn't completely won over by the Carlos record, "I thought, 'What the hell is this?' There was a picture of the thing it was played on, on the cover, and I wasn't too impressed to be honest, it sounded a bit boggy, too heavy sounding, too laboured. Then I heard that Mike Vickers had one of the first modular systems over here."

Mike Vickers heard about the Moog from friends in the business. He loved it and ordered one immediately but had to wait three months for it to arrive. By the time Keith got in touch with him he was reasonably familiar with the machine. "It's not a computer as many people think," Vickers explains, "And it's not an organ, as many people think. It's got a set of oscillators which are the basic sound forces and there are a series of envelope generators which basically shape the sound from the oscillators. There are various controllable filters and if you feed a complex tone into it you can make the filter sweep up or down, or both."

Very few people in the country owned such a device at the time, although George Harrison had one, and it had been successfully employed on The Beatles' *'Abbey Road'* album. "I went round to see it [at Vickers' flat]," Keith remembers, "And asked him if I could use it for one of my performances. He told me that it wasn't really meant to be moved around, it was really for studio rather than live performance [Vicker's original Modular system now resides in a museum]. Anyway, he was willing to have a go."

Even though Vickers was enthusiastic, he did have reservations which he reiterated to Keith. Sometimes the Moog wouldn't work even in a controlled environment, "I've never really taken this thing out on the road and I don't know how it would hold up. I've gone to studios to do sessions with some people and I've wired it up before I got there, and it hasn't done the thing I wanted it to. All the things like electricity and lights, they vary a hell of a lot." Keith remembered there was a lot of hit-and-miss about the whole thing, so he asked Vickers, "'Well, how can we work this?' And he said 'Well maybe I can hide behind the thing with some headphones on and while they're playing, I can make the necessary adjustments and tune it', and he was there giving me the thumbs up or the thumbs down, and I could play."

The Nice played both Festival Hall shows to sell out audiences of 3,000. Richard Green of the NME noted that the band just seemed to get better and better. "The Moog was introduced for the first time on a British stage during 'She Belongs To Me'," Green reported. "It's a weird thing, resembling a switchboard, and takes some playing. Mike Vickers, its owner, was on hand to programme it and Keith got laughs when he almost made the thing 'talk' *à la* 'Sparky's Magic Piano'. His silver suit, making him look like the urban spaceman, was a fitting prop for his outrageous acrobatics which, though becoming less violent these days, still go down well."

The band also played 'Hang On To A Dream', which included as many different styles as Keith could throw at Lee and Brian – both of whom coped admirably. The latter even afforded himself a laugh as they both took up the challenge and confirmed the impromptu nature of this section. Green paid attention

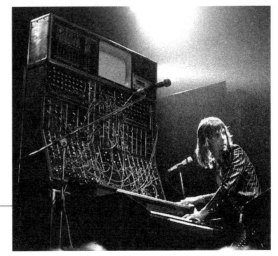

A huge machine that resembled
an ancient telephone exchange...
Keith with Moog in 1974

to the fact that Lee's playing was on top form and his voice sounded better too. The set also included a band version of 'Five Bridges' and 'Karelia Suite'. They even managed to dust off 'America', which was a track they played infrequently at that stage. Strangely, many fans ended up on the stage dancing to 'America'. There was a difficult moment at the end, due to the timing of the second show, when the band had to cut short proceedings in order to prepare for the next show. It took 15 minutes to persuade the crowd to leave the building. The second show Lee regards as his best gig.

After the show Keith admitted, with regard to the Moog, that the one show went better than the other. But there was more than enough potential in the Moog. Keith was convinced this was the future.

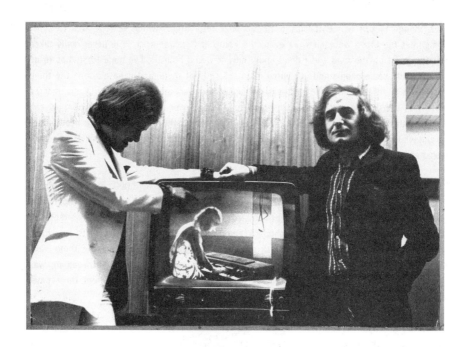

CHAPTER 12

CHIMES AT MIDNIGHT

"I want you on
that stage when
'Rondo' starts.
Come on Dave,
one more time!"

BAZZ WARD
to **'RONDO' DAVE**

THE NICE FLEW OUT to Los Angeles on Shrove Tuesday, February 10th 1970, to appear in a mixed-media programme for NBC television. The show was sponsored by the Bell Telephone Company and would be introduced by world famous singing star, Andy Williams. The Nice would appear with the Los Angeles Philharmonic Orchestra under the leadership of Zubin Mehta. The show, which was recorded over several days, was called 'Switched On Symphony' and was produced by Jack Good (who oversaw the famous British TV pop show, 'Oh Boy'). Good had heard about the trailblazing exploits of the band and had approached Keith directly. Other acts on the bill were Jethro Tull, Ray Charles, Santana, Daniel Barenboim, Jacqueline Dupré and Jerry Goodman of Flock - later to find new fame with the Mahavishnu Orchestra.

Mehta was an enigmatic character, eager to foster the idea of the temperamental 'genius'. As Keith explains it was an attitude that didn't go down well with the performers, "We were all practising in the corners of this one big arena when Jack Good came in and clapped his hands and said 'Listen everybody - Zubin Mehta!' And Zubin Mehta comes in and walks all the way through the studio with his head down... of course, we didn't get a good impression of him. He sort of stormed in and didn't really know what was going on. The whole thing was a sort of jumble, and Jack Good did marvels pulling it off."

As there were a lot of bands on the bill, the gear was piled in the corridors adjacent the stage. Santana's gear was next to The Nice's. The drum kits had been set up and, while they were waiting, Brian and Santana's Mike Shrieve started playing an impromptu drum jam. They were quickly joined by Santana's impressive percussion section. As Brian recalled, "They were shit hot!" They were able to play for about ten minutes before they were silenced for disturbing Mehta's preparations.

The band had a few days of rehearsals but Mehta's overbearing attitude really did get on everyone's nerves. "Mehta turned to Ray Charles at one juncture," Keith recalls, "And said 'Mr Charles you sang 'Suddenly' on the offbeat that time - will you be singing it that way next time?' 'I could put it anywhere next time', replied Charles, 'Just watch my body!'" Mehta got off to a terrible start when he asked Charles to follow his signal. There was a gasp from the assembled artists on the side of the stage who were all crammed in to see his performance. Mehta didn't know that Charles was blind. One of the violinists got up and whispered in Mehta's ear to tell him. Lee Jackson recalls the look of horror on the conductor's face. He was so shaken that he walked off and the orchestra followed Charles's cues with aplomb. Keith remembered that the timings of the event caused a little hassle, "Jack Good was great but we had some weird guy bugging us with a stop watch who expected everything timed down to the last note. We were a little disappointed in that, instead of fusing the orchestra and ourselves together it tended to be a bit of the group and then a bit of the orchestra."

The band also played with Jerry Goodman and Pinkas Zukerman, and were forced into a comical scene when they played 'America' with the LA Philharmonic. The producer lifted the whole band in the air with fork-lift trucks and placed them on sets that looked like theatre boxes. Brian's had a low parapet in order that his drums could be seen. It was one of the few times they were placed in such an artificial situation. The band also joined Santana, along with the orchestra, for Woodstock show stopper, 'Soul Sacrifice'. At the end of the show the band appeared in a 'sofa' interview, along with Ian Anderson, Jacqueline Du Pré and Daniel Barenboim. For all the talk of breaking down barriers, Lee remembers Barenboim spent most of the time looking with disdain at the group of rock musicians. Yet for all his temperamental loftiness, Mehta gushed that he had been so impressed with The Nice (especially the Bach/Dylan combination that was 'Country Pie') that he promptly invited them to Tel Aviv for a concert with the Israel Philharmonic in June. Unfortunately, this was a date The Nice would never keep.

In early 1970, Oldham's Immediate label was declared bankrupt. The company owed over $600,000. There was not a lot the Immediate artists could do about it. It's clear that some bands, The Nice included, never received any royalties from Oldham. The chaotic fall out of the bankruptcy has still not been fully resolved for some of the artists even today!

Worse still, sometime after the LA gig and before the resumption of the UK tour, Keith broke the news to Lee that at some point in the not to distant future, he would be breaking up the band. In the meantime, the band's demanding schedule meant that they carried on playing shows, but the end was moving into sight.

The constant gigging and the necessity of keeping sufficient revenue flowing into the organisation – partly because of the lack of any royalties having emerged from the now bankrupt Immediate label - meant The Nice were beginning to turn down some tempting and interesting offers. They had already been approached to do some film soundtrack work but they were forced to refuse due to live commitments. One film company was prepared to use existing material for Marianne Faithfull's film 'Girl On A Motorcycle', but the band didn't feel happy doing that. They wanted to be there when all this editing was done. They received another offer - while in Paris to do a Peter Ustinov film - but again they turned it down. "We have no time to work on film soundtracks," Lee explained. "It means cancelling gigs for quite a while and we thrive on live shows."

March 6th 1970 saw the band back at the Royal Festival Hall with the Royal Philharmonic Orchestra, conducted by Joseph Eger who was by now describing himself, only partly in jest,

---

copy of letter from R.I.O.

Dear Mr. S.S.,

This is to confirm that the programme for the 6th March will be as follows:-

Conductor: Joseph Eger
Soloists: Lee Jackson   Bass guitar, vocals
                  Keith Emerson Organ
                  Brian Davison Drums

Programme:

Beethoven   Overture Prometheus
Berlioz/Eger   Lelio
                  Symphonie Fantastique (excerpts)
Keith Emerson   'Five Bridges Suite'
R. Strauss   *   Theme & variations on '2001' Space Odyssey
Tchaikovsky *   Pathetique Symphony (excerpts)

* Arrangements by Keith Emerson and Joseph Eger.

You will have allready seen the poster and can I also confirm that the rehearsal for this concert will be as follows:-

5th March 1970   14.00 - 17.00   Morley College
6th March 1970   10.00 - 13.00   Royal Festival Hall

I have informed the Royal Festival Hall about John Neville and the Ambrosian Singers and hope that you can confirm their availability to me shortly.

We deeply appreciate your agreeing to finance John Neville, and any lighting, With regard to the latter I have given the Royal Festival Hall your telephone No. for any queries they might have.

We hope our leaflets will be ready by Friday morning this week and we will distribute these in the Royal Festival Hall; also any publicity you can give this concert from the platform at your own show would be wonderful.

With best wishes,

Yours sincerely,

Tom Petzal,
Concert Manager

as the fourth member of the band. Three hours of rehearsals were planned the day before at Morley College, London. On the day of the gig they had three hours to rehearse at the Festival Hall. They also had John Neville directing the Ambrosian Singers to complement the proceedings - the cost of the singers and the lighting were borne by the band, although following the success of the Fairfield Hall gig, funding was found for the orchestra.

The Festival Hall show saw Keith again using Mike Vicker's Moog. It was the last time Keith would play with a Moog which he'd borrowed. In keeping with the spirit of the times - space exploration was at its peak – The Nice's set included some music from Stanley Kubrick's masterwork, '2001: A Space Odyssey'; to wit, an excerpt from 'Also Sprach Zarathustra' written by Richard Strauss, cleverly interspersed this with Ligeti's 'Lux Aeterna'. During this number they used the Ambrosian singers and the Moog Synthesiser. After a rip-roaring version of Tchaikovsky's 'Pathetique' and the ubiquitous combination of 'Troika' and 'Rondo', the orchestra departed, leaving fans screaming for an encore.

When the band came back they asked the audience what they would like and they all seemed to scream back at them 'America'. They then proceeded to do a twenty-minute version with Keith throwing himself around and using the Moog again.

Keith felt that the Moog re-energised him. " I felt the new possibilities of the instrument," he said shortly after the Festival Hall show, "And that reminded me of the element of surprise."

A few days rest and recovery were set aside before the band started a short tour of Scotland. However, the secret that Keith and Strat had harboured for almost three months was about to officially see the light of day. Inexplicably, neither Keith nor Lee told Brian who, for some strange reason, was told last; even some of the crew knew before him. Lee's early warning from Keith of the impending end enabled him to make plans to form a new group sometime before the official announcement of the split.

The circumstances surrounding Brian finding out were odd, and quite cold and calculating. Brian recalls that it was a Sunday (probably March 8th). He was with his girlfriend, Maria (soon to be his second wife), and driver Alan Smith. At the end of the afternoon they went back to Brian's flat and played some records. Then at some point Alan said they had to go over to Tony's office for a meeting. Brian was confused, "Now? On a Sunday?" he asked Smith. On the journey Brian wondered what on earth could be afoot. But on entering the premises, Tony told him Keith was breaking up the band and was doing something new. Brian's reaction to this was, probably in a degree of shock, was, "OK, what do we do now?" Also, there was the sticky question of how they were get through their remaining gigs in this potentially explosive atmosphere.

The first gig of the Scottish tour was at the Usher Hall, Edinburgh, on March 11th. Lee remembers it was one of the few times they were mobbed by girls on stage. It was in Edinburgh that Bazz was told of the impending split. He was chatting to WEM owner Charlie Watkins, about the future of PAs and what the band could use on their next tour. That was when Alan Smith interjected with, "There isn't going to be another tour." Bazz thought he was dreaming. "You what?" His confirmation was crushing, "There isn't going to be another tour, the band is breaking up." In Bazz's stunned silence, Alan Smith went over the carefully pre-arranged plans. Looking at Bazz, he said, "Keith wants you to go with him." Bazz's reply was instant, "Where does that leave the other two?"

When Bazz asked why they were breaking up, Smith's reply was, "Keith has new ideas and wants a new direction." "What's he going to do then?" Bazz asked. Smith's reply was stunningly ironic, "He's going out with bass and drums!"

The next day the entourage went to Dundee. Needless to say, the atmosphere wasn't very good. Brian's girlfriend, Maria, verbally laid into Keith's wife, Elinor, in the lobby of the hotel, complaining at the shoddy treatment of the other musicians in The Nice. The gig in Dundee had an interval and when the band came into the dressing room, a row broke out between Keith and Brian. In fact, it turned into one of those 'fuck-you-well-fuck-you-too' arguments. Nobody can remember what it was specifically about but in general terms it was obvious. Lee remembers it very well because he was determined not to get involved. However, his hand was forced when there was a real doubt about whether the band would go back to complete the performance. Lee told them, "There are 2,000 people out there and we owe it to them to finish the show. It's not their fault!"

By now rumours were circulating in the music business that the band were splitting up which, inevitably, found their way into the music press. Just before the group returned to Croydon, the music press for that week splashed the headlines with news that all was not well. Disc and Music Echo, "Nice take it easy - but won't split." Strat was quoted as saying that the band was going to rest and solo projects would ensue but, on the same day, Melody Maker revealed the band was planning to split for good.

Croydon's Fairfield Hall on Sunday, March 22nd, was to be the band's last live gig in the UK. It was originally booked as one performance only, but a few weeks before the show Strat asked his personal assistant, Gail Coulson, to reserve one hundred seats for the press and families. Strat was perplexed to be told by Gail that the hall had completely sold out, and could have done so three times given the demand for tickets. There was only one thing to do. Strat asked if a matinee show could be arranged, which enabled the press to receive their allotted seat ration.

The mood at these last gigs was sombre. This was to be the last gathering of the legion of Nice fans who had loyally followed the band since its humble beginnings. This following was epitomised by what Bazz called the 'Marquee 12', which was made up of 'Rondo' Dave, Stella, Nicely, David Westrop (he later roadied for Gong with Brian), Gandalf, Amber, Sandy, Eve Diamond (who was later engaged to Bazz), Aragon, Elrond, Pat and Margot. Suzy and Pauline O'List were part of the inner circle of the band and not really part of the twelve. This hardcore support had followed the band from its early days. Dave Westrop who, back then, was very young recently recalled those days, "Bazz used to be my 'gig dad' and always looked. after us. He would put us on the guest list. He would give lifts in the back of the van, on top of the gear, to and back from out of town venues. If there was any sign of trouble it was always handy to have an ex-Liverpool docker on hand." This outfit began life as a small club/pub band yet even when they scaled the heights they always kept in touch with their roots. The existence of the 'Marquee 12' proves that.

Lee announced at the first performance that the band was breaking up in a few days. Amongst all the sadness it remained for Rondo Dave to have centre stage. Legendary for his idiot dancing to 'Rondo', the magnitude of the occasion got to him with his reluctance to go on stage. Bazz told him, "I want you on that stage when 'Rondo' starts. This is for you." In the end he had to be persuaded on stage by Bazz and Gail Coulson. As he went on stage for the last show at home, Bazz said, "Come on Dave, one more time." After the gig Bazz didn't go the dressing room where everybody was gathered, unable to confront the high emotion of the moment. He just got on with quietly packing up the gear. There were, however, three shows left.

Their last UK performance of all was in the quiet sanctuary of the Playhouse Theatre, Charing Cross, on March 25th 1970. It was the last session The Nice would record for the BBC. Keith turned up late and didn't

```
Monday 23 March
Off

Tuesday 24 March
Lee: 4p.m. Interview in the office with Roy Shipston (Disc)

Wednesday 25 March
2.30p.m. Play house Theatre, Charing Cross - Bernie Andrews

Thursday 26 & Friday 27
Off

Saturday 28 March
The Nice etc.
Please be at London Airport at 3.30p.m. You are booked
on Flight BE 610 dep: 4.05p.m. arr. Hamburg    where
you will be met by a representative from the Festival
who will take you to the hotel. You are on stage at
11p.m. supposed to be at the hall at 9p.m.

Bazz & John
Please be at Harwich at 3.45p.m. on Friday 27th. Boat
leaves at 4.30p.m. to Bremerhaven, equipment to be
in the hall by 7p.m..

Ernst Merck Halle,              Hotel: Hotel Larkhochhaus,
Juniusttrasse,                         Drehbahn 15
Hamburg.                               Hamburg

    Promoter: Hartmut K. Goetze,
              2104 Hamburg 92,
              Holtweg 49         Tel: Hamburg 701 92 97

Monday 30 March
Peace Festival,
Sportspalast,
Berlin                          2 shows

Bazz & John   Please be through the Berlin border early
Monday morning and go straight to the hall.
The Nice etc  Flights t.b.a. at Hamburg to be there at
12p.m.
Hotel: Pensione Berghoff - 9 people

Tuesday 31 March
Home
```

speak outside of the requirements of the music, he was remote and frosty. They recorded 'My Back Pages', a solo 'Five Bridges', 'Pathetique' and 'Country Pie'. When it was all over, Keith departed before the mixing was completed - an oblique indication of his feelings and something that, prior to the announcement of the split, would have been unthinkable in his capacity as the creative force in the band. This was a band that was limping towards its inevitable demise. Only time could put it out of its misery.

On Saturday, 28th March, the band flew out to Hamburg from London Airport for the gig on the same day. After the Hamburg gig it was off to West Berlin, to the Peace Festival at the Sportspalast. On the bill with them were The Greatest Show On Earth, Hardin & York, Free and Deep Purple. By this time personal relations between Keith and Bazz were poor, even though it had already been agreed that Bazz would go with Keith on his new project. The problem was with Bazz's devastation by the break up of The Nice - and it showed.

Bazz got into trouble at this gig when a local purloined his tambourine. Unable to get it back by fair means he walked up to the guy and head-butted him. The police arrived, truncheons drawn, at which point Brian intervened, "If you hit him I'm not going on." Faced with the prospect of an angry crowd the police backed down. However, shortly after this, Bazz made an appearance on the stage and was roundly booed by a large section of the crowd. As a result, he had to spend the rest of the gig out of view.

Strangely, not much can be recalled about that final gig. "The true point of departure for me was on that BBC session," Brian says. To Lee, the sadness of the last UK show at Croydon, had had the effect of blanking out the remaining German gigs.

When they came back from Germany they had to divvy up the gear - a painful process. They couldn't split the PA or the mixing desk so Bazz drove the van down to Townshend House, to Tony Stratton-Smith's flat, and left it parked in front of two speaker cabs. He locked the doors and walked away, not looking back.

Even though the band had split for all intents and purposes, they still had a new album in the can. With their third album reaching the top five there was every reason to believe that the new *'Five Bridges'* album would go even higher and sell more copies. In the press reports of the split just before the Croydon gig, it was stated that the album would be on Polydor Records. However, the reality was they hadn't actually signed to anybody. Strat wanted a Nice album for his fledgling label, Charisma. As it turned out he had a lot of leverage with Keith - the two were, after all, great friends. That Strat had initially had designs to be the manager of Keith's new band is undeniable, but Keith told him he didn't want the manager and record company to be the same - the memories of their situation with Andrew Oldham still fresh in his mind.

If Strat couldn't be Keith's manager in the future, he still wanted *'Five Bridges'* for Charisma and invited Keith to hawk the album around the record companies vowing to pay £100 more than the highest bidder. Strat got his album and Keith rode off into the sunset. But the arguments about *'Five Bridges'* didn't end there. Originally the inside sleeve was going to feature a photo of Joseph Eger and the orchestra but the only one to hand featured Keith as well, with Lee and Brian conspicuous by their absence.

By this stage things were very delicate causing hackles to be raised. Bazz suggested that they erase Keith out of the photo. Strat looked aghast at the suggestion. After much debate, Bazz got some individual photos of the band and cut out the heads and threw them on the desk and said, "Here, just put them on and everybody's happy." They didn't use those photos, they used others, but retained the idea.

It would have been too much to ask, considering the circumstances, for the band to break up amicably. They had all worked incredibly hard to be in a position where they were on the verge of making it big in America. They were a tight unit both on- and off-stage. They had all come up together from the basement and were about to embrace international success, which would mean financial security – something the band had lacked in spite of its sold-out shows and strong record sales. All the hard work that Lee and Brian had put in was now going to go to somebody else. It was a racing certainty that this new band of Keith's was going to be a success. However, the extent of the success was to take some by surprise.

CHAPTER **13**

FOR MOTHER, BAZZ & THE BEAST

"As brilliant
a fusion of sounds
as I've ever
witnessed!"

**RICHARD
'THE BEAST' GREEN**

129

JUST TWO WEEKS AFTER ambiguous headlines in the press about the situation with the band, the public were finally put out of their misery when the Disc and Music Echo confirmed the situation, "Nice split; and Keith Emerson forms group with Crimson Man." Many fans and sections of the press were devastated by this news.

Richard Green was shattered. "The demise of The Nice was one of the heaviest blows to fall on the beleaguered head of progressive pop for many a long day," he wrote in the NME on May 16th 1970. Green never really got into Keith's new band, and always hoped The Nice would get back together again.

Keith was keen to put the record straight as to why he'd broken the band up. As he outlined there were a number of reasons why he took the decision, "With The Nice we were working almost all the week," he explained, "And you get bored playing the same things. We never had time to rehearse." The financial pressures brought about by Immediate Records' lack of royalty payments and eventual demise meant the band were always living hand-to-mouth and they never got out of the habit of hard touring. Ironically, the only time they made real money was on the final Derek Block tour when Strat introduced merchandising and they booked the venues themselves. The fact that the band were so innovative and artistically ambitious didn't help the situation either. The mixed media festivals were extremely costly and there was no corporate sponsorship to take the sting out of large scale touring.

Keith had already stated he wasn't happy with Lee's singing. He was beginning to write more melodic material and yearned for someone to project it in a way that he felt would do it most justice. He also wanted someone with the extra talent to come up with the unexpected, "I'm not putting Lee down because what he plays is good but after nearly four years, I needed someone to come out of the blue with something."

Keith also suffered the pressures of being the group's creative force and confessed to mixed emotions about foisting the orchestras and choirs onto Lee and Brian. "Perhaps it was wrong of me go into all of this without considering the others, and the situation got a little uptight. Brian got a little disenchanted because he was left sitting on the stage waiting to do his little bit."

Yet another factor was that Keith didn't feel the band was theatrical enough. As he stated in Music Scene in 1974, it wasn't a sufficient spectacle for his taste, he wanted "A guy who could play a good drum solo. But it was always Brian's policy not to play drum solos because he considered them boring." The problem, as Keith saw it, was an emotional one - if Brian didn't feel right for a solo on one particular night, he would not play it. Keith's future band mate Carl Palmer (formerly of Atomic Rooster) has claimed that Keith developed the theatrical side of his performance because of the limitations of The Nice.

"[Keith] had a hard time at the end of The Nice because he had to drag the other two," Palmer told Best magazine in 1972. "For example, he was obliged to develop in extraordinary proportions all the spectacular gimmicks with the organ, just because the other two didn't 'fill up' any more." However, Palmer's assertion doesn't explain why Keith's new band, Emerson, Lake & Palmer, went on to develop the theatrics to 'extraordinary proportions' and make a great play of the fact?

Keith didn't want to alter the format of the band - he wanted to develop the old ideas more.

"I wanted to extend the possibilities of forming an organ trio, mainly because I wanted to use every person to their fullest extent," he told Music Scene in 1974.

King Crimson's Greg Lake had all of the elements Keith was looking for, he could sing and play bass, but he also played lead and acoustic guitar. He was a composer and had a good 'producer's' mind that he could apply to developing Keith's ideas. Keith had already established, even prior to playing with Greg, that they liked similar music. So there was a lot of common ground on which to base the partnership.

When the news of the split broke, Lee and Brian were keen to put the record straight. As Lee had known about the break-up for the longest, he was the most philosophical about it. Surprisingly, he wasn't too disappointed; he thought that a lot of the friendship had gone out of the band in the last six months anyway, "When things were going wrong with the band, towards the end, it was like watching your grandmother dying. It was a relief it was all over." It was then that Lee started looking on the positive side and thinking about what he could do afterwards.

Brian's ambivalent attitude to the split was shattered when he heard that Keith was taking the same format out, just with different personnel. There was no doubt he thought Keith had jumped the gun, as he stated to NME, "I didn't agree when the split came from Keith, that we had as a group achieved everything we could have musically. It was a bit premature. But Keith wanted to do it that way so he did it."

With Keith's new band looking like a copy of The Nice – at least in instrumental terms – Davison was clear that it would cast the status of the rhythm section in a poor light. The problem for Lee and Brian was that this stigma would be very durable.

The basis of this durability was also based on a plethora of articles in the aftermath of the split. Many were quite unfair and were presented without proper qualification. An article in the January 7th 1972 issue of Fusion was typical: "The inability of Jackson to challenge Emerson was one of the limitations of The Nice. Davison acted primarily as a time-keeper while Jackson tried to keep up with Emerson's quick and sometimes complex time shifts." It's remarkable to note that Brian's ability at keeping time could be somehow turned into a negative.

Yet another example was when Keith's new band ELP played the Isle Of Wight Festival of 1970. Within a very short time, journalists would tell how the festival was the biggest gig the three of them had ever played in their careers up to then. Which is strange considering The Nice had headlined the year before, as well as many other big festivals. Greg had played with King Crimson in front of 600,000 people when supporting The Rolling Stones in Hyde Park the previous year. And Carl Palmer's Atomic Rooster had also played at the 1969 Isle Of Wight Festival.

The aspersion cast upon the abilities of Jackson and Davison, based on Keith's rejection, still persists today. In a 1998 interview with the ELP magazine Impressions, Chris Welch recalled a Nice gig towards the end, "I remember going backstage (I think it was Dunstable) and being surprised to find Brian angry and complaining after the show, 'I can't play that fast anymore'." However, Brian can't recall saying anything along those lines. Later on in the interview Chris would only say that Greg was a better singer, no doubt about that, and that Carl could play rings around Brian in terms of speed or attack. It must be said it is a pretty selective summation.

Lee took a pummelling for his voice. He could never have been a great singer but he could have been better than he had been in The Nice. In those days Keith was unaware about the concept of letting the singer pick the optimum key. He thought a singer should be able to sing at any pitch. Many years after the split, when Keith and Lee were listening to The Nice BBC tapes prior to their release, only then did Emerson realise that Lee was singing in an inappropriate key. He apologised to Lee and said it was only when Greg forcefully suggested that the singer picks the key that he realised its significance.

With regard to Brian and Carl, there is no doubt Carl is a better technician and a faster player, but drumming is also about timing and feel, and Brian makes up the ground here. Brian was a highly rated drummer in his day. In 1968, in Melody Maker, Chris Welch put Brian in his Top 10 drummers of the year. The list included Jon Hiseman, John Bonham, Ginger Baker and Keith Moon, so he was in good company. Furthermore, in the 1980s, the author of a book titled 'A-Z of Rock Drummers' insisted, "When one hears the justified accolades heaped on drummers like Phil Collins and Bill Bruford - Brian Davison deserves to be considered in the same league."

Lee's subtle innovative bass style is worth mentioning too. His style of picking achieved a very percussive and staccato sound. This was a time when most bass players played with the fingers, rather than a pick, giving the sound too much depth and, sometimes, too much 'oomph'.

Of course, more than anything else, that both Lee and Brian effectively dropped out of the music scene after the demise of The Nice appeared to confirm the view that these two musicians weren't ever quite up to the job. And this despite their nine glorious months to follow with Refugee.

The huge global success enjoyed by Emerson's next band has naturally left The Nice overshadowed in the minds of many ELP fans, and it is difficult to think about The Nice without comparing them to what came after. But one should always remember that The Nice were compared by many critics - not just Richard Green and Chris Welch - to be as good as The Cream and anybody else around at the time.

Interestingly, it is only recently that Keith has been willing to talk about some of ELP's weaknesses. Keith confided to Brian Davison that one of the reasons that ELP played so much faster live than on record was that Carl was keeping bad time, so he had no choice but to follow him. Greg Lake was indeed a very good bass player and could play very fast, but sometimes he wasn't very adventurous. Many of his bass lines mimic what Keith was playing with his left hand (this is why some of his lines are 'hard to pick out on record). Also, as Keith revealed in a recent interview, there was something else about him, "Greg hated jamming. Particularly when it came to performing live. Before he went on stage he needed to know what we were playing. And if we did start to improvise... Greg would do it reluctantly."

Keith also revealed recently that even some of the perceived weaknesses of The Nice were also shared by ELP. As he candidly related to Record Collector, "It was a very tough relationship I had with Greg and, looking back on it philosophically, it was frustrating to write music and expect lyrics to be written just like that. I had the same frustration with Lee in The Nice." May it be that perhaps Keith, sometimes, expected too much of people?

Keith summed up recently another key difference between The Nice and ELP, "The Nice was very relaxed. We would go on stage and play whatever we wanted to play... It was very free and improvisational. ELP was more structured." They were, clearly, two completely different bands.

In retrospect the split was a messy affair but in some ways it was unavoidable. Keith's analogy was an accurate one when he likened the situation to a split with a long-term partner. Unfortunately in these cases there will always be a certain amount of acrimony. As Keith has stated, it wasn't personal, "If it hadn't been Greg and Carl it would have been somebody else". He felt the time was right to move on and, of course, had the right to do so. But perhaps if Lee and Brian had been told at the same time, that might have eased matters, or had Keith been more open about the split earlier. It didn't help either that Strat was embroiled in it all.

While Emerson would go on to much greater success with ELP, his new band never received anything like the same positive press enjoyed by his previous band. The reason why some of ELP's adverse press commentary stands out is because

YES FOLLOW NICE PATH

JON ANDERSON writes such powerful and dramatic themes, that I sometimes wonder if he was nurtured on such Broadway shows as "West Side Story." Whether he realises it or not, his music is very theatrical and exciting, indeed during some numbers one almost expects the audience to suddenly leap up and go into some wild choreographed routine.

However, the Marquee Club was so packed last Tuesday when Yes appeared that you could do little else but nod your head in time to the music.

It was obvious from the turn-out, that Yes are now drawing the same appreciative audiences that used to follow the Nice.

Yes play extended numbers, but unlike the majority of their contemporaries they never bore. Yes music has substance, it's not an endless string of uninspired solos and rehashed riffs.

On such popular numbers as " Everydays," " Then," and " Astral Traveller " they quickly build up the excitement on the main theme prior to shooting off into equally exciting second, third and even fourth interlocking themes and subsequent variations.

Amongst the newer material performed were a very short acoustic guitar feature for new man Steve Howe called " Clap," and a thundering workout that featured both Steve and The Jolly Green Giant, Chris Squires on bass guitars. Entitled the " Avengers " it proved a show-stopper.

The only thing that could follow it was the new Yes marathon Paul Simon's " America." After building the introduction to a crescendo, Jon sang the whistful lyrics before the group roared into various well arranged instrumental passages which heavily featured organist Tony Kaye, and the tight and precise drumming of Bill Brufford.

Performances like this can do nothing else but enhance their well earned reputation. — ROY CARR.

the media loved The Nice so much. It's very difficult to find a bad review. There's no doubt that some sections of the media hated ELP before they even heard them play a note. Whereas DJ John Peel loved The Nice, he memorably dubbed ELP as: "A waste of talent and electricity." Why was it that ELP provoked such extreme reactions? One of the reasons, of which Keith was aware, is that people didn't like it when he broke up The Nice so they took it out on ELP. That's probably why in the early days, they played press shows in the hope they would win the media over.

Yet another reason why the press didn't take to ELP is that the group was an ambitious band that immediately set out to take the musical world by storm. "ELP were undoubtedly a hard-edged super group for the new decade who would take no prisoners on the road to commercial success," Chris Welch recently conceded.

The Nice's ever loyal roadie Bazz remembers the very early days of ELP very well, as he was still Keith's roadie. Bazz didn't like the persona that ELP exuded, its management and even some of the band members. He didn't take too kindly to Greg's attitude. Of Lake, Bazz recalls, "I got the impression he wanted people to come running every time he snapped his fingers." Greg did indeed acquire a derogatory nickname based on his attitude. He became known as 'His Heaviness' among the ELP road crew so Bazz wasn't alone in his opinion. He couldn't - and wouldn't - work with Greg, but there was another reason why he was going to terminate his union with Keith.

Sadly after many years' loyal service, Bazz's relationship with Emerson came to an end in a dispute over a delay in back wages owed to him. Bazz got his money in the end but all calls to EG Management about his future in the organization were stalled. The Partnership with Keith was effectively over when he accepted an offer from Barry Dickens to do the Santana and then Johnny Winter tours of Europe. At a stroke Bazz doubled his pay. He felt at the time it was the right move and it's something he never regretted.

****

In the weeks after the split there was a lot of speculation in the music press as to who would fill the void let by The Nice. There were headlines like 'Yes Follow Nice Path' and 'Yes Move Into The Gap Left By Nice'. As NME's Roy Carr noted from a review of a Yes gig at the Marquee, "It was obvious from the turn-out, that Yes are now drawing the same appreciative audiences that used to follow The Nice." Coincidentally, Yes introduced a new marathon number into the show, Paul Simon's 'America'. Peter Banks of Yes even sent an open letter to Melody Maker acknowledging the important part that The Nice had played to bands like Yes. It's worth quoting in full, "The hippy 'mystique-filled' summer of '67 saw the birth of many freaked-out and musically precocious groups. There was also The Nice. To me, the Nice were unique in their ability to combine excitement and guts without losing their musical integrity. Their music has been a constant source of inspiration and, most important, enjoyment to the whole of pop music. Without sounding too much like an obituary, I would like to thank them for being such an incredibly good band and for being three of the nicest people I know. Good luck to Keith, Lee and Brian with their new bands."

Just after Keith had set the seal for his new band with the recruitment of Carl Palmer, Charisma finally released *'Five Bridges'* in June 1970, complete with a striking Hipgnosis cover. The band had a few problems in getting this album together. After recording it the tapes went missing for a few weeks. No one knew where they had gone but one day they turned up in the studio. This was an encumbrance as they had some free time just prior to the disappearance but after the tapes turned up they were back on the road and so were forced to mix them in between live dates. Even though Immediate Records had gone bust, its sister company, Immediate Music, was limping on and was listed as the publisher on the first pressings of the album.

Another problem was that they couldn't use the whole of the Croydon gig. The music publisher Boosey & Hawkes had warned them off using Prokofiev's 'Troika' because they owned the publishing rights. (The track was finally released by Sanctuary Records on a compilation in 2000.)

The album opens impressively with the title track. Split into five movements, it represents the musical 'friendly in-fighting' between the band and the orchestra. The subdued opening is purposeful as Keith explains in the notes the 'First Movement' he is building a musical bridge using old and new ideas. The 'Second Movement' is based more around 'rock rhythms and improvisations'.

The 'Third Movement' opens with Keith's piano solo which later brings in the orchestra. At this stage the band haven't made an appearance but that is put right in the 'Fourth Movement'. It opens with Brian's cymbals and Lee's bass. It isn't long before they're joined by Keith's choppy Hammond licks and the whole band bounces along and segues into the main melody that is the vehicle of Lee's lyrics. The words are no less interesting as the contradictions in society are intelligently brought out by Lee - the cost of industrial progress must be balanced against the ever-diminishing resources of nature. Creating wealth produces pollution. A whole section of society are excluded from the very wealth their labour has created but made dependent by their need to work to live. This is wonderfully summed up with the lines, "There's no good complaining of dirty air, cause there's nothing else to breathe / It's no good shouting from nine to five if you haven't got the guts to live." Newcastle may be the setting for this particular drama but the sentiments are universal.

After the general philosophical thrust of the 'Fourth Movement', the lyrics to the final movement run into the specifics and reveal vivid memories of Lee's home town. Keith returns to the piano and is joined by the band in a jazzy section. It is here that the brass join the fray. As Keith explained in the notes, he wrote the main riff for Chris Pine on trombone and Keith inserts some jazzy Hammond as the brass and the band get ready for the big finale. All in all it's a great performance and it's the culmination of everything they had strived for since 'Ars Longa Vita Brevis'.

Side Two opens with old favourite the 'Karelia Suite'. Keith plays bass pedals on the Hammond at the start of this track. In terms of musical integration with the orchestra this is probably the success of the album. This track contains one of the best sections of music the band ever recorded, even though it only lasts for under a minute and half. It starts at four minutes into the cut and is loose and free with the band swinging. There then follows an interval of Hammond feedback shortly after - Keith accidentally pulls the lead out of the fuzz box and all goes quiet. One can hear Keith say, "Yeah!" What one doesn't hear - because it was edited out - is Bazz shouting "Oh, fucking shit!" as he reconnects the lead.

The next track is the last from the Croydon gig. 'Pathetique' is an adaptation of the 'Third Movement Of Tchaikovsky's Symphony No.6' and is probably the least successful of the Croydon tracks, though interesting none the less. Starting off with the orchestra Keith comes in with a particularly fluid Hammond line and towards the end it does contain some very good moments of fusion between the band and orchestra.

Keith had had a brilliant idea on the second American tour. He realised that Dylan's 'Country Pie' and Bach's 'Brandenburg Concerto No.3' were very similar in structure and outlined to Lee that he could play Dylan's piece with his left hand and with his other hand play the 'Brandenburg'. So they hurried down to the Scene club, where there was a piano, and worked it out there. That's when Keith decided that 'Brandenburg No.6' would fit better. It's a triumph of fusion and became a live staple.

The final track is 'One Of Those People'. It had started out as 'I'm One Of Those People My Father Tells My Sister Not To Go Out With', a song written by Lee from experience! The song, given its full title, had been premiered in an earlier BBC Radio session. It was recorded at Trident studios in the same sessions as the third album.

The album got to No.2 in the UK charts and received rave reviews. It is certainly one of the highlights of Keith's career. Chris Welch gave them a good send off in Melody Maker, "Here is a Nice farewell... the last album by a great group," he began. He saw it as their best album and it is apt, as to Welch and many others, as they always projected themselves best live.

However, Keith wasn't very happy with the album. He felt a couple of the live tracks were just not good enough for release. He wasn't consulted on the track selection, and outlined his anger in Sounds: "It's quite a shock - in fact it's plain arrogance not to at least consult the artist before releasing tapes like this." His anger was heightened by the fact that 'Country Pie' had been released as a single without his knowledge and Charisma had another album in the can. Obviously, Strat felt he owed nothing to Keith. The thrust of Keith's complaints was that the public was being conned by cheap nostalgia. Then he makes a remarkable statement, "There's a lot of bread to be made from nostalgia that people may feel for The Nice, but I'm not a nostalgic person. My music is now not then!" This may sound like a fair point but when it emerged that Keith was going to play Nice numbers with ELP – something they did for years – it becomes more questionable.

It has been said that in releasing posthumous records by The Nice, Tony Stratton-Smith was cashing in on the success of ELP, but that was ridiculous. Even if Keith had formed a broom handle and washboard band there still would have been a demand for work by The Nice. Besides, *'Five Bridges'* made number two in the charts before ELP ever played a note!

April 1971 saw Charisma release another album by The Nice, appropriately titled *'Elegy'*. This basically comprised all the left over tracks from the studio and some of the best live work from the Fillmore gigs of 1969. Keith was not involved in compiling the album but Lee and Brian had an input.

Andrew Oldham has latterly accused Stratton-Smith of starting Charisma Records with stolen tapes. The two studio tracks from *'Elegy'* which were started during the Immediate era never got into the hands of Immediate's liquidators because they were then classed as unfinished work. They ended up being the property of Charisma when they were finished. The live tapes were paid for by the band. Around the time of Immediate Records going bankrupt, Strat had to have a bodyguard outside his office. As Strat's employee Gail Coulson recalled recently, "We were getting anonymous threatening phone calls but we were sure who was responsible."

The opener of *'Elegy'* is an extended version of Tim Hardin's 'Hang On To A Dream'. This augmented 'jazzed-up' arrangement gives Keith a chance to showcase his many talents. Most of which are employed in a jazz idiom. "The interplay between bass and piano becomes very complicated then Keith drops in a boogie riff and goes off on a little journey through New Orleans," Richard Green wrote of the middle section. "This is Keith's track and one of the best examples of his playing I've heard." Brian doesn't have much to do here. The track was recorded at the final Fillmore East gigs.

'My Back Pages', another Dylan cover, was considered for *'Five Bridges'* but was left off at the last minute. Again from Richard Green, "The intro features excellent drumming, both forceful and positive. When Lee begins singing it is at once evident that without being a great vocalist he fitted in with The Nice like a mortice and tenon joint." This is the first of the two tracks recorded at Trident studios. Even though 'My Back Pages' is a classic, it has that under worked feeling to it. It hasn't been rehearsed into oblivion. After the piano intro, Keith comes in with the Hammond and it's a dramatic moment. This second section features a wonderful 'walking' bass line and Lee also gets the obligatory violin bow in as well. It's interesting that Lee's bass line is well up in the mix and is as prominent as Keith's Hammond. In fact, the track also features a few licks that Keith later used in 'Blues Variations' off ELP's *'Pictures At An Exhibition'*.

Side Two opens up with a studio version of the 'Third Movement of Tchaikovsky's Pathetique'. They had featured this in the classical concerts and it did appear on the previous album. However, this is just the band. The opening provides Keith with the opportunity to demonstrate once again he is one of the great Hammond Organ players. However, in this one Lee and Brian take much closer order and it's a lot tighter than 'My Back Pages'. That could be because they played it live more and had much more of a feel for the piece. Once again Lee's playing is given a lot of freedom and he makes his mark with a number of fast runs. Brian manages to get in a stunning drum solo at the end of the piece.

The final track is a live version of Bernstein's 'America'. It's in a much faster tempo than in the early days. Keith's playing was, at times, speeding up and he carried that on to the ultimate degree with ELP. "The drama created by Keith, Lee and Brian playing together is rarely approached by anyone else..." Richard Green wrote of this track. "The Hammond is raped, the drum kit is subjected to rapt attention and the bass guitar is played with persistent forcefulness. On record, the sound created by Keith's physical abuse of the organ often resembles musique concrete but it revives memories of happy nights at home and abroad when The Nice reigned supreme. The final minute or so of the final track of the final album is as brilliant a fusion of sounds as I've ever witnessed."

This album was, as Green described it at the start of his review 'For Mother, Bazz and the Beast', three of The Nice's closest allies. Green began his piece by outlining the meaning of the word Elegy – 'Lamentation of the dead'. Green also used the review to continue to pine for a reunion.

The album made No.5 in the UK charts.

CHAPTER **14**

REFUGEES

"I don't regret
The Nice split except
from the money
point of view.
The amount of money
people were paying us
was incredible."

LEE JACKSON

THERE WAS NEVER ANY DISCUSSION about Lee and Brian staying together. As Lee had had more notice of the upheaval, he shrewdly put the wheels in motion to get his band off the starting line early.

He called it Jackson Heights. It was Strat who suggested the name as he had visited the suburb of Jackson Heights some years before while he was in New York. From his home town of Newcastle, Lee recruited drummer Tommy Sloane and guitarist Charlie Harcourt.

Lee didn't want to play bass and felt he would like a try out on acoustic guitar - he had already decided that Jackson Heights was going to be an acoustic band. His split from The Nice bolstered the desire for him to leave the bass to someone else for a while; he was "Sick of being judged by what I couldn't do."

A lot of pressure was lifted from Lee's shoulders now, "We are quietening the whole thing down, and getting away from the hysteria, we are about to play pleasant music," he explained. Now it was all over there was only one thing he missed from The Nice, "I don't regret the Nice split except from the money point of view. The amount of money people were paying us was incredible."

Charlie Harcourt, formerly of the Newcastle band The Junco Partners, taught Lee a few chords so he could get his acoustic playing off the ground. Melody Maker described Charlie as a "witty, fast-talking, fast-drinking Geordie." Charlie was going to handle the difficult stuff, anyway. Lee had always kept in touch with Tommy Sloane and he was keen to reiterate that his old mate's fame had had a positive effect on him, "Lee hasn't changed a bit, but after The Nice there are quite a few things he can tell me. Things that I don't know."

The final member of the band was from nowhere near Newcastle. Mario Enrique Covarrubias Tapia's first encounter with Lee was rather strange, as Lee explains, "I first met Mario when I sat down having a meal in town. This Spanish guitarist came up behind me, and played 'America'. I turned round and told him I recognised the number, and after a chat I found out he could play bass." From that moment he was in the band. Mario was actually a Mexican and had played in several bands in Central America.

With the line-up complete they got down to writing, rehearsing and then recording. However, due to the instrumentation of the band they found they had to do some fine tuning with the sound levels, as Lee explains, "We found during early practice that to raise the level of the vocals above the acoustic (guitar) led to annoying difficulties that were better done away with. So now we're electric, but whenever we can use acoustic, we use it." They had already decided to concentrate on songs and this would give plenty of opportunity to develop vocal harmonies. Lee was relishing his bandleader status and he was looking forward to easing some of the pain of the recent past, as he outlined, "I think I will enjoy singing much more with the new band. I don't claim to be a great singer, but there were some songs I could sing all right. But I had to do some amazing conjuring tricks on Keith's music. I like songs that have emotion rather than vocal cleverness."

Lee's new band recorded their debut album jointly at IBC and Advision studios. The engineer at IBC was Damon Lyon Shaw, with Eddie Offord doing the honours on one track at Advision. Of course Offord was to be the future ELP engineer who played a major part in the studio sound they achieved on the three studio albums they made with him. Lee didn't actually ask for Offord, he came with the studio. The album was called *'King Progress'* and was released on Charisma on September 18th 1970, and what a good album it turned out to be.

The opening song 'Mr Screw' features a terrific percussion platform on which Charlie Harcourt delivers some interesting spiralling lead guitar licks, with a good solo at the end to boot! The atmospheric 'Since I Last Saw You' features some good interplay on acoustic guitar and bass guitar, and a great melody. This would perhaps have made a better choice for a single than 'Doubting Thomas'. It is obvious even after only two tracks that Lee's voice is used to greater effect. There is no doubt that having the decision on how the material was presented was having a positive effect on his vocal contribution. 'Sunshine Freak' sees the band in Moody Blues mode. It's exactly what the title suggests, music for a sunny day. Mario's bass is great here again and the band is really together. Closer to the first side of the album is the title track. Violins and a recorder are used to great effect here and it's interesting to note they used a small chamber orchestra but because of the deadline for the record sleeve, they weren't given a credit.

Side Two opens with the single 'Doubting Thomas'. This is the cut where the band unveiled their new instrument - Tommy Sloane's beer belly! He is 'playing' his bare stomach with his hands and this achieves the slapping sound heard on the track. Tommy was a prodigious beer drinker and it had the effect of swelling his stomach out to resemble a drum. Another dimension was added to the sound as he sucked in gulps of air to change the pitch. Lee's jaunty lyrics tell the story of a toilet jape. It's a strange subject but it's delivered with humour. The jape concerns something they used to do back home in Newcastle. There used to be cufflinks on sale that were in the shape of a Derringer pistol and really did make a bang when they were 'fired'. The trick was to tie one end of a piece of string onto the trigger and the other to the toilet chain and when someone pulled the chain, it would pull the trigger and literally frighten the shit out of them. Lee plays the harmonica on this cut. The next cut is 'Insomnia' and this was a contender for the best track. Even though the band was looking for good melodies and harmonies, they play some really good music here (probably the best music on the album).

The final track of the album is the old Nice number 'The Cry Of Eugene' (the music publisher was still Immediate Music). This was the only track recorded at Advision and it raises some questions as to the validity of going over old ground. Lee and Brian had already bemoaned that Keith was going out with the same format, and playing old Nice numbers too, but the comparisons are unfair. Keith was playing the Nice numbers in ELP in exactly the same way, whereas the version of the Nice song here is completely rearranged with different instrumentation. Also, it was the other members of the band who wanted to do it. On this version the melody is enhanced to great effect and it illustrates another nuance to the song. There are some great backing vocals and a great solo by Charlie Harcourt.

Looking back, Lee stated recently that he really should have got someone else to mix the album. In those days he was still stuck in the same mind set as The Nice had, i.e. they did not spend much time on the post-production of albums. That was an area that Lee subsequently felt had been neglected by The Nice and so for Jackson Heights. One of the things he did manage to put right with this band was his vocals. The songs were arranged, in tandem with the band, to the optimum pitch for Lee. In later albums with Jackson Heights if a track couldn't quite accommodate his vocal range, someone else would sing it. In The Nice he didn't have that luxury! *'King Progress'* is their best album. It was also the only one with Strat, who parted company with the band afterwards.

In early 1971, Jackson Heights and Brian Davison's post-Nice project, Every Which Way, briefly united at a gig at the Lyceum, London, where the Nice had enjoyed some great moments.

Jackson Heights continued with the new line up and they had some success in Europe but the album didn't make much impact at home. As time went on Lee was became dissatisfied with the band. He decided to end the acoustic experiment because he finally admitted to himself it wasn't working and he was losing his own money keeping the band going. One of the problems with having a drummer with an acoustic line-up was that he drowned out the rest of the band. This was especially apparent at the larger open air festivals.

By the end of the recording of Jackson Heights second album, *'5th Avenue Bus'*, Lee thought the band had really got into gear. The first incarnation of the band seemed more like a knee-jerk reaction to the breaking up of The Nice. As he pointed out, "Getting all my old drinking mates from Newcastle down, that was a complete mistake." Also, as the band progressed, Lee was coaxed back into more bass playing, which he didn't really relish. But he was big enough to admit his limitations, "I'm a word writer and in the end all the words were piling up with no music to go with them." That was to be a prerequisite in the new Jackson Heights - plenty of song-writing ability.

With Strat out of the picture, Lee recruited The Nice's old booking agent Johnny Toogood, who remained as manager until the end. Lee added guitarist, John McBurnie and keyboard player, Brian Chatton. They made two more albums, *'Ragamuffins Fool'* and *'Bump 'N' Grind'.* Despite a lot of good music they never had success with their albums, though they did make money touring.

Jackson Heights
Newcastle City Hall, 1972

Lee Jackson plays 'bowed' bass

Keith Emerson became a fan of the band, "Keith would come to the London shows," Brian Chatton recalls, "And that always became a nerve-wracking experience, because I thought he was the greatest keyboard player, having seen him a number of times in both The

Nice and ELP. He would be the first to applaud at the end of the songs, and if I wasn't so totally star struck, I'd say they would have been the proudest moments on stage." Keith was keen to see the band do well and he even provided some help on their final album by loaning and programming his Moog. Keith also loaned Chatton his piano for a gig in Germany in 1973, when Jackson Heights were on the bill with ELP.

On *'Ragamuffins Fool'*, at the suggestion of Chatton and McBurnie, they covered the 'Chorale' from *'Five Bridges'* album and Keith Emerson helped to transcribe it for piano. Actually, the choice of the 'Chorale' neatly sums up the differences between the first line-up of Jackson Heights and the subsequent ones. The first line-up asked for 'The Cry Of Eugene' off the first album. The latter band preferred the classical side of the Nice.

Jackson's work with The Nice re-surfaced when Charisma released *'Autumn 67 – Spring 68'* in 1972. The project was put in the hands of Lee Jackson by Strat. As Lee explains, "In 1972 we used the Phonogram Studio in the Bayswater Road. The project was to remix original recordings from the early period of the band. The only recording we made was when Keith and I did the voices for 'Daddy Where Did I Come From?'. Keith was only in the studio for a few hours. I was in there for two weeks. I produced and chose the running order for the album."

In the summer of 1973 Lee renewed another, albeit brief, Nice acquaintance when he bumped into Patrick Moraz in London at the Speakeasy. Moraz had been in a band called Mainhorse whose live work was hampered by Patrick's work permit problems but Lee jumped at the chance of bagging him for Jackson Heights. Before Lee had a chance to think of how Patrick would fit in, John McBurnie and Brian Chatton departed and with them, the end of Jackson Heights.

Of course, with their instrumentation they were never going to set the world alight and this was especially true at large festivals. As Brian Chatton recalled recently, "It was hard to keep the attention of audiences of 20,000 or more when our line-up consisted of acoustic piano, acoustic guitar and Lee on congas. We were so quiet when we played outdoor arenas, if there was a strong wind, the cows in the next field could hear us better than the crowd." In spite of these shortcomings *'King Progress'* and *'Ragamuffins Fool'* are two very good albums and their back catalogue deserves some recognition (only one of the albums is available on CD). Jackson Heights was a bold experiment and they left four studio albums as a legacy. Even though they have been forgotten today they did make some good music.

****

In the aftermath of The Nice split, Brian Davison decided he would take a short holiday to think out his future plans. Unlike Lee, Brian needed time to think things over. One thing was certain - he wanted to pursue a different direction to The Nice. Like Lee, he didn't want to go down the same path again. When he did come back he outlined the plans to Melody Maker, "The new band will be forceful as well as soft. It will be a lot different from The Nice. We want to embrace everything. I wouldn't put a tag on it yet. It's something fresh and we will find our own personality." The initial name for the band was Brian's, Hamara Pran, which is Indian for 'Our Life'. However, Strat came up with the name they settled on, Every Which Way. It was a name that neatly summed up the musical directions the band was about to embark on. It also suggested that the band wouldn't linger on a particular style for very long.

The first person Brian signed up was Graham Bell, whom he had known for a number of years. Formerly in Skip Bifferty, Brian wanted Graham because of his song writing and singing abilities. He knew he could be a bit of a handful but the creative potential swung it. Another musician he'd known for a while was tenor saxophonist and flautist, Geoff Peach. Roadie Alan Smith suggested former Manfred Mann bass player, Alan Cartwright. The final slot took quite a while to fill. For some reason they couldn't find the right lead guitarist. They deliberately looked for an unknown. Brian remembers they hired a hall and auditioned many young hopefuls. Some of them came in with the line, "I play like Jimi Hendrix!" That wasn't what Brian was looking for. Eventually, Graham Bell said he had a friend who played lead guitar. He had never played professionally but he was more than useful. His name was John Hedley. He was very nervous, the basis of which was a shocking lack of self-belief.

They decided to record before gigging, as Brian stated to Melody Maker, "It's nice to give people something to judge you on." It was a decision he would come to regret. In the same interview, Brian gave an indication of just how an important acquisition Graham Bell was, "It's difficult to describe the music. The best thing is to listen to us. Probably the main change will be that the new band will be much more melodic than The Nice. There will be more accent on the vocals." With the prospect of live work looming, Brian was eager to outline another facet of the band. It's an aspect that showed how similar his thinking was with that of Lee's outlook with Jackson Heights, "Another thing is that I won't have to play so loud. Now I will be able to get quality out of my drum kit instead of volume. In the Nice I had to get up to a certain volume because the organ was very loud. I knew I was losing quality, but there wasn't much I could do about it. I hope the new band will allow me to get back to crisper playing again."

With the new band assembled, they went straight into rehearsal with a view to going into the studio to record the album. It is interesting to note that, like Lee in Jackson Heights, Brian was now a bandleader. But it was a title he was keen to clarify to Melody Maker, "I don't really regard myself as leader. All the guys in the band have done their bit. I am just letting the whole thing come together, exploring other people's thoughts. I think you lose respect if you try and dominate, you lose what each individual has to offer." Even though Brian was letting everyone have their space it was obvious that if things didn't go right in any area, he would have to mediate.

The new group adjourned to Trident studios, planning to record the album very quickly; there was no money to do anything but. However, the decision to record before gigging soon backfired on Brian. Guitarist John Hedley was very nervous and had to be given many pep talks. Brian was always having to 'put an arm on his shoulder'. Another problem was that Brian and Graham Bell started to argue over musical direction. Brian had gone to great trouble to pick his band but he had misjudged some of the personalities badly!

They managed to record the album in a few weeks and it was released in October 1970 on Charisma. The album boasted six tracks and, like Lee's band, was a complete departure from The Nice. The opening cut is 'Bed Ain't What It Used To Be'. The acoustic guitar opening soon gives way to the band in full flow, with John Hedley playing some good lead and Geoff Peach blowing away like mad on saxophone. There are a few things that stand out immediately. The first thing is that the playing is very good, with very few overdubs. Also Graham Bell has a great voice, really soulful. It's difficult to pinpoint who they sound like on this first cut - Every Which Way perhaps? The second cut, 'Castle Sand' is the best track on the album. Geoff Peach's flute opening lends the track a great atmosphere, sounding a little like early King Crimson. There's some great guitar from Hedley, which is surprising considering he was suffering a chronic lack of confidence. The third track 'Go Placidly' quietens down proceedings somewhat. Geoff Peach plays an important role in the band because his constant switch from sax to flute opens up a lot of possibilities for the band. It's interesting to note that Brian's drumming is very precise and never intrudes into the space of the lead instruments.

All the songs so far have been penned by Bell until Side Two opens with the Niforos composition 'All In Time'. The song is credited to Brian's then girlfriend, and future wife, Maria Niforos. In fact, it was Brian who composed the song, but the drummer was so besotted, he decided to give her all his credits on the album. 'All In Time' is a funky little number with some great sax and guitar. The lead instruments compliment each other towards the end of the cut, snaking in and out of the lead line. The penultimate track is 'What You Like' and is a Bell/Niforos composition. Brian remembers this track very well as this is what he played to Stratton-Smith as an introduction to the band. Strat's reaction to this was, "Oh, I didn't know you were going down that road." He didn't like it and was getting very nervous about this project. It didn't seem to him to have any commercial potential. It got worse for Brian - he played Strat a track off Pharaoh Sanders' (ex sax, John Coltrane) album and told him that would be the direction for the new album, only freer! That put the seal of fate on the band in Strat's mind.

It's difficult to categorise the music of Every Which Way. Sounding very jazzy at times and soulful elsewhere it is hardly what would be called 'rock'. But there is no doubt that Brian gave everyone a chance to express themselves and much credit should be given for that. The album was produced by Brian and engineered by Roy Baker and Malcolm Toft; the latter having engineered some of The Nice material. In terms of the brief Brian set himself, the album was a success.

With the album in the can they set about putting a show together. Ex-Nice roadie Alan Smith was working for the band. During his tenure with The Nice, Alan actually did very little technical work and really became the driver for the group. In this new situation, he needed some technical advice about the PA they were using and so turned to Bazz. In the aftermath of the Nice split Brian had decided, because no-one else was using it, to purloin the Nice's PA. He reasoned that, as it was gathering dust, he would find a use for it. Bazz would help at gigs when his schedule allowed and would also help at rehearsals in the Fishmongers Arms public house at Hornsey, London.

Then things started to go from bad to worse. The album labels were pressed on the wrong side. The band also had trouble in getting regular gigs. Brian decided to change agencies and signed to the famous NEMS, surmising that many of the bands problems would be eased with regular live work. For example, John Hedley's problem with his nerves would be helped immeasurably with less time in between gigs. Serious troubles were created by the lack of activity. Brian remembers they would turn up for rehearsal but wouldn't play music. It wouldn't take long before Brian and Graham would argue about musical direction, so they would smoke a joint and have a few drinks - a major problem for Brian as band-leader. The buck stopped with him but as the pressure mounted he would have another drink. Obviously the rehearsal rooms were expensive, even more so with no revenue coming in. Amazingly, in amongst all the chaos, the recording of the second album was pencilled in for early 1971.

It was no surprise when Graham Bell left. Brian recruited Mike Storey as replacement and for a brief time the band was re-energised. There looked like every chance they might even get some gigs abroad. Things were looking on the up but then John Hedley departed. Shortly after that, Strat called Brian into his office and told him he didn't approve of the direction the band were taking. As a result, Brian lost his manager and his record label. There was no alternative left but to disband the group. The headline in Melody Maker was 'Every Which Way Crashes' and Brian was quite forthright in what he wouldn't be doing next, "I will not be forming a new band of my own. There are too many hassles."

Shortly after Every Which Way folded in Spring 1971, Brian signed up for a short stint with a German band called Et Cetera, after a call from an old acquaintance from The Nice era. He joined them for a month of touring with Welsh band, Man. In Et Cetera, Eberhard Weber played bass, Gary Boyle played guitar, American Fred Bracewell played amazing percussion (using everything but the kitchen sink) and Wolfgang Dauner played keyboards. In fact, Wolfgang was years ahead of his time as he used to feed tapes of other people's music in gigs, stuff like The Beatles. As Brian recently testified, "He did it all so seamlessly. It was a wild and wonderful experience." It was the only band that Brian was in that used Quadrophonic sound.

There is no way that anybody could say that Jackson or Davison were trading on former glories. The music of both Jackson Heights and Every Which Way were significant musical departures from The Nice and for this, they should both be given credit. Sadly for them, neither outfit was ever going to gain the kind of wealth and fame that their former colleague would achieve.

CHAPTER **15**

THE BIGGEST
SHOW
IN TOWN

"Greg was adamant that
it shouldn't be like
a 'New Nice' but,
at the back of my mind,
that's exactly what
it was going to be."

KEITH EMERSON

BY THE TIME *'Elegy'* was released Emerson, Lake & Palmer had been on the scene for just over six months and were well on their way to major success. The level of interest in ELP was virtually assured well before they played their first gig. King Crimson and Atomic Rooster fans followed Greg Lake and Carl Palmer, but most of the interest was on the keyboard player - Keith Emerson was now a very big name in the rock world - thanks to the success of The Nice. Greg Lake was very aware, not to say concerned, of the baggage that Keith was bringing with him. As Keith related in an interview with Classic Rock, "It was very tricky in the early days deciding what we could play. Greg was adamant that it shouldn't be like a new Nice, but at the back of my mind that was exactly what it was going to be."

The band had several record companies after their signature but in the end signed for Island Records. Rehearsals were going well but the fact that they had signed to do the upcoming Isle Of Wight Festival sharpened the nerves. They were going in cold, they had no records behind them and they only had one gig booked beforehand in Plymouth, 23rd August 1970. As they rehearsed, they also started recording their debut album.

Keith was in confident mood at the Plymouth gig as he told the audience, "This is what we sound like!" Six days later they journeyed to the Isle Of Wight for the ill-fated festival, which was promoted by one of Keith's old associates, Rikki Farr (brother of Gary, ex of the T-Bones). Emerson, Lake & Palmer made their appearance on Saturday, 29th August 1970. They played Mussorgsky's 'Pictures At An Exhibition'. The piece was packed with lots of fast runs which would be the band's trademark for the future, especially live. As well as 'Pictures' their short set also comprised of 'The Barbarian', 'Take A Pebble', the old Nice favourite 'Rondo' and 'Nutrocker'. As the shape of things to come in terms of theatrics, cannons were fired off at the end of the Mussorgsky piece.

ELP's debut album was finally released in November 1970 and mapped out similar territory to that which Keith had trodden with The Nice. There were the classical adaptations and even a short concept piece. It was the final cut that gave Keith the chance to do something completely different. A shortage of material manifested itself as studio time was running out. Asked for any ideas, Greg Lake offered up 'Lucky Man'. It was attempted but was not satisfactory until Lake suggested Emerson add the Moog. No less than Dr. Robert Moog was impressed with the result, exclaiming, "That's a real pile-driver!" Keith's solo remains an important milestone in the the the Moog Synthesiser's development.

Importantly, Emerson came to realise that he could get the Moog to work on a musical rather than the novelty level at which it had operated during its brief on-stage appearances with The Nice, and determined to take it on the road.

ELP started touring in earnest, first at home and then Europe. However, as with any band there was a 'bedding down' phase. In Keith's case it turned out to be a very painful 'baptism of fire' as Greg's forceful personality was creating problems that he hadn't envisaged. In the later days of The Nice he liked to take his wife, Elinor, on tour. However, as Keith explained in the early 1990s, Greg caused problems in this area, "He basically wanted it to be his band, and I felt a bit of an ego problem there right from the beginning. I'd never played in this kind of set-up with anyone else before. Whereas I thought if one of us had some suggestions to make we should listen to that. Greg would just order us to do this and that like saying 'Don't bring your girlfriend or wife on tour' and so on. He was really difficult to deal with." Storm clouds were brewing and things would get worse before they got better. The preparation for the second album would be a watershed for the band.

Early 1971 was spent rehearsing and recording material for the second ELP album; which was recorded very quickly. 'Tarkus' was a piece written and developed by Keith on the piano. When he premiered it to Greg and Carl he got a big surprise. Greg was adamant, "If that's what you want to play then I think you should find someone else to play with." Keith was crestfallen, he never had this reaction to his music before. For all Keith wanted another creative element within the band, he realised that this also meant devolving power. However, the management persuaded Greg and Carl to go into the studio on the basis that the time was already booked. It's astonishing that the 'Tarkus' suite was recorded in just six days! Judging by Keith's subsequent comments he never really totally got used to this arrangement. Keith stated in Classic Rock magazine (amazingly forgetting why he'd broken The Nice up in the first place), "Quite honestly we could have saved ourselves a lot of time and money at the beginning if I'd said 'I am the band leader. I'm writing the music'."

'Tarkus' was released in June 1971 and was ELP's only UK chart topper. By now the voice of Greg Lake was making its mark on ELP's overall sound. He had a superb voice and was able to project it with bags of feeling. The album has a jazzy feel to it and Emerson has cited Frank Zappa as an inspiration in the writing. On the first album Keith used the Moog sparingly but here he uses it more consistently, unleashing its potential with spectacular success, though is careful to keep it subordinated to the Hammond.

After the Spring UK tour, ELP headed to the United States for a successful clutch of dates, climaxing in a gig at Carnegie Hall. In a way they toured as relentlessly as The Nice, which is strange as comments by Keith at the time of the break-up of The Nice suggested that that was one of the things he wanted to change; wanting a little more breathing space to be able to step back and take stock. It certainly wasn't happening that way. In an interview with Classic Rock magazine, Keith gave an insight into why, when asked why there were four albums in just under two years, "I suppose Greg was the instigator of the 'We've gotta keep going' policy."

In 1971, ELP had a serious stab at introducing props into the act. For the Winter tour of the UK they used a host of them, including creatures on wires flying over the audience and a full size replica of the Tarkus. There were of course a few teething problems. Halfway through the piece the crew were supposed to shoot polystyrene from the Tarkus's guns into the crowd. However, the direction went awry and the foam ended up in Keith's piano! The gig had to be halted while the roadies vacuumed it out!

ELP rounded off 1971 with the release of Mussorgsky's *'Pictures At An Exhibition'*. Emerson had ambitiously combined the classics with original music to create one of the ultimate concept pieces and demonstrated his talents on both Moog and Hammond. In an interview given to a French magazine, he gave this response when asked why he appeared to be using the Moog more, "What is important to me is to give a specific colour to the band's music and the Moog is ideal to add colour. When you do a concert and you have to keep up the interest level for two hours, it is important to use the biggest possible variety of nuances." The album justly was recognised by rock fans as one of the best live albums of the 1970s, along with The Who's *'Live At Leeds'* and Deep Purple's *'Made In Japan'*. The album was released at a budget price as a *quid pro quo* to the record company for not letting them release it with *'Tarkus'* as a double album.

By mid 1972, ELP were one of the world's top acts and gear and gizmos were being added to their stage show at an ever increasing pace. In the summer they went to Japan, where the acclaim bordered on hysteria. They even chartered their own plane, a novelty in those days! The weather was causing havoc and it brought it into conflict with another important aspect of the band's act. As Keith recalled the plan was to have three limos - one for each member of the band - to enter the stadium. The problem was that he was still trying to fix the Moog, "Everyone was saying 'Come on, lets get going, get in the limo' and I'm saying 'Leave me alone, I've got to get the instrument going, I've got to get my instrument going. I don't care about your fancy entrance schemes'." Keith never forgot the main reason why they were all there in the first place.

ELP went into the New Year unstinting in their desire to take the show even higher in the theatrical stakes. In an early interview with NME's Nick Logan, Greg told him they were going to "Take the concept of live appearances one step further. A lot better and more interesting than most are now." With that interview being before they even played a note in public, they were proving to be as good as their word. Their Spring 1973 tour of Europe wasn't called 'Get Me A Ladder' for nothing. They had their own proscenium stage-set built and planned to take it around with them – the first band to do so. However, the problem was it was massive, by the standards of the day, and required three articulated lorries to move it. This was really the beginning of the 'overkill' that so many people despised.

Even in the middle of all the excess that made up an ELP show, it was Keith who got most of the headlines, and it sometimes grated with him. By now he was distancing himself from the theatrics because people were placing too much importance on them. When asked by a French magazine how important his stage act was, he went on the offensive but also gave a clue as to why he never dropped it from the act, "It's not important at all, it has no influence on the music. I could play the organ with my feet, it would make no difference to me. But I think it makes a difference to the public."

One of the most publicised of these excesses was the expensive Persian carpet on which Greg Lake stood. It was originally only acquired to cover the rubber mat that protected him from electric shocks. Greg told the roadie to go and find something that looked better to hide the mat and the roadie came back with the persian carpet. However, the press latched onto this luxurious item and there's no doubt Lake playfully encouraged the hype by having the roadies vacuum it on stage before each gig.

The year was punctuated with long bouts of touring and recording. ELP invested more time in making the next album than any other to date. It was mooted for September but wasn't released until December 1973. *'Brain Salad Surgery'*, was the band's fifth effort. Featuring striking HR Giger artwork, the curious title alluded to a sexual act, fellatio - they'd heard the term in a Dr John song.

Keith's partnership with Dr Robert Moog was still paying dividends and it showed on one of the cuts on the album. The commercial success of the Moog company (in which Keith had played a big part) ensured a stream of new inventions and the latest was a godsend to Keith. The Polyphonic Moog gave the sound more depth as it enabled him to play chords as opposed to the hitherto limiting single notes. The vehicle that Keith chose came all the way from South America. Argentinean composer Alberto Ginestera's '1st Piano Concerto' provided Emerson with the inspiration and he used it to the full. Keith first heard the piece in 1970 when he was at the 'Switched On Symphony' with The Nice. Only last minute permission by Ginestera to use his music kept it on the album, in fact he even endorsed it on the sleeve. ELP called it 'Toccata' and it remains one of Keith's best adaptations.

The album closes with the thirty minute long futuristic 'Karn Evil 9'. Split into three 'Impressions' its scope is massive; technology out of control being one of the themes of the latter part. It was a stroke of luck that ex-King Crimson lyricist Pete Sinfield was taken on by Lake as he used to work for IBM in the '60s. His insights fully complement the trumpeting fanfares of Keith's aggressive Moog, and the jazzy Hammond interlude convincingly represents the struggle between man and computer. The climax of the show on this tour was yet another eye catcher - an exploding computer! The album was the first to be released on ELP's own Manticore label.

To promote the album, the band kicked off a United States tour in late 1973. By now the show was even bigger than the 'Get Me A Ladder' tour of only nine months before – they'd even added Quadraphonic sound. The tour continued into 1974 and concluded with a massive outdoor gig at the California Jam, held at the Ontario Speedway just outside LA, on April 6th 1974. Co-headlining with Deep Purple, just to smooth egos they tossed a coin as to who would have the prime slot. Deep Purple won and went on early evening, leaving ELP to finish their set well after midnight, and in freezing conditions.

At that gig Keith used his latest prop, the revolving grand piano, designed by illusionist Bob McCarthy. Keith went to see him in Long Island where it was demonstrated in his back garden. Though Keith had a few accidents on it (broken nose and finger) he carried on using it for the really big gigs in the USA. He even had fireworks attached to the piano legs to give the effect of a catherine wheel!

Next ELP played a short tour of their homeland, including four shows at the prestigious Wembley Empire Pool (now known as Wembley Arena). By Autumn 1974, if the band were showing signs of fatigue, subsequent interviews confirmed it. They had become very rich and there was a feeling, if not said, that they wanted a rest and the opportunity to enjoy their wealth.

Just before they signed off in August 1974, they released a massive triple album, *'Welcome Back My Friends, To The Show That Never Ends ~ Ladies And Gentlemen, Emerson, Lake & Palmer'*. Encapsulating their current show, the album was recorded at Anaheim Convention Centre, California, on February 10th 1974. One section stands out that is not the usual ELP fayre. Occurring during 'Tarkus', 'Aquatarkus' is a master stroke - this is the best section of music found on any of their live albums, featuring some of Keith's most free flowing and restrained playing. One critic observed that Emerson "drew some feeling out of the mechanical monster." The band were playing at a furious pace as opposed to the tempo in which the studio tracks

were recorded. For example, the album opener, 'Hoedown', is played too fast and invites the opinion - actually confirmed by Keith - that the band was in competition with one another.

In 1975 Keith went to Ronnie Scott's in London, to see the Indo-Jazz Fusions. Wanting to work with John Mayer again - the last time was 1969 - he asked him to help him orchestrate the pieces of work that he was writing. It had been over five years since he had worked with an orchestra. During the time he worked with ELP, John Mayer visited Keith's home in Chiddingly and his home in Bishops Avenue, London. Keith would visit John's house in Maida Vale, London.

A lot of preparation was put in and they got to know each other very well. In all, Mayer worked for about six months for ELP, travelling to both Montreal and Montreux. Keith Emerson had come full circle and returned to where The Nice left off.

In early 1977, ELP announced their return with a double album and orchestra tour. The radical change was realised. 'Works Volume 1', with its stark black artwork, was their most eclectic album. Keith's 'Piano Concerto No.1', recorded with the London Philharmonic Orchestra, occupied all of Side One. It is a very satisfying piece of work and a successful return to the orchestra. But there was yet another motivation for writing this piece. By this time he had become a little insecure about his previous work with ELP, "You get to the stage where you do things like 'Tarkus' and 'Karn Evil 9' and they come out, and records eventually get deleted, and you think ,what the fuck is it all about?" he told Chris Welch in a Melody Maker interview in early 1977. "It's just not lasting."

Keith felt he still had something to prove by doing something 'substantial'. John Mayer was well connected in the classical world and was able to use this to facilitate the booking of the orchestra. Initially, the recording sessions were held at the Kingsway Hall, London. As it was an old church, the acoustics were not right and the session was abandoned and re-recorded at CTS studios. Keith was pleasantly surprised how well the 'Concerto' was received. BBC Radio Three even played it a few times!

Opposite:

ELP at
Tuscaloosa, AL
20 January 1974

The band side saw Keith ringing in the changes. Keith had discovered a new toy - the Yamaha GX1. He had also discovered a new anthem - Aaron Copland's 'Fanfare For The Common Man' - the GX1 fitting the track as comfortably as the Hammond had fitted 'Rondo'. Godfrey Salmon conducted the trumpets at Mountain Studios, Switzerland. The track includes a timely intervention by Greg who, still wearing his producer hat, did a lot more production on the album than he is given credit for. Keith was playing the straight arrangement in the studio. Realising the commercial potential of the track, Greg suggested adding the famous bass shuffle riff. He asked the engineer, John Timperley, to record a two-track version. They'd hit on something spontaneous and exciting and were so pleased with the finished track they had to change the sleeve of their long awaited release. Keith had to plead with Atlantic Records boss, Ahmet Ertegun, to include it for the new album and not 'Works Volume 2', as was originally planned. Keith won and the rest is history. Interestingly, Keith recorded, with John Mayer, (also at Kingsway Hall) an orchestral version of 'Fanfare' but decided to re-record it with ELP.

Including their newest album, Works, Volume 2.
On Atlantic Records and Tapes.

Available at "Record People" and "Bach to Rock."

Keith's next plan was to take a full orchestra on the road. Greg and Carl had some serious misgivings about the project - it was risky and extremely expensive. However, it transpired later that Keith was going to go his own way if the project didn't come to fruition. The tour of North America started on 24th May 1977 at the Freedom Hall, Kentucky. Prior to that the band had got in the mood by going to see the 'King of Rock 'n' Roll' himself in concert, Elvis Presley.

At first things went well. However, it wasn't long before the logistics of the operation made bankruptcy a certainty. After three months of rehearsals and the extensive work on assembling the stage set, over one million dollars had been spent before the lights went down on the first show. The expenditure to keep an entourage of 120 people on the road was over $20,000 a day! The margins were so tight that the cancellation of one big outdoor gig exposed the precarious finances of the project. Lack of research also caused a problem, the musicians union declared the members of the orchestra couldn't travel more than 250 miles a day. In the light of this no wonder the project was doomed. In ELP's attempts to take the theatrical experience of a rock show further than anyone else, they had overstretched themselves with drastic repercussions.

Planned Christmas shows in England were abandoned. In order to pay off their debts, ELP continued to tour into 1978 without the orchestra, but in an atmosphere of disillusionment. On several occasions Keith apologised to audiences for the lack of the orchestra. Limping on until March 13th, they played their final gig at the Civic Centre at Providence, Rhode Island. ELP had been sucked dry by the experience, though Keith had no regrets. He felt that the only way the 'Works' album could be toured was with an orchestra. Lake and Palmer had different opinions.

In the aftermath of the tour, Atlantic Records insisted on another studio album to fulfil the contract. The band reluctantly adjourned to Nassau in the Bahamas in the summer of 1978 to make a record. The results were horrendous. The band hated 'Love Beach', splitting immediately after its completion, though this decision wasn't to be made public until the release of the disappointing 'In Concert' in late 1979.

While Keith maintained touring 'Works' with an orchestra was the right thing to have done at the time, he did have other regrets about the full on nature of the ELP experience. "We could be in Japan one minute, America the next and Canada after that," he reflected. "The sad part about it was I never got the chance to see my first son grow up. There never was a chance to get your personal life together. Not only that but your financial life as well. We entrusted everything to accountants and lawyers because when you are touring as industriously as we were, you have to trust it to other people... You can't do everything at once and I think the destruction of ELP was because we tried to do everything at once."

However, by the time ELP split, Keith had achieved the things he set out to do when he broke up The Nice. ELP had taken the theatrical experience as far as any other band could. Keith complained sometimes that the fans only remembered the exploding computers, the flying pianos, the organ wrestling, the Persian carpets, Moog and rotating drum kits, but the band must bear some of the blame for this themselves. That was the risk they took when they piled on the many distractions to the music.

By the late 1970s, Keith Emerson was at the height of his fame. The 1980s would prove less successful for the keyboard player and in some ways it was an intentionally low-key period. He started working on film scores and in the early '80s produced some good music. 'Nighthawks' was his best score. However, the problem was that, in the main, the films were of a secondary nature. No matter how good the music is, the film has to have a profile. Some of the films were made in Japan and Italy and had limited distribution potential. To prove the point, Keith had a No.1 album in Japan and hardly anybody at home knew about it!

In the middle of the decade, Keith reunited with Greg Lake and made a very good album with new drummer Cozy Powell, the initial of whose surname meant the three musicians were still able to retain the ELP name, but the new alliance didn't last long enough to establish any lasting success. ELPowell toured the US and continued a trend of ignoring their homeland.

Emerson, Lake & Palmer briefly reunited in 1987 but all that was established was that they really didn't want to play with one another again. An injury to Keith put the project out of its misery. Keith then teamed up with Carl Palmer and, along with American singer-guitarist Robert Berry, formed a band called Three. That didn't last long either – nor did they tour at home. So by the end of the '80s Keith Emerson didn't seem to have any direction regarding his career. The '90s, however, would be different.

Lee and Keith, at Keith's home, 1989

CHAPTER **16**

THE DEATH
OF
MOTHER

"I came over
from the States
just to be at
Strat's memorial.
Everybody loved him."

LEE JACKSON

WHILST LEE WAS PERSEVERING with Jackson Heights, Brian was embarking on a few years in the wilderness. His alcohol problems were escalating out of control and often kept him from playing. His first marriage to childhood sweetheart Maureen had broken down during the early days of The Nice, and his second marriage to Maria, who he met on The Nice's 1968 US tour, was also in trouble.

In late 1972 Brian made a rare appearance on Roy Harper's album, 'Lifemask', including the memorable 'Lords Prayer', alongside such luminaries as Jimmy Page. Brian also slotted in a session for the Incredible String Band. However, sessions were generally few and far between but by late summer of 1973 his exile was about to end, and how!

Meanwhile, Lee Jackson and Patrick Moraz were lining up their next move, "Initially, we started off with a plan to do an extension of Jackson Heights," Lee explains. "But directly we started writing material and it was obvious it was going to be much heavier than that. It was obvious too that we needed a really hefty drummer." There was, in fact, only one man for the job, Brian Davison! But before that, Lee and Patrick went to the Speakeasy to see Strat with a view to getting a record deal. As they walked in they could see Strat who saw them bearing down in him. Before they had time to say anything Strat said "Yes, if it's what I think you want. Come and see me in the office in the morning."

It was clear that people would start to make comparisons with The Nice. Nonetheless, it has to be remembered that Patrick was taking the most pressure. If people made the connection to The Nice, as they did, then Patrick would be compared to Keith, and that would test the mettle of any musician. It wasn't an easy move for Lee and Brian neither. But Lee was unflinching in his honesty, as he confided to Sounds, "I suppose in a way you could say it's an admission of failure that Brian and I are back where we left off two years ago. We couldn't get our own bands off the ground. Brian went through a very bad patch when his band never took off and Heights was a failure." However, Lee astutely turned the argument back on the critics by arguing that if they could discern The Nice in the new band then it was proof that the rhythm section did make a contribution to that band.

The new band would be called Refugee. On the first day of rehearsal Brian, was nervous and nursing a serious hangover. Lee wasn't aware how bad Brian's drinking had got. As Brian confesses, "I was in a mess." After the rehearsal, Brian got drunk and fell over in Lee's flat! But the good thing was it didn't get any worse. Refugee was a hard working band and as long as they were gigging or rehearsing, Brian's drinking was under control. After signing to Charisma they invited Gail Coulson to come and see rehearsals at Chalk Farm in London. Gail was blown away when she heard the band and wasn't expecting anything of that calibre. It was amazing that a musician of Patrick's calibre was so unknown.

Refugee continued to rehearse furiously and were determined they would gig before recording. It turned out to be a wise decision. Lee and Brian were revelling in playing with such a talented musician as Patrick – something neither had experienced for over three years. Strangely, the three of them could have got together earlier as Keith had suggested Patrick as a replacement in The Nice when he left to form ELP. Unfortunately Lee and Brian were mentally exhausted by the break up and it just wasn't the right time. Chris Welch interviewed the band and remembered Brian cracking a joke about Patrick, "He's not bad... for a foreigner!"

After a couple of month's rehearsals they played their first gig at
The Roundhouse in London, 2nd December 1973. It was the first
of a dozen or so gigs that were mainly on the University circuit.
Their repertoire consisted of the material that was scheduled for their
first album and a few Nice numbers, including 'The Diamond Hard Blue
Apples Of The Moon' (which The Nice never played on stage) and
'She Belongs To Me'. Like The Nice they interspersed touring and recording. Consequently,
the album took three months to record but, according to Lee, represented only about three
weeks of studio time.

**Refugee at The
Marquee, 1974**

Brian Davison
and Lee Jackson

The band then continued gigging in relatively small venues, building a reputation; they continued to return to the studio until the spring when the album was finally finished. It was still difficult for the band to break out from the shadow of Lee and Brian's former group. In an interview on a radio show, Extravaganza, in April 1974, to rebut the charge that Refugee were 'The Nice Mark Two', Brian gave a cutting riposte to their detractors, "It would be a waste of time to do the classics as Patrick is such a great writer!"

"The music is more symphonic than The Nice used to be," Patrick insisted, "So it's really up to date. Most of the music is more emotional in its entity. The solos, the singing, everything expresses our emotions. And although it could be very fast and technical in places like 'Credo' and 'Grand Canyon' everything we play expresses an emotion."

The eponymous debut album was produced by John Burns and recorded at Island studios. As Brian remarked recently, John didn't really produce the album as they were "Quite self contained in that area," but he did get Brian a great drum sound. The basic album was recorded very quickly - twelve hours quickly! They decided that Patrick would choose the lead instrument and then the band would record the basic track. The problem was, when Patrick started laying down the overdubs, he didn't know when to stop. On more than one occasion Brian was heard to say, "But Patrick we'll have no room for the bass guitar!" There was a bewildering choice of lines to choose from, which made the editing and mixing process fraught. Keen to avoid such scenes, John Burns would call up Brian and ask him, "Have you got any time for mixing? The whole thing is getting too fucking confusing!"

Out of the chaos, came a very strong album. The tone was set with the fiercely played opening instrumental, 'Papillon', titled because the band felt the Moog flurry sounded like a butterfly's wings, and because the record coincided with the recent Steve McQueen movie of the same name.

'The Grand Canyon' is the first of the two concept pieces on the album (on the inner sleeve and record label the track is called 'Canyon Suite').

CREDO

I BEILIEVE IN MIDNIGHT MADNESS
AND SHIPS THAT PASS IN THE NIGHT
AND I STILL BELIEVE IN LOVE
LIKE A CHILD IN SANTA CLAUSE
AND THE KING WHO HAD NO CLOTHS
WASN'T THE ONLY ONE EXPOSED.
THE QUEUE FORMS BESIDE ME
AS I SING MY CREDO TO A LOST CAUSE

I BEIEVE IN CONSTANT PA
LIKE A ROMAN HOLLIDAY
I OFTTEN STOP FOR AIR
AS I CLIMB THE SPANISH STAIRS
AND THE KING WHO'S TOUCH WAS GOLD
WAS SUPPRISED AS HE GREW OLD.
THE QUEUE FORMS BEHIND ME AS I
AS I SING MY CREDO TO A LONG PAUSE

I BELIEVE, AND YOU BELIEVE, AND WE BELIEVE WE SE
BUT THE NR DON'T COST A THING
TO A BIRD WITH A BROKEN WING
AND THE WIS'EST KING OF ALL
LEFT HIS WISDOM ON THE WALL
THE QUEUE FORMS BESIDE ME

CREDO

I BEILEAVE, THE LIFE YOU L
CANT CONCEAVE, AN EXTRE
FROM NEAR TIMES FAR, W
WE STAY. TO PLAY A
STAGE AND LEAVE. TO
AND HALF FORGOTTON LI
A SONG IN PRAISING
THE WORD'S

I BELEAVE, THE LIFE YOU
CANT CONCEAVE THE EXRT
FROM NEAR THE STARS,
HEAR THEY'RE YOURS, TO
THE UNIVERSE, AND SM
WE CHASE, THE WIND, A
AND PLAY A WHILE THE G

160

Patrick wrote the music after seeing a BBC documentary about the famous natural landmark and asked Lee to come up with some lyrics. After an initial block, Lee saw another TV show featuring the canyon, and that night he dreamed he was flying over it using his arms as wings. He woke up at four o'clock that morning and wrote the lyrics there and then. The track begins with Lee's violin bow coupled with Patrick's opening chords which help to set an eerie scene. Patrick even manages to play a little bit of Alpine Horn - this was his trademark at the gigs. Lee used to say that anyone who could fill it with hash could have the horn - leaving the hash for them! Brian's drumming really comes to the fore here and in the 'Second Movement' he combines well with Patrick on great form on the Moog. Lee's bass is a lot more 'toppy' than it was in The Nice. The 'Third Movement', 'The Journey', evokes the piece's compositional process, "When you go home and sleep this night / Dream of wings and astral flight." It features some great piano by Patrick - a strange combination of speed and feeling, but it works. It's exactly how Patrick described the music on the radio show - full of emotion. The 'Fourth Movement', 'Rapids' is dominated by Brian's steamrollering playing and some extremely fast electric piano runs by Patrick. The last Movement is 'The Mighty Colorado' which comes to a tremendous, and ironic, conclusion with Brian's timpani and Patrick slamming the Hammond down with the reverb producing a crashing sound and giving it an 'à la Keith Emerson' climax. The 'Grand Canyon' suite is a breathtaking concept piece. Lee remembers that Patrick employed some brilliant strokes on the track. He particularly recalls the way he put both the Hammond and the electric piano through a Binson echo machine to achieve some of the special sounds. "There's some clever shit on that!" Lee concluded.

Side Two opens with the funky instrumental 'Ritt Mickley' – named for Patrick's foreign pronunciation of 'rhythmically'. The next track, 'Credo', a rumination on Lee's attitude to his strict Catholic upbringing, is the second concept piece on the album. Brian remarked in a radio interview that 'Credo' was his favourite track because it was as far removed from The Nice as it could possibly be. The album included 'Someday', a very personal song about the break-up of Lee's first marriage.

Though not a huge seller, the album was well received, and things were looking good for the band. There was already talk of a second album and a possible United States tour supporting Eric Clapton. Then, in the late summer of 1974, disaster struck. Brian picked up Melody Maker and saw the headline that Rick Wakeman had quit Yes. He went straight over to Patrick's flat in Earls Court, London. He showed the Melody Maker it to Patrick and said, "They're going to come for you!" Moraz's reply was emphatic, "I'll turn it down." Brian was worried though; he knew a man of Patrick's calibre was going to be ripe for recruitment to a more successful group.

After Yes unsuccessfully tried out Vangelis as a replacement for Wakeman, their manager, Brian Lane, invited Patrick to a rehearsal - it was very early August 1974 - to see how things worked out. Patrick was offered the job, and in spite of his initial reluctance to quite Refugee, he accepted. Patrick called a meeting with Lee and Brian and informed them of his decision to quit the band. Tony Stratton-Smith was at the meeting and it was at this time that Patrick expressed a desire for his move to remain unannounced until after the final gig - they had a number of bookings to fulfil.

Refugee played their final gig at the Roundhouse in London on the 13th August. It just happened to be Strat's birthday so Patrick played a stunning rendition of 'Happy Birthday' in which he spectacularly improvised around the main theme. For a farewell show the atmosphere was a lot better than at the final gigs of The Nice. However, Patrick didn't get his way with regard to keeping his departure under wraps. Lee introduced the band and announced that it would be Refugee's last show as Patrick was leaving to join Yes.

For Lee it was the end of the line in top-flight music. He would never play in a front-line band again until The Nice reformed in 2002. He'd had enough. Brian was gutted at how history had repeated itself but is not bitter, explaining recently, "What a lucky man I've been. To have played with two of the greatest keyboard players in rock history."

Even though Refugee only made one album, there is no doubt it's a classic. The album drew a lot of critical and fan acclaim. One person who was impressed was Keith Emerson. When the album was finished, Lee took an acetate round to Keith's house where, in Lee's words, Keith was 'blown away' by what he heard. Furthermore, they both agreed that this was Brian's best drumming ever. The standard of musicianship on the album as a whole is stunning but Brian's contribution is as good as drumming gets. Lee is no slouch either. His bass work is good too and his vocals are strong. There is no doubt that having the luxury of choosing the optimum key made a marked improvement to his singing.

Chris Welch witnessed Refugee in concert a couple of times and rated them highly. Chris interviewed Patrick recently, "He was always torn and upset about giving Refugee up for Yes... He wasn't really happy in a 'super group'. He would have been better off as a bigger fish in a smaller sea, I think."

Shortly after Refugee split, Brian joined Gong in February 1975, taking over the drum stool from the departing Bill Bruford. He enjoyed playing with the band, managing to remain reasonably sober, but when leader Daevid Allen left and Steve Hillage took the helm, Brian didn't like the new musical direction and quit in July 1975. That was when his problems really started. By now his second wife had gone back to the States. He lost his flat and, after storing his drums at a friend's restaurant, for a period of about nine months he was sleeping rough, sometimes bedding down on a Thames barge, other times in Paddington Station – occasionally managing to bunk down in a train's sleeper compartment. It would be a few more years until Brian would emerge out of the dark tunnel in his life.

Sadly, Gong was the last time Brian would play in a front-rank band for 27 years. Keith Emerson told Brian's wife Maria that he felt especially bad about the way things turned out for him.

****

One of the myths that has attached itself to The Nice is that Lee and Brian took years to forgive Keith for breaking up the band. There's no doubt that Keith has encouraged such perceptions, deliberately or not. Even as late as 2001 he was talking about getting The Nice back together, Lee and Brian having 'forgiven him'. However, except for the naturally difficult period just after the break up, the three men have always been mates. When ELP played a gig at the Royal Festival Hall on October 25th 1970, Brian went along as Keith's guest. Hanging out backstage he noticed a different vibe from the ELP entourage than that of The Nice. Brian didn't like all the 'hangers on', and he found the music "Dry, boring and very clinical." However, that opinion never affected his and Keith's friendship.

One thing that did annoy Brian, and Lee, was how Keith would play old classics from The Nice era with his new band. It was understandable for Keith to do this in the early stage of ELP as the new group didn't have enough material to fill a show. It does seem strange that Greg and Carl went along with this as they had made it very clear that they were keen to avoid comparison with The Nice. Keith appeared unable or unwilling to let go of The Nice's music. Even by the time ELP got to the fourth album, 'Trilogy', he was still persevering with those old tunes. Up until 'Fanfare For The Common Man', 'Rondo' was still one of the central highlights of the show.

For a while after The Nice split, Lee didn't have any contact with Keith. He was busy with Jackson Heights and Keith was tied up with ELP. Lee remembers the first time he spoke to Keith after the break up. Keith called him out of the blue to excitedly tell him about the birth of his first child, Aaron. What struck Lee the most was that Keith spoke as if The Nice split had never happened. It was almost as if Keith might have said, "Oh, by the way, there is a band rehearsal at the weekend." So there never really was a time that Lee and Brian were estranged from Keith. Consequently, in the intervening years the three of them crossed paths a number of times.

In the summer of 1983, Keith was in LA scouting for a singer, and looked up his old buddy Lee, asking him for any suggestions. One evening they went along to the Central club for a 'Jam Night' run by old Nice roadie Keith Robertson. Al Kooper, ex of Blood Sweat & Tears and many other legendary sessions, was performing. Keith suggested to Lee that, "We should do this next week!" Lee was surprised as he hadn't played the bass for four years. However, on the 5th of July 1983, Keith and Lee appeared on the same stage for the first time in 13 years. They also had Ian Wallace on drums as well as a guitarist. Usually on 'Jam Night' there was little advance publicity but when Lee arrived and saw the queue going around the block he knew the word had got out. They played 'America', 'Fanfare For The Common Man', 'Nutrocker' and 'Rondo'. Ian Wallace took advice off Lee on how to play 'Rondo' and all-in-all it worked. Not bad, considering they only had a short rehearsal. Keith Robertson closed the evening by expressing the hope that The Nice would play the upcoming 25th Anniversary of the Marquee later in the year.

Initially Keith was up for the anniversary gig, but according to Brian and Bazz, wanted the show to take place at the larger, more prestigious (and more lucrative) Hammersmith Odeon (now Apollo). Clearly it was difficult to celebrate the anniversary of The Marquee at a different venue. It certainly wouldn't have had the intimate atmosphere of The Marquee, which the event was supposed to recreate. Perhaps Keith had played in so many big arenas, he couldn't contemplate playing in such humble surroundings. Negotiations continued for a while but faltered, to Lee and Brian's great disappointment.

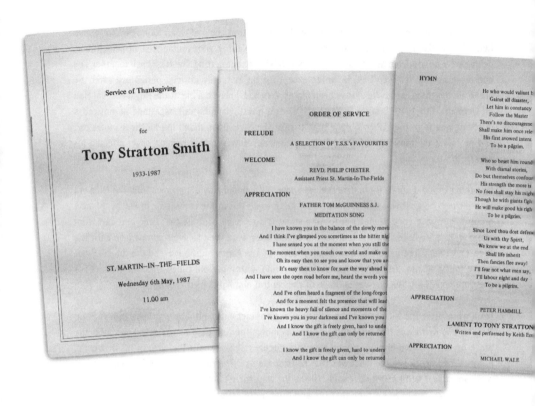

The order of service documents read:

Service of Thanksgiving

for

Tony Stratton Smith

1933-1987

ST. MARTIN–IN–THE–FIELDS

Wednesday 6th May, 1987

11.00 am

ORDER OF SERVICE

PRELUDE

A SELECTION OF T.S.S.'s FAVOURITES

WELCOME

REVD. PHILIP CHESTER
Assistant Priest St. Martin-In-The-Fields

APPRECIATION

FATHER TOM McGUINNESS S.J.

MEDITATION SONG

I have known you in the balance of the slowly movi
And I think I've glimpsed you sometimes as the bitter nig
I have sensed you at the moment when you still the
The moment when you touch our world and make us
Oh its easy then to see you and know that you ar
It's easy then to know for sure the way ahead is
And I have seen the open road before me, heard the words you

And I've often heard a fragment of the long-forgot
And for a moment felt the presence that will lead
I've known the heavy fall of silence and moments of the
I've known you in your darkness and I've known you
And I know the gift is freely given, hard to unde
And I know the gift can only be returned

I know the gift is freely given, hard to unders
And I know the gift can only be returned

HYMN

He who would valiant b
Gainst all disaster,
Let him in constancy
Follow the Master
There's no discourageme
Shall make him once rele
His first avowed intent
To be a pilgrim.

Who so beset him round
With dismal stories,
Do but themselves confoun
His strength the more is
No foes shall stay his might
Though he with giants figh
He will make good his righ
To be a pilgrim.

Since Lord thou dost defend
Us with thy Spirit,
We know we at the end
Shall life inherit
Then fancies flee away!
I'll fear not what men say,
I'll labour night and day
To be a pilgrim.

APPRECIATION

PETER HAMMILL

LAMENT TO TONY STRATTON
Written and performed by Keith Em

APPRECIATION

MICHAEL WALE

1987 was a sad year for close associates of The Nice. On March 19th 1987, Tony Stratton-Smith died of cancer of the pancreas. He was just 53. His Charisma Record company was, by the '80s, a reputable label and its roster included artists as diverse as Monty Python, poet Sir John Betjeman and Peter Gabriel. The huge diversity of the Charisma line-up was pure Strat - he took risks. He took risks with his health too. 'Burning the candle at both ends' was a lifelong occupation. He was always seen propping the bar up at The Marquee, La Chasse or The Ship.

Bazz was the first of the inner crew of The Nice to hear the distressing news. A colleague at his works told him that one of the big figures of his past had died, but details were sketchy. For some reason Bazz thought it was Jack Barrie. So he phoned up the Marquee and was astounded when Jack answered the phone. Poor old Jack had to break the news, "So you haven't heard then? It's Strat who's passed away." Bazz couldn't believe it. That's how quick it happened, he didn't even know he'd been ill. He pondered what to do for a while. He phoned Brian, who was out, and then he phoned Lee in LA (he didn't know Keith's number). Just after that, Brian phoned and the two men unashamedly wept as Bazz related the details to him.

On Wednesday 6th May, Tony Stratton-Smith's Service of Thanksgiving was held at St Martin-In-The-Fields, London. Prior to the event, Gail Coulson, Strat's old PA, phoned Bazz and asked him to roadie one more time. So he went down early and set up some gear, as a friend of Strat was going to play a song. The service was conducted by the Rev Philip Chester and included appreciations by Lee, Graham Chapman and Peter Hammill. Keith played a number he'd written especially for Strat called 'Lament To Tony Stratton-Smith'. Keith related to Keyboard magazine how it was a very difficult thing to do, "I'd never played at a memorial service before. It's not an easy gig, quite honestly. You get up there and perform, and nobody claps. Everybody cries." Tony's favourite hymns were also sung, including 'Jerusalem'. The Monty Python team broke the funereal mood by singing 'Always Look On The Bright Side Of Life'. At the end of the service there was a collection for The Mother Theresa Mission Of Charity, Calcutta, India. Bazz remembers it was a very emotional event.

Davy O'List turned up too, but his arrival with a repackaged copy of a 20th Anniversary edition of the first Nice album with his above-the-band credit didn't go down too well with the rest of the band.

Afterwards the mourners decamped to the Marquee where Gail Coulson, Jack Barrie and Harold Pendleton were drinking Bucks Fizz. Bazz thought, "Fuck this, I'm going round to The Ship. That's where Strat would be." Richard Green accompanied him. One by one, the party adjourned to The Ship, Strat's spiritual home. This was an emotional place for Bazz apart from The Strat connection as this was where he first heard about a job going for The Nice from Mel Baister. Before long all the band were there. Lee had especially come over from LA. Brian remembers, "Lee paid for my meal because I was flat broke." By the end of the afternoon most of the entourage staggered home, drunk out of their heads and reflecting how much emptier life would be without Strat.

Strat's Memorial, The Marquee

Left-right:
Davy O'List,
Keith Emerson,
Brian Davison,
Elinor Emerson,
Gail Coulson,
Lee Jackson

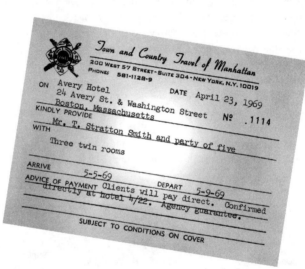

CHAPTER **17**

THE NICE
ROAD HOME

"What have I
been doing
all these years?"

KEITH EMERSON

The Return of the Legendary
EMERSON, LAKE & PALMER
ELP

OCTOBER
ROYAL ALBERT HALL
MANCHESTER APOLLO   FRI 2 /SAT 3 /MON 26
NOVEMBER   SUN 25   071 589 8212
BOURNEMOUTH INT. CENTRE   061 236 9922
NEWCASTLE CITY HALL   WED 25
BIRMINGHAM SYMPHONY HALL   THUR 26   0202 297297
BRISTOL COLSTON HALL   FRI 27   081 261 2606
                           SAT 28   031 212 3333
EDIT CARDS ACCEPTED   0272 223686
£15 and £13 except Royal Albert Hall £17.50, £15 and £12.50
Affairs of the Heart out now taken from the new album Black Moon

IN 1991, THE NEWS BROKE that ELP were recording again. *'Black Moon'* appeared the following year. Lee Jackson helped Keith on one of the tracks. Lee explains, "He had a piece called 'Close To Home' [According to Lee, this started life as the piece that Keith played at Strat's memorial], I sat with him when he was playing it. I said 'Hold it back, think about how Debussy or Chopin would have played something like that'. I worked with him the whole afternoon. I said 'Forget about it being in time, let it flow'. I feel quite proud of helping him with that."

ELP's world tour of 1992/1993 was a great success and put the band back on the map much to the delight of their fans. However, the triumph was marred by the appearance of the disastrous *'In The Hot Seat'* in 1994. This record was afflicted by in-fighting, record company politics and a career-threatening arm injury to Keith. Fortunately after surgery, Keith made a complete recovery. Also around this time Keith got divorced, after 23 years of marriage to Elinor. It was time for a complete break so he moved to Santa Monica in the USA. As he recalled to The Guardian, it was a time for reflection, "I wrote film scores, customised a Harley Davidson and began writing my autobiography, 'Pictures Of An Exhibitionist' [yet to see the light of day]."

ELP returned to the stage, touring with Jethro Tull in 1996 and Deep Purple in 1998, after which they broke up over arguments about producer credits for the next studio album. It would now appear that ELP may never even play live again.

****

Brian Davison had endured a terrible time since the mid '70s. In 1980 he managed to secure a job teaching percussion at Clapham College in London, on the strength of his background, but was still having problems with drinking. Fortunately he was popular with the Principal of the college and so Brian had more leeway than he might otherwise have had. He made a big effort to succeed but in the end he lost his job. Soon after that Strat helped him out and bought him a car but by the time of

Strat's memorial he was still living in limbo.

Lee had gone to LA in 1977 to seek his fortune in interior designing. By 1979 he'd started up his own business and was making a very good living out of it. He married an American and happily settled down there. With regard to his new career of design and commercial interiors, he remarks, "I'm lucky – I was able to do something else which I love just as much. The visual arts are a lot of fun to me." Occasionally the past caught up with him. He'd just finished designing a bank in Santa Ana and turned up at the opening. Unbeknown to him the staff had found out who he was and he entered the building to the strains of 'Rondo'. Lee returned to the UK to live in 1994.

Brian, Lee,
Par Lindh

On returning to Britain, Lee recorded a version of Ravel's 'Bolero' with keyboard player Andrew Marlow. Lee was a friend of Andrew's brother, Duncan. It has been suggested that Brian was involved in this project but he never was. Lee just went over to Andrew's house and put down a bass line. Andrew even suggested that they tackle 'Riverdance'!

In September 1994, Lee and Brian were approached by Norwegian keyboard player, Par Lindh, with the idea of forming a trio. They rehearsed and gelled quite well. The material was originally to be a combination of Lindh's, The Nice and, surprisingly, ELP, as well as a Swedish folk song (which Lee loved). Less surprisingly, Lee and Brian were adamant they wouldn't play any ELP material. What was the point? There was no connection with any member of the band. The project eventually fizzled out due to the lack of financial backing, "The idea was to tour Scandanavia but we would only have the gig money," says Lee. "It appeared to us the finances needed more working out. Par impressed us both with his ability, but it was not to be."

****

After a long gestation period, an album of The Nice's BBC sessions, *'America'*, was finally released in 1996 on Trojan Records. According to Brian Davison, one of the reasons why the process had dragged on for so long was that "Davy thought he'd written most of the material." It was also claimed that O'List wanted all of the payment for the record, believing that his bandmates had withheld royalties from him from previous Nice albums. Davy saw things differently. In a letter to an American friend on 18th March 1993, Davy wrote, "The Nice BBC CD seems close to a release, only Lee and Keith are holding back and behaving very illusively about signing a deal." Around about this time he contacted Q Magazine in the UK and provided them with a piece

ELP, Birmingham
Symphony Hall
27th November 1992

on the band called 'Where Are They Now'. In the piece, Davy's name appears first, thus actually creating the impression, as he had with the first album's 20th Anniversary release, that he was the leader of the band.

Keith's 50th Birthday, 2nd November 1994, with Pat Arnold and Lee Jackson

Trojan certainly had a lot of material to choose from, but the opener 'America' was a truly dreadful way to start, as Brian acknowledges, "If someone would have heard the first track as a decider on whether to buy it they would have run a mile... It was the worst version of 'America' they had!" The fact the band didn't have any input into track selection wasn't the only problem. The tracks needed more technical polishing to bring them up to a releasable standard. If only Trojan had cleaned up the source material, it would have been a good album, whichever tracks they selected. Having said all that, there are some gems. There's a band version of 'Five Bridges' and some rare stuff played at the gigs at the time, like 'Sombrero Sam' (wrongly titled 'Sombrero King'), 'St Thomas' with Roy Harper and the old barnstormer, 'Aries - The Firefighter'. And at least the members of The Nice got paid for the record - that hadn't happened for a long time. Brian bought a car with his advance.

In late 1996, Lee went over to LA to visit his children. He met up with Keith who put an interesting proposition to him. Keith handed Lee a cassette he had done from a mix off a DAT tape. On the cassette was Keith's recent attempt to rework Bob Dylan's 'Man In The Long Black Coat'. Keith told Lee that when ELP had covered it on 'In The Hot Seat', Greg had done it in operatic mode and Keith was keen to redo it more satisfactorily, suggesting that Lee's voice would suit the track better. Keith also wanted Brian to play on the new recording. Keith left the tape for Lee to take away and record his parts and Brian's. It would be the first studio recording by the The Nice since 1969.

When Lee got home, he booked a studio near his home and Brian came up to record. Both of them had spent some time working out their parts. Keith's backing stretched the track a lot more than the ELP arrangement, so the two musicians had a lot of scope. Although Lee and Brian weren't sure what Keith's aim in all of this was, they had waited a long time for the opportunity. The recording went very well and they were happy with the end result.

Keith was pleased with the work too. He came over to England and a studio was booked on March 1st 1997, to accommodate the final bit of post-production. Lee wanted to have another crack at the vocal. He had delivered the vocal pretty much in the same style as Dylan had on the original. When they got to the studio at Clarkenwell, they found that Keith had brought along a session guitarist who turned out to be very good and the recording went very well. The final version of the track features a more complex arrangement than the ELP version, and is extremely musically invigorating with a great ambience. Sadly, following the sudden death of the session guitarist, any potential of live performances petered out. Still, Lee and Brian both think Keith's motivation in this was to see if they could still do it. On the evidence of this track, there is no doubt about that.

In June 1998, Keith met up with some of the original T-Bones, Stuart Parkes and Winston Weatherall, and Brian Walkley turned up as well. Keith was in England, visiting his mother, when he heard they were playing at the Connaught pub in Hove. So he went along and surprised them. They were still playing well as Keith commented, "It was great to have the chance to watch Winston and Stuart playing live again. They were fabulous – really knock-out – and still true to that bluesy feel of old." It was on the eve of ELP's US tour with Deep Purple and Keith made a remarkable confession to Brian, "I don't really enjoy playing live any more." Apparently tired of ELP shows, Keith appeared to be searching for something to get his enthusiasm back.

Keith with ELP,
Hamburg, July 1997

There was another reunion for The Nice on Saturday, 6th March 1999. Keith called up Lee and Brian and asked them if they would play a surprise gig for his mother's birthday. Dorothy Emerson had always preferred The Nice to ELP and one of the lasting memories that Lee has of her was seeing her in tears at the end of the last Fairfield Hall gig. It was actually the idea of Keith's friend, comedian Jim Davidson, to get this thing together. Keith had booked a big band to play at the party but the reunion element was kept a secret. They discussed over the phone what they were going to play and decided on 'Rondo', 'America' and 'Little Arabella'. Keith had some new chord changes for Lee to learn for 'Little Arabella'. Lee and Brian travelled down to Worthing and checked into the hotel that Keith had booked for them.

On the day, Jim Davidson brought his own PA to help out. Lee remembers carrying the mixing desk with Jim out of the van into the hall. There were a couple of lads standing outside and as Lee went past he heard one of them say, "One of those roadies is the spitting image of Jim Davidson." The big band had set their gear up on stage but behind that was a Hammond Organ, bass guitar and drums. It wasn't the total surprise they hoped for, for Dorothy had recognized her 'second son' – as she always called Lee. Aaron Emerson approached Lee, excitedly telling him, "I'm going to see The Nice. They split up before I was born!"

The Nice proceeded to play for over half an hour. Lee remembers it was just like the old days as they would respond to Keith's body signals. It was as if thirty years had never passed. When they finished, as Brian got off his drum stool he heard Keith say, "What have I been doing all these years?"

The Nice Reunion, 1999

Note comedian – and roadie for a day – Jim Davidson, disappearing far right

****

There is a happy ending for Brian, who is well established at a college in Devon, teaching various kinds of percussion including African drumming. He hasn't had a drink for thirteen years – the turning point was when he met his current partner, Teri West (a professional storyteller). It was Teri's support that got him back on track. It wasn't easy for him at first, but he is now enjoying life to the full and is very happy living by the seaside.

Keith is currently working to release a batch of archive material, including The Nice's Fillmore gigs. A good start has already been made with the 1967 concert recorded by Swedish broadcasting, released by Sanctuary Records in October 2001. It's a valuable piece of work from the O'List era, if anybody needed evidence just how potent the band was, even in those early days. The third track 'Sombrero Sam' is fantastic, with every member playing wonderfully. Keith has also remastered the BBC sessions to be released as a double CD on Sanctuary in September 2002. It is hoped that these will be the first of many archive releases to create a more complete concert history of the band.

CHAPTER **18**

YOUR FRIENDLY
NEIGHBOURHOOD
GROCERY STORE

"Well, we're back!"

KEITH EMERSON

PEOPLE HAVE OFTEN COMPARED The Nice to ELP but that is not really a viable concept, just because Keith Emerson was in both groups. The music they played, although similar on the surface, was executed in two completely different ways. The Nice were a loveable band and their freer music generated a degree of warmth. ELP, on the other hand, were more rigid and calculating. Watching The Nice live could possibly result in a little bit of secret foot tapping. With ELP you watched with jaw-dropping awe. Also, and most critically, The Nice came first and blazed the trail that made audiences receptive to the kind of music with which ELP enjoyed overnight massive success.

In the three years between the formations of the two bands, studio and recording technology took a quantum leap in development. Stereo was firmly established by the very early '70s, ushering in the appearance of the 24-track mixing desk. The stereo imperative in the studio drove the industry to produce better stereo systems for home consumption. Another implication of all this was that bands spent more time in the studio. The Nice didn't do that. The sound revolution also permeated live performance. Of course, The Nice developed their own unique sound system and built up a great reputation on the back of it, but they were also one of the first bands to recognise the necessity for great sound, albeit because they lost a guitarist. They were also a major force in thrusting the keyboard to the fore. Of course a lot of that was due to Keith but he still needed a band to pull it off.

The onset of ELP seemed to coincide with a change in the way music was presented live. The venues got bigger and bands lost contact with their fans. Some fans of The Nice didn't follow Keith's new career, including many of the 'Marquee 12'! The culmination of this remoteness was when bands of the '70s, ELP being one of the main culprits, blatantly ignored their home fans to play for big bucks in the States. When the USA's greatest film maker, Orson Welles, was presented with a lifetime achievement in 1975 he said, "In the age of supermarkets, I'm your friendly neighbourhood grocery store!" The Nice were always the friendly neighbourhood grocery store to ELP's Hypermarket, neatly encapsulating the '60s and the '70s.

When The Nice started out they had to build their audience. They had to contend with people dancing instead of listening to them; they didn't know how far they or how long they could go on playing this kind of genre-busting music. They compiled their musical act on the hoof, without any previous 'set of instructions' from any other band. They were creating something unique and Keith Emerson was at the forefront.

Their first album is one of the most progressive albums ever made, without actually formally falling into the category which is now called 'prog rock'. In fact, the term 'prog rock' is something of a misnomer. As Chris Welch remarked recently, "All the rock music that was happening – up until 1977 – was regarded as progressive. It was the current way of regarding contemporary music as forward thinking, experimental and looking for ways to improve." So to Chris it was all progressive music, "It was all rock until it became unprogressive – i.e. punk, pub and other dismal aberrations that eventually destroyed the credibility of most forms of British music."

Even though 'Sgt Pepper' was the major defining moment of the era in terms of ambitiously expanding rock's musical palette, Keith Emerson had already taken tentative steps towards his own progressive path. But it all came about by serendipity. In an interview with Disc given just after The Nice had split, he explained to Penny Valentine, "At rehearsals I'd always played classical and jazz piano, just messing around, and everyone said: 'Why don't you do that on stage?' I thought they were joking. Then I realised I didn't have anything to lose anyway."

After 'Sgt Pepper' smashed many of the restrictions and rules as to what was acceptable in popular music, helping to ensure that the album was rock's key medium, progressive groups ambitiously took in a number of influences to expand the rock sound. Led Zeppelin drew on blues and folk to create their unique sound. Colosseum drew heavily on jazz. The Nice was drawn more to the classics. It is from this inspiration that they were to find themselves at the vanguard of a new genre of music, justly revered by the musicians who were inspired by their particular brand of trail blazing.

But there were other factors that contributed to this explosion of creative music. There was the prevalent use of drugs which had the effect of increasing experimentation – although The Nice was less affected by this than other bands. There was also the great liberating social and cultural shifts that the '60s had ushered - not only was there liberation in music it spread all through the arts. The least acknowledged factor in all of this, however, was probably the passive role of record companies. As Keith Emerson remarked, "In the '60s-'70s record companies didn't question anything." By the early '70s 'uncommercial' music such as Pink Floyd's 'Atom Heart Mother' and ELP's 'Tarkus' scaled the pinnacle of the album charts. The fact there were few fetters on the creative artist was crucial.

In order to ascertain what was the first 'prog rock' album, the latest wave of journalists who have written serious books on 'prog rock' (Paul Stump: 'The Music Is All That Matters', Bill Martin: 'Listening To The Future' and Ed Macan: 'Rockin' The Classics') have all made the same mistake by classifying the genre only when it can be recognised in its stereotypical form. In the final analysis they all rule out any band who started out in the formative stage of what Chris Welch called progressive music.

Consequently, King Crimson's debut 'In The Court Of The Crimson King' is usually cited as the first proper 'prog rock' album and, by implication, King Crimson the first 'prog rock' band. But when Crimson made the album, The Nice had been going for over two years. In fact, the vast majority of their back catalogue had already been signed, sealed and delivered before Crimson's debut was released. Furthermore, there was one member of King Crimson who was more than aware of The Nice. Future drummer Michael Giles remarked in 1967 just why the band he was in at the time had broken up. He felt Trendsetters Ltd. were not living up to their name. His statement is remarkable, "There's The Beatles, there's The Nice, there's The Rolling Stones, there's Bob Dylan. Why aren't we doing something?"

There is no doubt that by 1969, The Nice had made progressive strides in driving music forward. The Nice's back catalogue is, in fact, the story of progressive music's development into what is more genuinely accepted as 'prog rock', i.e. Yes, ELP, King Crimson, Jethro Tull, etc. They heavily influenced two of the most successful bands of that genre, Yes and Emerson, Lake & Palmer, and had some sort of influence on most of the others! When these bands started out, they could map out where they were going; The Nice had already taken most of the risks.

In 2001 there was a significant step for The Nice in their quest to reclaim the lost royalties of the Immediate years. They signed a deal for back payment of royalties with Sanctuary, who now

hold the catalogue. Unfortunately this deal only goes back five years but is a step in the right direction. It seems incredible to most how this situation could have continued for so long. Davy was also part of the deal and will receive his payment for the first album. This might help O'List finally acknowledge that the band were not filtering away his share of the royalties.

****

On April 9th 2002, The Nice made an historic return to the stage. The 100 Club provided a wonderful ambience for a band that hadn't played in public for over 32 years. Chris Welch and roadie Keith Robertson also turned up at an event which was actually set up to promote Keith's new album, 'Emerson Plays Emerson', a delightful collection of old and new piano cuts. In the dressing room prior to the gig, Keith turned to his old friends and said, "Well, we're back!" With that the three men embraced as one.

Dressed in black, Keith took to the stage and played three piano numbers, including the impressive, if flippantly named, 'A Cajun Alley'. Keith introduced the besuited Lee and Brian to the stage and the three musicians played sprightly versions of 'Honky Tonk Train Blues' and 'Summertime'. Bazz was even roadying again – though this time just for Lee and Brian. (In the sound check Keith did fire a few questions at Bazz about a couple of Hammond problems he was having – he was using a C3.)

The highlight of the evening was when Keith introduced guitarist Phil Hilbourne, who joined the band for a segued version of 'America' / 'Rondo' (ex-Soft Machine guitarist John Etheridge was invited but couldn't make it). At times, Keith took a back seat while Hilbourne delivered some tasty, mainly restrained licks. Lee was confidently providing a solid base with some nifty fingering of his own to boot! Brian's playing was aggressive at times - the years of teaching percussion seem to have imbued another dimension into his playing and with spectacular results! Considering the musicians only had a few hours in which to rehearse at John Henry's, plus an hour in the sound check, it was impressive stuff.

Some timely additions to the audience lent the evening an even greater edge. Even though it was by invitation only, there was a liberal sprinkling of lucky fans - the winners of an internet ticket ballot. As long-standing fan Robert Ashmore observed at the conclusion, "If this is what they can do after a few hours, what would they sound like after a month's touring! I've been a lifelong Keith Emerson fan but I missed The Nice, but they were the best versions of America and Rondo I've ever heard." Lee simply summed up the evening by remarking, "It's been special for all of us."

The band reconvened in the dressing room after the gig. Briefly the old quartet was reunited in splendid isolation. Bazz looked at Keith, Lee and Brian and announced,

The Nice Reunion, 100 Club, 2002

Opposite:
Keith Emerson,
Brian Davison,
Lee Jackson
with guitarist
Phil Hilbourne

Below: A break
from rehearsals at
John Henry's

Bottom:
Keith Emerson

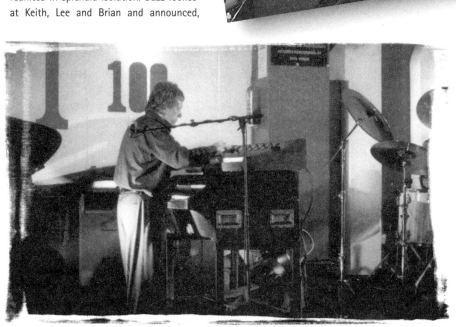

"Well I've seen you perform again so now I can retire." There was a slight pause before Keith brought the conversation to a satisfactory conclusion. He looked at Bazz straight in the eyes and said, "You bloody well better not!"

Indeed, the reunion is scheduled to begin in earnest on 2nd October 2002, at the Wolverhampton Civic Hall. This heralds a short UK tour with the highlight being a date at London's Royal Festival Hall, where they played some of their most important gigs. Foreign trips are also mooted.

But one thing's for sure, Bazz will be getting his suitcase out as The Partnership rides again.

****

The last word is from Bazz. In all the years travelling the world and seeing hundreds of the best bands around, he is convinced of their supremacy, "When they were flying, and that was often, there was NO-ONE to touch them."

APPENDICES

WHERE ARE THEY NOW?   180

DISCOGRAPHY   185

BBC SESSIONS   208

LIST OF GIGS   209

REFERENCE SOURCES   212

INDEX   215

WHERE ARE THEY **NOW?**

LEE JACKSON

For the last few years, Lee has played with the wonderfully named The Ginger Pig Boogie Band. The band was formed in 1980, Lee joining in 1994. Bass player Mark Griffiths knew Lee was in town and invited him to join the band, Griffiths switching to lead guitar. They play all types of music - including trad jazz - but in their own inimitable style. The band has a varying line-up but usually features trumpet, trombone, two saxophones, Latin American percussion, piano, bass, guitar and two vocalists. They play a lot of gigs in Europe, especially festivals. They also take regular trips to Bermuda. "The band kicks like shit. We don't have rehearsals. It can get a bit raggy at the end of numbers. In Europe we're known as the bad ending band," says Lee.

BRIAN DAVISON

Now part of a very lively band of local musicians, most of whom have been around for a while and can really kick. They call themselves Basil's Blues Band and within their ranks are the splendidly named Ranald Macdonald on sax, flute, waffle and vocals; Stuart Knowler on guitar and vocals and Bert Slee (Basil) on bass and vocals. Brian describes them as - and how wonderfully accurate it is - "A weird and wonderful band which can turn blues into funk at the drop of a drumstick."

KEITH EMERSON

Though Keith has a lot of projects on the back burner it is frustrating for his many fans that things can be so slow in coming forward. He had hoped to record his 'Piano Concerto No.2' with the London Philharmonic Orchestra but that is now on hold. His first piano album, entitled *'Emerson Plays Emerson'*, was released in May 2002 on the EMI Classic label, featuring both originals and standards.

Keith is planning to move back to the UK, telling The Guardian recently, "I have this dream of retiring to an old cottage by the sea in Cornwall."

BAZZ WARD

After having roadied for the Johnny Winter, Santana and Every Which Way tours in the early '70s, Bazz toured with many other bands. An old friend, Bruce McCaskill, had organised a charity show at the Lyceum, featuring Eric Clapton and friends. Bazz went to see the gig and ended up working for them as there were problems with the Hammond and PA Monitors. The very next day, he was approached to tour with the resulting band. Their name? Derek and The Dominoes! That lasted till early 1971 after which he toured with bands like the Spencer Davis Group, Medicine Head, Sweet Sensation and The Sex Pistols. The latter gig happened only because no other roadie would work with them, but Bazz had a marvellous time! As he stated recently, "Great fun, a hippie roadie with a Punk band!" In 1979, after a British tour with The British Lions (a merger of Medicine Head and Mott The Hoople) Bazz joined a PA company, Liveware, and did gigs with Stiff Little Fingers (he has two of their silver discs on the wall in his flat).

Bazz came off the road in 1983 but still works in the business. He agreed to help at John Henry Enterprises (now John Henry's Ltd, a rental/PA/studio complex in North London) for a month. That month turned into 18 years! Emerson, Lake & Powell rehearsed there and Bazz was able to offer Keith's techie, Spencer Allen, some sound Hammond advice. He runs the highly successful 'Pro Shop' supplying all the necessary bits and bobs for touring. Supplying the technical requirements of the old and the new, he is able to draw on extensive knowledge. The past is never far away, as he outlines, "This young lad came into the shop and he was hustling for a discount as his dad knew my colleague, Will Wright. It turns out his dad is my old mate Bob Young from Status Quo, and there is his son starting out on the road. Another band, Vent, features Morgan Nicholls, son of Billy from Immediate Records."

Bazz Ward with the American flag, showing knife damage by Keith (see also photo on Page 69)

Now in his 60th year he is still in contact with Lee and, especially, Brian. Bazz regularly helps Brian with equipment for his college and he helped Lee with a recent purchase of a new Bass combo. There is still a bond between them that is illustrated by the following story. On the night of the tragic Kings Cross fire on the London Underground, in which many people lost their lives, Bazz received a call at his flat. It was Brian checking he was alright, knowing Bazz lived fairly close to the station.

Thinking back to the days with The Nice, he remarks, "There was a lot of wheeling and dealing but it was the days when musos and crews would go out drinking together. There was a lot of camaraderie amongst crews." Sadly those days no longer exist. He still regrets the incident at the last Nice gig in Berlin although, as he explains, he still feels he was in the right, "What you have to understand is it was the LAST gig of MY band and this geezer had nicked my LAST tambourine. I told him he could have it after the show but he wouldn't give it back to me, so... I hit him."

He still keeps an extensive archive of the band and he also has a gold (250,000 sales) disc of *'Five Bridges'* hanging on his wall. Lee and Brian had no idea he had compiled an archive of the band but were very glad he did.

DAVY O'LIST

Things did not go well for Davy following his sacking from the band in 1968. Not long after this, Mick Abrahams was to leave Jethro Tull, so Davy went to audition for the vacant post. But, as he outlined to Terrascope in 1994 he wasn't ready, "I couldn't get The Nice out of my system. I was emotionally strung out on their music, it was The Nice I wanted to be with and not Jethro Tull. I couldn't get my head into it." He then formed his own band, Opal Butterfly, but that didn't last long. Joining a more promising group, Misunderstood, they even performed a couple of tracks in a film, 'Super Group Sessions', which also included Led Zeppelin and Cream. But there were problems in the group and Davy found himself on his own again. Misunderstood changed their name to Juicy Lucy with moderate success.

In 1970, he tried to form another group, Cody's Glider, but that too had disaster stamped all over it. Davy's Rickenbacker guitar was stolen and, not being a wealthy man, that put an end to that until an insurance policy taken out with the Musicians Union soon provided him with a replacement. He then formed a group, Nasty, who supported Leon Russell but that came to a nasty end when, after a gig in a London pub, they were beaten up by a gang of skinheads.

In October 1971, Davy placed an advert in Melody Maker, playing on his successful tenure in The Nice. He was contacted by an unknown singer who asked him to come down and try out for his band. That singer was Bryan Ferry and that band was Roxy Music. Ferry was delighted in Davy as he had always been a big fan of The Nice. Years later Ferry commented, "He joined us for about three months, the only evidence was on our first BBC session which was very good. It was the first time we'd been into a studio of any sort." At the time Davy was the biggest name in the band and they used his studio experience at that BBC session. Davy was there during the process of being signed to EG Management. Richard Williams of Melody Maker gave a glowing review of one of their gigs. But there were rumours of personality clashes and, the next thing he knew, Davy was out (on February 12th 1972 to be precise). The rift with Ferry couldn't have been too serious as Davy was to appear on a number of his solo tracks, including 'The In Crowd'.

Times became hard for Davy as he outlined to Melody Maker's Chris Welch, circa 1973, "I've been on Social Security, you know. I was very ill. I was so ill, that's why I had to leave Roxy Music although I didn't know it at the time. Apparently I'd be all right one day, and hard to get on with the next. So I had to go into hospital for anti-depressant injections. To keep going, I worked in restaurants at the bar, and I had sickness benefit." It was on one of those bad days that led to his departure from Roxy. Though, according to Andy Mackay, he had a few of those, "O'List was quite troubled, quite difficult to deal with." Phil Manzanera, originally a roadie for the band, had auditioned earlier but had been rejected. He was there when they auditioned for EG Management and describes what happened next, "On come the band, then Davy O'List and Paul Thompson proceed to have a punch up." Manzanera claims it was EG that decided to get rid of Davy.

Things got worse, Davy ending up working in a factory. The rest of the '70s was spent in various bands but he would never again have the same success. In 1974 he joined a group called Jet, supporting Ian Hunter and Mick Ronson for their 1975 tour of the UK. They made an album, produced by Roy Thomas Baker, without success. Davy later supported ex-Velvet Underground guitarist, John Cale, on his European tour. Not much would happen for him in the '80s, searching for that elusive break. What else could he do but change his name to The Big Seal; this was around the time he purloined a copy of the Nice's first album and engineered the '20th Anniversary' release in 1987.

Davy turned to film production in the early '90s. In 1994 he made an effort to get together a tour of the US but couldn't get enough interest in the project. Then in 1997, he released an album, 'Flight Of The Eagle', featuring Davy on an array of instruments with more than a few tasty licks. Davy still hopes to one day get back into top-flight music. He still plays live music and occasionally tours the UK. There is no doubt Davy brought a lot of things on to himself but if there is anybody that deserves a bit of luck it's him. There is a part of Davy that is still stuck in those days with The Nice.

P.P. ARNOLD

Pat Arnold is a true survivor. In the early '70s she formed a band with Ashton, Gardner & Dyke. When that fizzled out she supported Eric Clapton on the Delaney and Bonnie tour. By the mid '70s, as punk rock took hold, she found the opportunities in the UK even more limited and so returned to the States. In 1977, her daughter Debbie was killed in a motor accident, leaving Pat totally lost and disillusioned. What followed was a string of projects that could only be filed under 'near misses'. She almost worked with Barry Gibb but ended up recording with younger brother Andy. Trying her hand at acting, she appeared in a string of hit shows like 'Quincy', 'Knots Landing', 'Fame' and 'St. Elsewhere'.

By the early '80s she resolved to go back to the UK and, in 1984, found herself starring on roller skates in Andrew Lloyd Webber's musical, Starlight Express. Her London return was a triumph! She later worked with Boy George and sung the title song for the 'Comic Strip' movie.

In 1986, after working with Billy Ocean, she was badly injured in a car accident. Her legs were so badly hurt she couldn't do any conventional work and so began a very successful TV jingles career, singing on campaigns for some of the biggest companies, including Coca-Cola and Peugeot. She signed off the '80s by recording with the KLF. By the early '90s her association with Immediate Records would initiate a reappraisal of her work, the basis of which was the Brit Pop movement, led by Oasis and Ocean Colour Scene who cited The Small Faces, The Beatles and The Kinks as their main inspiration. In the wake of this, Pat was invited to work with Ocean Colour Scene, backing them on their UK tour. Their guitarist Steve Craddock was mooted to produce her solo album but all that came of it was the excellent single, 'Different Drum', which she promoted on various television shows.

1999 became a better year for her, being invited by ex-Pink Floyd mentor Roger Waters to join his world tour. She was very excited about this project, and had a great time as she stated recently, "Roger is a gentleman and treats his artists with respect." The money she earned from the tour has enabled her to make a solo album, recorded in London in 2001. The album has contributions from Chip Taylor and ex-Blockhead Chaz Jankel and contains a song dedicated to her daughter Debbie, 'I'll Always Remember You'. She toured once again with Roger Waters in early 2002. An official web site keeps her fans informed. Pat is writing her autobiography and a video is currently being shot, showing her at work. Not before time, things are looking good for P.P. Arnold!

ANDREW LOOG OLDHAM

In 1974, Andrew Oldham met a Colombian actress, Ester Farfin. On St. Valentine's Day 1975, they married and went to live in Bogota, Colombia. In the '90s Oldham toyed with the idea of reclaiming the Immediate Master Tapes, ownership of which had been a bone of contention ever since the liquidation of the original company. However, Oldham has a problem in presenting himself as a 'knight in shining armour' as many of the artists under him never received any royalties. Interestingly, as he recently described one of the most crucial parts of his life, "The fact is that sometime between 1967-69, I went 'out to lunch' and did not return until the summer of 1995." He is now a follower of Scientology, to which he attributes the re-energising of his career, "It jump-started my ability to return to productive life after thirty years out there in the cold."

However, at a final court ruling in February 2002, he finally lost any claim to the Immediate tapes.

IAN HAGUE

After The Nice, he joined Herbie Goins and The Nightimers for about a year. Goins offered him the job by saying, "We're going to Rome. Do you want to come?" Touring Europe extensively, it was a great band, full of good musicians. Goins was a black American and very talented. The band also included, at one stage, guitar legend John McLaughlin (Hague sat in once while he was in the band). After he left Herbie Goins he almost joined Arthur Brown but the band leader changed his mind. He then joined J.J. Jackson's Greatest Little Soul Band but was seriously injured when, returning from a gig, the band coach was blown off the motorway and into a bridge. This kept him off the music scene for a while.

He still plays semi-pro in many modern jazz bands, in and around Cambridge where he now resides. Unfortunately he recently suffered a broken leg and multiple fractures of the ankle after falling over in a restaurant. His drumming career is on hold for a while but he is trying his hand at serious tenor singing in a choir. His latest project is to start a band that will perform songs from the 1940s, a period he has always loved.

TONY STRATTON-SMITH

Still greatly missed by all the band, crew and many in the business. As Bazz said recently, "I can recall Strat in my head any time I like."

DISCOGRAPHY

COMPILED BY ANDY WILSON

Keith Emerson - Organ, Piano, Harpsichord & some Vocals; Lee Jackson - Bass & Vocals; Brian Davison - Drums; Davy O'List - Guitar, Trumpet & Vocals (until late September 1968)

SINGLES & EPS

● **THE THOUGHTS OF EMERLIST DAVJACK /**
Azrial (Angel Of Death)
UK 1967 7" Single, Immediate IM 059 mono
UK 1967 7" Single Demo, Immediate IM 059
Germany 1967 7" Single, Immediate C 23662
Denmark 1967 7" Single, Immediate C7 1007
Denmark 1967 7" Single, Immediate IM 059
France 1967 7" Single, Immediate IMF 501
USA 1968 7" Single Promo, Immediate ZS 7 5004
Holland 1968 7" Single, Stateside HSS 1232
Australia 7" Single, Stateside OSS 290
THE THOUGHTS OF EMERLIST DAVJACK /
Sampler for The Thoughts Of Emerlist Davjack LP
UK 1967 7" Single Promo, Immediate IM AS 2
THE THOUGHTS OF EMERLIST DAVJACK /
Daddy Where Did I Come From
UK 7" Single, Muza S 586

● **AMERICA** (America / 2nd Amendment) / America
UK 7" Single, Immediate ZS7 5008
USA 1968 7" Single Promo, Immediate ZS7 5008
AMERICA / The Diamond Hard Blue Apples Of
The Moon
UK 1968 7" Single, Immediate IM 068
UK 7" Single, Immediate ZS7 5008
Italy 1971 7" Single, Immediate 2C 006 92654
Holland 1968 7" Single, Immediate IM 068L
Germany 1968 7" Single, Immediate IM 23921
Australia 1968 7" Single, Immediate IM 8597
France 1968 7" Single, Immediate IMF 513
Japan 1968 7" Single, Immediate IR-2348
UK 1982 7" Single Reissue, Castle
AMERICA / Diary Of An Empty Day
Italy 1971 7" Single
AMERICA / Hang On To A Dream
Germany 1977 7" Single, Immediate 103460
AMERICA / Rondo
Belgium 1978 7" Single, Golden Hit Parade 79 755Y
Belgium 1978 7" Single, Golden Oldies GOS 316

● **INTERMEZZO FROM 'THE KARELIA SUITE'**
UK 7" Single, Philips 6000 004 Serie Parade

● **HANG ON TO A DREAM /** Diary Of An
Empty Day
Japan 1969 7" Single, Immediate
Holland 1969 7" Single, Immediate 5C 006 90903
France 1969 7" Single, Immediate C006 90 903
Germany 1969 7" Single, Immediate C006 90 903
HANG ON TO A DREAM / Have A Nice Day
Holland 1999 CD, Neon Records

● **BRANDENBURGER**
UK 1968 7" Single Demo, Immediate
UK 1968 7" Single White Label Promo,
London Disc CC LTD
BRANDENBURGER / Happy Freuds
UK 1968 7" Single, Immediate IM 072
UK 1968 7" Single Demo, Immediate IM 072
USA 1968 7" Single, Immediate IM 072
Denmark 1968 7" Single, Immediate IM 072
Holland 1968 7" Single, Immediate IM 072
Sweden 1969 7" Single, Immediate IM 072
Germany 1968 7" Single, Immediate IM 23 988
France 1968 7" Single, Immediate IMF 515

● **SHE BELONGS TO ME /** She Belongs To Me
(alternative version)
UK 1969 7" Single, Immediate IM AS4
UK 1969 7" Single Promo, Immediate IM AS4

● **FINALE 5th BRIDGE /** Country Pie
USA 1970 7" Single Promo, Mercury 73272

● **COUNTRY PIE /** One Of Those People
UK 1970 7" Single, Charisma CB 132
USA 1970 7" Single, Mercury SP 61295
Holland 1970 7" Single, Philips 6000 007 mono
COUNTRY PIE / Pathetique
Japan 1970 7" Single, Philips SFL-1289
COUNTRY PIE / Brandenburger
UK 1970 7" Single Promo, Mercury DJ 274
UK 1970 7" Single, Mercury DJ-274 (73114)
COUNTRY PIE / Brandenburger / 5th Bridge
UK 1970 7" Single, Mercury 73272

● **TANTALISING MAGGIE /** Bonnie 'K'
Poland 1977 7" Single, Muza S 587

ALBUMS

■ **THE THOUGHTS OF EMERLIST DAVJACK**
UK 1967 LP, Immediate IMLP/IMSP 016
UK 1967 LP 1-sided Promo, Immediate AS 2
USA 1967 LP, Immediate 52004
UK 1978 LP Reissue, Charly CR 300021
Germany 1982 LP Reissue, Line
1988 Germany CD, Line IMCD 900228 0
1992 CD Repertoire REP 4238-WY
UK 1993 CD, Charly CD IMM 010
UK 1998 CD, Castle ESM CD 647 (with bonus
tracks: The Thoughts Of Emerlist Davjack (single
A-side) / Azrial (Angel Of Death) (single B-side) /
The Diamond Hard Blue Apples Of The Moon
(single B-side))
Tracks: Flower King Of Flies / The Thoughts Of
Emerlist Davjack / Bonnie 'K' / Rondo /
War And Peace / Tantalising Maggie / Dawn /
The Cry Of Eugene

■ **ARS LONGA VITA BREVIS**
UK 1968 LP, Immediate IMSP 020
USA 1968 LP, Immediate 52020
Italy 1974 2LP, 3 C154-52123/24

UK 1975 LP, Charly CR 300019
UK 1987 CD, Castle Classics CLACD 120
1992 CD Repertoire REP 4289-WY
UK 1998 CD, Castle ESM CD 646 (with bonus
tracks: Brandenburger (single version) / Happy
Freuds (single B-side))
Tracks: Daddy Where Did I Come From / Little
Arabella / Happy Freuds / Intermezzo from 'The
Karelia Suite' / Don Edito El Gruva / Ars Longa
Vita Brevis (Prelude / 1st Movement: Awakening
/ 2nd Movement: Realisation / 3rd Movement:
Acceptance "Brandenburger", 4th Movement:
Denial / Coda - Extension To The Big Note)

■ **NICE**
UK 1969 LP, Immediate IMSP 026
1969 LP, Immediate 52022
UK 1973 LP, Columbia Special Products P 11635
UK LP, Immediate SBA 16016
UK 1978 LP, CHARLY CR 300014
1992 CD, Repertoire REP 4290-WY
UK 1998 CD, Castle ESM CD 645 (with bonus
tracks: Hang On To A Dream (mono) / Diary Of
An Empty Day (mono))
Tracks: Azrael Revisited / Hang On To A Dream /
Diary Of An Empty Day / For Example / Rondo
(69) (live) / She Belongs To Me
Also released in the US as **EVERYTHING AS
NICE AS MOTHER MAKES IT**
USA 1969 LP, Immediate IMOCS 102

■ **FIVE BRIDGES**
UK 1970 LP, Charisma CAS 1014
UK 1970 MC, Polygram 830 291-4 M-1
USA 1970 LP, Mercury SR 61295
Japan 1990 CD, Virgin VJCP-23029
UK CD, Virgin CASCD 1014 (with bonus tracks:
The Thoughts Of Emerlist Davjack / Flower King
Of Flies / Bonnie 'K' / Diary Of An Empty Day /
America (America / 2nd Amendment))
Tracks: The Five Bridges Suite (Fantasia 1st
Bridge / 2nd Bridge / Chorale 3rd Bridge / High
Level Fugue 4th Bridge / Finale 5th Bridge) /
Intermezzo from 'The Karelia Suite' / Pathetique
(Tchaikovsky's 6th Symphony, 3rd Movement) /
Country Pie / Brandenburg Concerto No.6 /
One Of Those People

■ **ELEGY**
USA 1970 LP, Mercury SR 61324 LP
UK 1971 LP, Charisma CAS 1030
US LP, Mercury SR 61324
Japan 1990 CD, Virgin VJCP-23030 CD
UK 1990 CD, Virgin CASCD 1030 (with bonus
tracks: The Diamond Hard Blue Apples Of The
Moon / Dawn / Tantalising Maggie / The Cry Of
Eugene / Daddy Where Did I Come From / Azrial
(Angel Of Death))
Tracks: Hang On To A Dream / My Back Pages /
Pathetique (Tchaikovsky's 6th Symphony, 3rd
Movement) / America (America / 2nd Amend.)

___**COMPILATION ALBUMS** (selected)___

■ **ABSOLUTELY THE BEST**
USA 2001 CD, Fuel 2000 Records
Tracks: Rondo / She Belongs To Me / Diary Of An
Empty Day / For Example / Azrial (Angel Of
Death) / America (America / 2nd Amendment) /

Happy Freuds / The Thoughts Of Emerlist Davjack
/ Hang On To A Dream / Flower King Of Flies /
Bonnie 'K' / America (live) / Rondo (69) (live)

■ **ALL ABOUT THE NICE,
FEATURING KEITH EMERSON**
Japan 1986 2LP, Immediate IP93015B

■ **ALL THE BEST**
UK 1999 CD, Repertoire REP 4822-WG
Tracks: The Thoughts Of Emerlist Davjack /
Azrial Angel Of Death) / America (America / 2nd
Amendment) / The Diamond Hard Blue Apples
Of The Moon / Acceptance "Brandenburger" /
Happy Freuds / Hang On To A Dream / Diary Of
An Empty Day

■ **AMERICA**
UK 1969 CD, Laserlight 12 334
Tracks: Azrial (Angel Of Death) / America
(America / 2nd Amendment) / The Diamond Hard
Blue Apples Of The Moon / The Thoughts Of
Emerlist Davjack / Rondo / The Cry Of Eugene /
Dawn / War And Peace / Daddy Where Did I
Come From / Little Arabella

■ **AMERICA - THE BBC SESSIONS**
UK 1996 CD, Receiver Records RRCD 224
Tracks: America (America / 2nd Amendment) /
One Of Those People / Azrael Revisited /
St. Thomas / Five Bridges Suite / Pathetique
(Tchaikovsky's 6th Symphony, 3rd Movement) /
Little Arabella / Happy Freuds / Better Than
Better / Sombrero King / Aries / Diary Of An
Empty Day / Ars Longa Vita Brevis

■ **AMERICA & OTHER CLASSIC TRACKS**
UK CD, WMCD 5526

■ **AMOENI REDIVIVI**
UK 1976 LP, Immediate IML 1003
Tracks: Rondo / Hang On To A Dream (first
version) / The Thoughts Of Emerlist Davjack /
Intermezzo from 'The Karelia Suite' /
America (America/ 2nd Amendment) (single) /
The Cry Of Eugene / The Diamond Hard Blue
Apples Of The Moon / Ars Longa Vita Brevis (3rd
Movement: Acceptance "Brandenburger" / 4th
Movement: Denial)

■ **ATTENTION! KEITH EMERSON AND THE NICE**
Germany 1972 LP, Fontana 9299 032

■ **ATTENTION! THE NICE**
Japan 1973 LP, Fontana/Charisma PAT-20

■ **AUTUMN '67, SPRING '68**
UK 1972 LP, Charisma CS 1
Tracks: The Thoughts Of Emerlist Davjack /
Flower King Of Flies / Bonnie 'K' / America
(America / 2nd Amendment) / The Diamond
Hard Blue Apples Of The Moon / Dawn /
Tantalising Maggie / The Cry Of Eugene /
Daddy Where Did I Come From

■ **AUTUMN TO SPRING '67-'68**
US 1973 LP, Charisma CAS1 0598
US 1973 MC, Charisma
US 1973 8 Track Cartridge, Charisma
Japan 1973 LP, Charisma 598

■ **THE BBC SESSIONS**
UK 2002, Sanctuary CMRCD457

■ **THE BEST OF THE NICE**
UK 1971 LP, Immediate C 048-90674
Germany 1971 LP, Immediate C048-90 674
THE BEST OF THE NICE
Germany 1983 LP, Line OLLP 5278 AS
Tracks: America (America / 2nd Amendment) (single) / Little Arabella / The Diamond Hard Blue Apples Of The Moon / Intermezzo from 'The Karelia Suite' / The Thoughts Of Emerlist Davjack / War And Peace / The Cry Of Eugene / Acceptance "Brandenburger"
THE BEST OF THE NICE
UK 1993 CD, Charly CD IMB 501
Tracks: The Thoughts Of Emerlist Davjack / Rondo / War And Peace / The Cry Of Eugene / America (America / 2nd Amendment) / Intermezzo from 'The Karelia Suite' / Acceptance "Brandenburger" / Hang On To A Dream
THE BEST OF THE NICE
1995 CD, Griffin
UK 1998 CD, Castle ESM CD 629
Tracks: The Thoughts Of Emerlist Davjack / America (America / 2nd Amendment) / Little Arabella / Acceptance "Brandenburger" / Tantalising Maggie / Intermezzo from 'The Karelia Suite' / Happy Freuds / War And Peace / The Cry Of Eugene / Diary Of An Empty Day / Hang Onto A Dream / She Belongs To Me / Rondo

■ **CASTLE MASTER COLLECTION**
Switzerland 1992 CD, Castle Comm. CMS 3077

■ **FIVE BRIDGES / AUTUMN '67, SPRING '68**
UK 1983 MC, Charisma 163

■ **GREATEST HITS**
UK 1977 LP, Immediate IML 2003
UK 1977 8 Track Cartridge, Immediate Y8IM 2003
Holland 1981 LP, Philips HO 25
Germany 1989 LP, Big Time 2615511
Germany 1989 CD, Big Time 2615512

■ **HANG ON TO A DREAM**
UK 1967 LP, Emidisc 6E 048-50722
Holland 1970 LP, EMI C 048-50722
Germany 1994 CD, Music Reflexion LC-4912

■ **HERE COME THE NICE - THE IMMEDIATE ANTHOLOGY**
UK 2001 3CD, Sanctuary CMETD 055
Tracks: CD1: The Thoughts Of Emerlist Davjack / Azrial (Angel Of Death) / Sampler for The Thoughts Of Emerlist Davjack LP / Flower King Of Flies / Bonnie 'K' / Rondo / War And Peace / Tantalising Maggie / Dawn / The Cry Of Eugene / America (America / 2nd Amendment) / The Diamond Hard Blue Apples Of The Moon / Daddy Where Did I Come From / Little Arabella / Happy Freuds / Intermezzo from 'The Karelia Suite' / Don Edito El Gruva
CD2: Ars Longa Vita Brevis / Brandenburger / Azrael Revisited / Hang On To A Dream (long version) / Diary Of An Empty Day / For Example / Rondo (69) (live) / She Belongs To Me (live)
CD3: America (live) / Rondo (live) / The Thoughts Of Emerlist Davjack (long version) / Flower King

Of Flies (alternative version) / Bonnie 'K' (alternative version) / America (alternative stereo version) / Dawn (alternative version) / Tantalising Maggie (alternative version) / The Cry Of Eugene (alternative version) / Daddy Where Did I Come From (alternative version) / Brandenburger (demo version) / Pathetique Symphony 4th (live) / Lt. Kije (The Troika) (live)

■ **IN MEMORIAM**
UK LP, Immediate 2C 054-91.951
France LP, Immediate 2C 054-91.151
UK CD
Tracks: America (America / 2nd Amendment) (single) / Rondo (69) (live) / The Diamond Hard Blue Apples Of The Moon / Intermezzo from 'The Karelia Suite' / The Thoughts Of Emerlist Davjack / Azrael Revisited / Hang On To A Dream / Brandenburger

■ **INTERMEZZO**
Spain 1989 LP, Soundwings 101.1021-1
UK CD, AAD 101.1021-2

■ **ITS ALL A DREAM - NICE BERLIN**
UK 1996 CD

■ **KEITH EMERSON AND THE NICE**
UK 2LP, Mercury SRM 2 6500
UK LP, Armando Curcio Editore GSR-15
Poland LP, Polskie Nagrania SX 1235
Italy 1983 MC, S.I.A.E
Tracks: America (America / 2nd Amendment) / Intermezzo from 'The Karelia Suite' / Country Pie / Brandenburg Concerto No.6 / Hang On To A Dream

■ **KEITH EMERSON WITH THE NICE**
Italy 1970 LP, Philips GDA 1115/6
1971 LP, Mercury 830 457
France 2LP, Philips 6499 393
France 1972 2LP, Philips 6641 119
Italy 1981 LP, Philips 9279 526
UK 1987 CD, Polygram 830 457-2 M-1
Germany 1987 CD, Mercury 830 457-2
Tracks: Five Bridges Suite / Intermezzo from 'The Karelia Suite' / Pathetique (Tchaikovsky's 6th Symphony, 3rd Movement) / Hang On To A Dream / America (America / 2nd Amendment) / My Back Pages
KEITH EMERSON WITH THE NICE
UK 8 Track Cartridge, Mercury MCT 8 26500
Tracks: Five Bridges Suite / Intermezzo from 'The Karelia Suite' / Pathetique (Tchaikovsky's 6th Symphony, 3rd Movement) / Country Pie / Brandenburg Concerto No.6 / One Of Those People / Hang On To A Dream / My Back Pages / Pathetique / America (America / 2nd Amendment)

■ **LEGENDARY - THE NICE**
Germany 2LP, Bellaphon CR 3042

■ **NICE HITS, NICE BITS**
UK 1999 CD, Dressed To Kill METRO303
Tracks: America (America / 2nd Amendment) / War And Peace / Dawn / The Cry Of Eugene / Happy Freuds / Hang On To A Dream / For Example / Bonnie 'K' / Daddy Where Did I Come From / Tantalising Maggie / Azrael Revisited / Diary Of An Empty Day / Little Arabella

■ **THE IMMEDIATE COLLECTION**
UK 1999 2CD, Recall SMDCD 203
Tracks: CD1: The Thoughts Of Emerlist Davjack /
Azrial (Angel Of Death) / Flower King Of Flies /
Bonnie 'K' / Rondo / War And Peace /
Tantalising Maggie / Dawn / The Cry Of Eugene /
America (America / 2nd Amendment) /
The Diamond Hard Blue Apples Of The Moon /
Daddy Where Did I Come From / Little Arabella /
Happy Freuds (mono) / Brandenburger (demo)
CD2: Intermezzo from 'The Karelia Suite' /
Don Edito El Gruva / Ars Longa Vita Brevis /
Azrael Revisited / Hang On To A Dream / Diary Of
An Empty Day / For Example / Rondo (69) (live) /
She Belongs To Me (live)

■ **THE IMMEDIATE STORY**
USA 1975 2LP, Immediate/Sire SASH-3710
UK CD
Best of the first two albums plus unreleased
version of Daddy Where Did I Come From

■ **THE IMMEDIATE YEARS**
France 1987 CD, Accord 139239 CD
Tracks: America (America / 2nd Amendment)
(single) / Hang On To A Dream (first version) /
Rondo / Tantalising Maggie / War And Peace /
The Thoughts Of Emerlist Davjack /
Intermezzo from 'The Karelia Suite' / Bonnie 'K' /
Diary Of An Empty Day / Ars Longa Vita Brevis
(3rd Movement: Acceptance "Brandenburger")
THE IMMEDIATE YEARS
UK 1995 3CD, Charly CD IMM BOX 2
Tracks: CD1: Flower King Of Flies / The Thoughts
Of Emerlist Davjack / Bonnie 'K' / Rondo /
War And Peace / Tantalising Maggie /
Dawn / The Cry Of Eugene / The Thoughts Of
Emerlist Davjack (remix) / Flower King Of Flies
(remix) / Bonnie 'K' (remix) / America (America /
2nd Amendment) (single)
CD2: The Diamond Hard Blue Apples Of
The Moon / Dawn (remix) / Tantalising Maggie
(remix) / The Cry Of Eugene (remix) /
Daddy Where Did I Come From (early version) /
Azrael (version one) / America (America / 2nd
Amend.) / Daddy Where Did I Come From
(second version) / Little Arabella /
Happy Freuds (mono) / Intermezzo from 'The
Karelia Suite' / Brandenburger (demo)
CD3: Don Edito El Gruva / Ars Longa Vita Brevis /
Azrael Revisited / Hang On To A Dream /
Diary Of An Empty Day / For Example /
Rondo (69) (live) / She Belongs To Me (live)

■ **THE LONG VERSIONS**
UK 1999 CD, Double Classics DC 31025

■ **THE NICE 1967-69**
Germany 1972 2LP, Immediate 148-93 603/04

■ **THE NICE**
1976 2LP, Bellaphon/Charly CR 3003
Germany LP, Bellaphon CR 3029
Tracks: Rondo / Hang On To A Dream
(first version) / The Thoughts Of Emerlist Davjack
/ Intermezzo from 'The Karelia Suite' /
Ars Longa Vita Brevis
THE NICE
UK 1972 LP, Pickwick SHM 917
UK 1980 LP, Oxford OX 3170

Germany 1987 CD, Line IDCD 900233 0 CD

■ **NICE / ARS LONGA VITA BREVIS / THE
THOUGHTS OF EMERLIST DAVJACK**
France 1977 3LP, Charly 3XD 2676 210

■ **THE NICE COLLECTION**
UK 1985 2LP, Castle CCSLP 106
UK 1985 2LP, Castle Collector Series CCSLP106
UK 1985 CD, Castle CCSCD 106
Tracks: America (America / 2nd Amendment)
(single) / Happy Freuds / The Cry Of Eugene /
The Thoughts Of Emerlist Davjack /
Rondo / Daddy Where Did I Come From /
Little Arabella / Intermezzo from 'The Karelia
Suite' / Hang On To A Dream /
The Diamond Hard Blue Apples Of The Moon /
Azrial (Angel Of Death)
THE NICE COLLECTION
Germany 1989 CD, Line IDCD 9.00720
Tracks: (America / 2nd Amendment) (single) /
Daddy Where Did I Come From /
Rondo / The Thoughts Of Emerlist Davjack /
Brandenburger / War And Peace /
Intermezzo from 'The Karelia Suite' /
Don Edito El Gruva / Azrial (Angel Of Death) /
Hang On To A Dream (first version) /
For Example / She Belongs To Me

■ **THE NICE FEATURING KEITH EMERSON**
UK 1971 LP, Philips 9279 525
THE NICE FEATURING KEITH EMERSON
Holland 1990 CD, Woodford Music WMCD 5526

■ **THE NICEST OF THE NICE**
Japan 1985 LP, Immediate IP 9540

■ **THE SWEDISH RADIO SESSIONS**
UK 2001 CD, Sanctuary CMRCD349
Tracks: She Belongs To Me / Flower King Of Flies
/ Sombrero Sam / You Keep Me Hanging On /
The Thoughts Of Emerlist Davjack / Rondo

■ **20TH ANNIVERSARY OF THE NICE**
UK 1987 LP, Seal Records SLP 2
1988 CD, Bite Back BTECD 2
Re-release (by Davy O'List) of The Thoughts Of
Emerlist Davjack with extra track: Daddy Where
Did I Come From (original version wirth O'List)
Billed as 'The Nice Featuring Davy O'List' with
sleeve notes by The Big Seal (a.k.a. Davy O'List)

SESSION APPEARANCES (selected)

■ **P.P. ARNOLD** – See P.P. ARNOLD section

■ **ROY HARPER** – Flat Baroque And Berserk
UK 1970 LP, Harvest SKAO-418
1970 LP, Harvest SHVL 766
UK 1997 CD, Science Friction HUCD028
The Nice play on the track Hell's Angels

VARIOUS ARTISTS COMPIL. (selected)

■ **ACID DROPS, FLYING SAUCERS & SPACE DUST:
PSYCHEDELIC CONFECTIONERY**
2001 4CD Box Set, EMI 5350782
The Nice track: Flower King Of Flies

■ THE AGE OF ENLIGHTENMENT –
PROG ROCK, Volume 1
1995 CD, Alex 5078
The Nice track: Flower King Of Flies

■ BEAT CLUB – LIVE RECORDINGS
Germany 1995 2CD, Repertoire REP 4527-WR
The Nice tracks: Hang On To A Dream / America

■ THE BEST OF THE NICE, The Small Faces,
Humble Pie, Eric Clapton & John Mayall
Germany LP, Immediate 1C148-92661/662
The Nice tracks: America (America / 2nd Amend.)
/ Brandenburger / Hang On To A Dream

■ BLITZ OF HITZ
Germany 2000 2CD, Charly CDBOOK 101
The Nice tracks: America (America / 2nd Amend.)
/ The Diamond Hard Blue Apples Of The Moon

■ CHARISMA DISTURBANCE
LP, Charisma TSS1
The Nice tracks: Intermezzo from 'The Karelia
Suite' / She Belongs to Me

■ CLASSIC ROCK – WHERE LEGENDS LIVE
UK 2000 CD, CR 23/14/00
The Nice track: America (America / 2nd Amend.)

■ DISRAELI YEARS
UK 1998 CD, Dressed To Kill 69
The Nice tracks: America (America / 2nd Amend.)
/ Little Arabella

■ THE FAMOUS CHARISMA BOX
1993 4CD, Virgin 39084
The Nice track: Intermezzo from 'The Karelia Suite'

■ GIGANTES DEL POP, VOL 52
Spain 1981 LP, Philips 92 79 525

■ HAPPY TO BE A PART OF THE INDUSTRY OF
HUMAN HAPPINESS
LP, Immediate 1106
The Nice track: Hang On To A Dream
2000 CD, Sequel 324
2000 CD, Castle CMUCD065
The Nice tracks: The Thoughts Of Emerlist Davjack
/ Azrial (Angel Of Death) / America (America / 2nd
Amendment) / The Diamond Hard Blue Apples Of
The Moon / Brandenburger / Happy Freuds

■ HISTORIA DE LA MUSICA ROCK NO.25
Spain 1982 LP, Philips 68 41 150

■ IL ROCK VOLUME 57
Italy 1989 LP, De Agostini IGDA 1115/116

■ I MAESTRI
Italy 1973 LP, Immediate 3C-064-94693

■ IMMEDIATE As & Bs: The Singles Collection
1981 LP, Compleat 672010
The Nice track: The Thoughts Of Emerlist Davjack

■ THE IMMEDIATE COLLECTION
UK 1995 CD, Charly SUMCD 4036
The Nice tracks: Hang On To A Dream / America
(America / 2nd Amendment)

■ IMMEDIATE LETS YOU IN
1968 LP, Immediate IMLYIN 1
The Nice tracks: Happy Freuds / Rondo

■ IMMEDIATE PLEASURE
2002 2CD, Castle Pulse CMDDD425
The Nice Tracks: The Thoughts Of Emerlist
Davjack / America

■ THE IMMEDIATE SINGLES COLLECTION, Vol.1
UK 1994 CD, Castle CLA353
The Nice tracks: America (America / 2nd Amend.)
/ Brandenburger
THE IMMEDIATE SINGLES COLLECTION, Vol.2
UK 1994 CD, Castle CLA
The Nice track: The Thoughts Of Emerlist Davjack
THE IMMEDIATE SINGLES COLLECTION, Vol.4
UK 1994 CD, Castle CLA
The Nice track: Azrial (Angel Of Death)
THE IMMEDIATE SINGLES COLLECTION
2000 6CD Box Set, Sequel NXTCD324
The Nice Tracks: The Thoughts Of Emerlist
Davjack / Azrial (Angel Of Death) / America / The
Diamond Hard Blue Apples Of The Moon /
Brandenburger / Happy Freuds

■ THE IMMEDIATE SINGLES STORY, Vol.1
2000 2CD, Charly CDBOOK101
The Nice Tracks: America / The Diamond Hard
Blue Apples Of The Moon

■ THE IMMEDIATE STORY
UK 1980 LP, VIRGIN V 2165
The Nice track: America (America / 2nd
Amendment) (single version)

■ LEGENDS OF ROCK
CD, Bigtime 3415022
The Nice tracks: America (America / 2nd
Amendment) / Acceptance "Brandenburger"

■ THE PROGRESSIVE '60s
Holland 3LP, Philips 6685 106

■ A PROGRESSIVE AND ART ROCK PRIMER
UK 1997 CD, Virgin Choice Cuts CDOVD497 7243
8 44701 2 8 LC 3098

■ SPIRIT OF THE AGE
UK 1997 CD, Castle RENCD 118
Renaissance RENCD 118
The Nice track: America (America / 2nd Amend.)

■ STARS OF BRITISH ROCK
1993 MC, K-Tel 3120
1993 CD, K-Tel 3120
The Nice track: America (America / 2nd Amend.)

■ SUPERNATURAL FAIRY TALES: THE
PROGRESSIVE ROCK ERA
1996 CD, Rhino R 2 72451
The Nice track: America (America / 2nd Amend.)

VIDEO & DVD APPEARANCES (selected)

➤ BBCTV
UK 1968, 4 minute Video clip
The Nice: America (America / 2nd Amendment)

➤ **BBCTV - HOW IT IS**
UK 1968, 5 minute Video clip
The Nice: America (America / 2nd Amendment)

➤ **FAIRFIELD HALL, CROYDON 29.9.68**
UK 1968
Tracks: America / Rondo / Ars Longa Vita Brevis

➤ **DICK CLARKE TV SHOW**
USA 1968, Video clip

➤ **GRANADA TV**
UK 1968, Video clip

➤ **REUNION JAM**
7.5.83 at The Central
Tracks: America / Rondo / Nutrocker
Keith Emerson - Keyboards; Lee Jackson - Bass

➤ **BEAT CLUB - BEST OF '68**
2000 Germany DVD
The Nice performance: Hang On To A Dream

➤ **BEAT CLUB - BEST OF '69**
2000 Germany DVD
The Nice performance: America

BRIAN DAVISON

SESSION APPEARANCES

■ **THE INCREDIBLE STRING BAND - Earthspan**
1972 LP, Island 9211
1972 LP, Warner Brothers 2122
1994 CD, Demon 360
Brian Davison - Drums

■ **ROY HARPER - Lifemask**
1973 LP, Chrysalis 1162
1973 LP, Harvest SHVL 808
1994 CD, Griffin Music 232
1995 CD, Science Friction 005
1997/98 CD, Resurgence 4057/4067
ROY HARPER - Work Of Heart
1986 LP, Awareness 1002
Brian Davison - Drums

AS A MEMBER OF OTHER BANDS

THE MARK LEEMAN FIVE

*Mark Leeman (John Ardrey) - Vocals; Alan Roskams -
Guitar; Terry Goldberg - Organ; David Hyde - Bass;
Brian Davison - Drums*

SINGLE & ALBUM

● **PORTLAND TOWN** / Gotta Get Myself Together
UK 1965 7" Single, Manfredisc
with Paul Jones - Harmonica

■ **THE MARK LEEMAN MEMORIAL ALBUM**
UK 1991

Tracks include: Got My Mojo Working +11 others
from 1962 Pye Marble Arch sessions

EVERY WHICH WAY

*Graham Bell - Vocals; Alan Cartwright - Bass;
Brian Davison - Drums; Geoff Peach - Flute;
John Hedley - Guitar*

SINGLE & ALBUM

● **GO PLACIDLY**
UK 1970, Charisma BD 1

■ **EVERY WHICH WAY**
UK 1970 LP Promo, Mercury SR 61340
UK 1970 LP, Charisma CAS 1021
Tracks: Bed Ain't What It Used To Be, Castle Sand,
Go Placidly, All In Time, What You Like, The Light

VARIOUS ARTISTS COMPILATION

■ **THE FAMOUS CHARISMA BOX**
1993 4CD, Virgin 39084
Every Which Way track: Go Placidly

DAVY O'LIST

SINGLE & ALBUM

● **FALLOUT LOVE** / Talking Pictures
UK 1982 7" Single, Underground Music UMA 004
Davy O'List - Guitar; Brian Davison - Drums

■ **FLIGHT OF THE EAGLE**
UK 1997 CD, Jet Records JETCD 1013
Tracks: Girls In My Cars / Outside Broadcast /
Fax / Gone To The Beach / Sealed With A Kiss /
I Wish I Had You On My Side / You And I / Nuke
/ Walking Talking / Flight Of The Eagle / Pale Pale
Girl Of The Neat White Uniform

SESSION APPEARANCES

■ **BRYAN FERRY - Another Time, Another Place**
UK 1974 LP, Island ILPS
UK CD, Virgin EGCD14
UK CD, Virgin FERRYCD2
Davy O'List - Guitar
BRYAN FERRY - Let's Stick Together
UK 1976 LP, Island ILPS 9367
UK CD, Virgin EGCD24
UK 1999 CD, Virgin 7243 8 47602 29
UK CD, Virgin FERRYCD3
Davy O'List - Guitar on Chance Meeting

■ **TONY ASHTON - Live In The Studio**
1984 LP, EMI 176358-1
Davy O'List - Guitar

AS A MEMBER OF OTHER BANDS

THE ATTACK

Richard Shirman - Vocals; Gerry Whitehead - Bass; Davy O'List - Guitar; Bob Hodges - Organ; Alan Whitehead - Drums

SINGLES & ALBUM

- TRY IT / We Don't Know
  UK 1967 7" Single, Decca F 12550

- HI-HO SILVER LINING / Any More Than I Do
  UK 1967 7" Single, Decca F 12578

- ■ MAGIC IN THE AIR
  1990 LP, Reflection MM08
  UK CD, Aftermath AFT1001
  Tracks: Magic In The Air / Colour Of My Mind /
  Mr. Pinnodmy's Dilemma / Hi-Ho Silver Lining /
  Try It / Freedom For You / Any More Than I Do /
  Strange House / Neville Thumbcatch /
  Feel Like Flying / Lady Orange Peel /
  We Don't Know / Too Old / Go Your Way

MISUNDERSTOOD

Guy Evans - Drums; Remi Kabaka - Conga; Chris Mercer - Alto Sax; Davy O'List - Guitar; Steve Whiting - Bass

EPS & ALBUM

- CHILDREN OF THE SUN
  UK 1969 EP

- NEVER HAD A GIRL LIKE YOU
  UK 1969 EP

- YOU'RE TUFF ENOUGH
  UK 1969 EP

- ■ THE LEGENDARY GOLDSTAR ALBUM /
  GOLDEN GLASS
  1997 CD, Cherry Red 142
  Blues With A Feeling / Who's Been Talking /
  You Got Me Dizzy / You Don't Have To Go Out /
  Goin' To New York / Shake Your Moneymaker /
  I Just Want To Make Love To You / I'm Not
  Talkin' / Never Had A Girl Like You / Golden Glass
  / I Don't Want To Discuss It / Little Red Rooster /
  You're Tuff Enough / Freedom / Keep On Running
  / I'm Cruising

JET

Andy Ellison - Vocals; Martin Gordon - Bass; Davy O'List - Guitar; Peter Oxendale - Keyboards; Chris Townson - Drums

SINGLE & ALBUMS

- NOTHING TO DO WITH US / Brain Damage

UK 1975 7" Single, CBS S CBS 3317

- ■ JET
  UK 1975 LP, CBS 80699
  1975 LP, Pacific Arts 129

- ■ NOTHING TO DO WITH US - A GOLDEN
  ANTHOLOGY OF JET
  Holland 2CD, 2002 Fan Mael Records

LEE JACKSON

AS A MEMBER OF OTHER BANDS

JACKSON HEIGHTS

Personnel on King Progress album and Doubting Thomas single: *Lee Jackson - Guitars; Harmonica & Vocals; Charlie Harcourt - Guitar; Keyboards & Vocals; Tommy Sloane - Drums & Percussion; Mario Enrique Covarrubias Tapia - Guitar, Bass & Vocals* Personnel on other albums and single: *Lee Jackson - Vocals, Guitar, Bass, Percussion & Harmonica; John McBurnie - Vocals, Guitars & Keyboards; Brian Chatton - Vocals & Keyboards; also featuring: Michael Giles, Ian Wallace & Ian Paice - Drums & Percussion; Godfrey Salmon - Violin*

SINGLES

- DOUBTING THOMAS / Insomnia
  UK 1970 7" Single, Charisma JH1

- MAUREEN / Long Time Dying
  UK 1972 7" Single, Vertigo 6059 068
  US 1972 7" Single, Verve VK-10706
  US 1972 7" Single Promo, Verve VK-10706

ALBUMS

- ■ KING PROGRESS
  UK 1970 LP, Charisma CAS 1018
  UK 1970 LP, Mercury SR 61331
  UK CD, Repertoire REP 4714-WY
  Tracks: Mr. Screw / Since I Last Saw You /
  Sunshine Freak / King Progress / Doubting
  Thomas / Insomnia / The Cry Of Eugene

- ■ THE FIFTH AVENUE BUS
  UK 1972 LP, Vertigo 6360 603
  UK 1972 LP, Vertigo 6360 067
  UK 1993 CD, Repertoire REP 4365-WP
  Tracks: Tramp / Autumn Brigade / Long Time
  Dying / Sweet Tunnel Hill / Laughing Gear /
  House In The Country / Rent A Friend / Luxford /
  Pastor Roger

- ■ RAGAMUFFIN'S FOOL
  UK 1973 LP, Vertigo 6360 077
  Tracks: Maureen / Oh You Beauty / As She Starts
  / Bebop / Catch A Thief / Ragamuffin's Fool /
  Chorale (Five Bridges Suite) / Chips & Chicken /
  Poor Peter / Bellyful Of Water

■ **BUMP 'N' GRIND**
UK 1973 LP, Vertigo 6360 092
Tracks: I Could Be Your Orchestra / Spaghetti
Sunshine / Long Necked Lady / Public Romance /
Bump 'n' Grind / Cumberland County / It's A
Shame / Ladies In The Chorus / Whatever
Happened To The Conversation
Moog loaned & programmed by *Keith Emerson*

■ **JACKSON HEIGHTS**
US 1973 LP, Verve V6 5089

■ **ATTENTION! JACKSON HEIGHTS**
Japan?/Germany? 1973 LP, Fontana 6424 085

VARIOUS ARTISTS COMPILATION

■ **THE FAMOUS CHARISMA BOX**
1993 4CD, Virgin 39084
Jackson Heights track: Doubting Thomas

LEE JACKSON & BRIAN DAVISON

AS MEMBERS OF ANOTHER BAND

REFUGEE

*Patrick Moraz - Keyboards; Lee Jackson - Bass &
Vocals; Brian Davison - Drums & Percussion*

ALBUM

■ **REFUGEE**
UK 1974 LP, Charisma CAS 1087
LP, Charisma FC 6066
UK CD, Si-Wan Records SRMC 6024
Tracks: Papillon / Someday / Grand Canyon (The
Source / Theme For The Canyon / The Journey /
Rapids / The Mighty Colorado) / Ritt Mickley /
Credo (Prelude / Believe / Theme / The Lost
Cause / Agitato / I Believe (Part II) / Variation /
Main Theme Finale)

VARIOUS ARTISTS COMPILATION

■ **THE FAMOUS CHARISMA BOX**
1993 4CD, Virgin 39084
Refugee track: Ritt Mickley

KEITH EMERSON

SINGLES

● **HONKY TONK TRAIN BLUES** / Barrelhouse
Shakedown
UK 1976 7" Single, Manticore K13513
Italy 1977 7" Single Juke Box Promo, Manticore 111
Spain 1976 7" Single, Manticore 16964 A
Germany 1976 7" Single, Manticore K16964 AT

Italy 1976 7" Single, Manticore MAN 5406
Japan 1976 7" Single Promo, Manticore P-32M
HONKY TONK TRAIN BLUES / Afrika Man
Italy 1977 7" Single Juke Box Promo, Manticore 111

● **MAPLE LEAF RAG** / The Sheriff
1977 7" Single, Ricordi MAN 5409

● **ODEON RAG** / Illusione
Italy 1977 7" Single Juke Box Promo, Ricordi JB121
ODEON RAG / The Sheriff
Italy 1977 7" Single, Dischi Ricordi MAN 5409

● **TAXI RIDE (ROME)** / Mater Tenebrarum
1980 7" Single, Atlantic K11611
TAXI RIDE (ROME) / Mater Tenebrarum
Holland 1980 7" Single, Atlantic K1161

● **MATER TENEBRARUM** / Inferno
France 1980 7" Single, Barclay 620580
MATER TENEBRARUM / Cigarettes Ices etc
Italy 1980 7" Single, Cinevox Record MDF 130

● **SALT CAY** / Taxi Ride (Rome)
1980 7" Single, Cinevox Record MDF 129

● **I'M A MAN**
UK 1981 7" Single, MCA 697
1981 7" Single, MCA 103 126-100
Argentina 1981 7" Single, MCA 9307
12" Single, White Label Test Pressing

● **RUM-A-TING** / Big Horn Breakdown
1982 7" Single, Bubble BLU 9321
RUM-A-TING / ?
Italy 1982 7" Single, Bubble BLU 61002
Italy 1982 12" Single Promo, Bubble BLU 61002
RUM-A-TING / Ci Siamo Anche Noi
Italy 1982 7" Single Juke Box Promo, Bubble JB70

● **CHILDREN OF THE LIGHT** / Challenge Of The
Psionic Fighters
Japan 1983 7" Single, Canyon 7Y00 39

● **UP THE ELEPHANT & ROUND THE CASTLE**
1983 7" Single, Red Bus RBUS 85
with Jim Davidson - Vocals

● **WE THREE KINGS** / Captain Starship Christmas
UK 1988 7" Single, Emerson Records Keith 1
1988 7" Single, Priority Keith 1

● **THE CHRISTMAS SINGLE**
UK 1995 CD Single, Amp Records AMP-CDS001
Troika / Captain Starship Christmas /
I Saw Three Ships

● **TETSUI 1** / Tetsui 2
1998 CD, Import 58669
with Rosemary Butler - Vocals

ALBUMS

■ **INFERNO**
1980 LP, Ariola 202 079-320
1980 LP, Atlantic K50753
1980 LP, Barclay BA-253
Italy 1980 LP, Cinevox CIA 5022 LP
Italy 1997 CD, Cinevox Record CD-CIA 5022

Tracks: Inferno (Main Title Theme) / Rose's Descent Into The Cellar / Taxi Ride (Rome) / The Library / Sarah In the Library Vaults / Bookbinder's Delight / Rose Leaves The Apartment / Rose Gets It / Elisa's Story / A Cat Attic Attack / Kazanian's Tarantella` / Mark's Discovery / Mater Tenebrarum / Inferno Finale / Cigarettes Ices etc

■ NIGHTHAWKS
1981 LP, MCA BSR 5196
1981 LP, MCA MCF 3107
2001 CD, NetEvent
Tracks: Nighthawks / Mean Stalkin' / The Bust / Nighthawking / The Chase / I'm A Man / The Chopper / Tramway / I'm Comin' In / Face To Face / The Flight Of A Hawk

■ HONKY
Italy 1981 LP, Bubble BLU 19608
UK 1985 LP, Chord Records Chord 002
Italy CD, Chord Records Chord CD 002
1992 CD, Chord Records JICK-89038
USA 1999 CD, Gunslinger GSR-612000
Tracks: Bach Before The Mast / Hello Sailor / Salt Cay / Green Ice / Intro-Juicing / Big Horn Breakdown / Yancey Special / Chic Charni / Jesus Loves Me
Keith Emerson - Keyboards; Kendal Stubbs - Bass; Frank Scully & Neil Symonette - Drums & Percussion; Mott - Guitar; Andrew Brennan, Dick Morrissey & Pete King - Saxes

■ HARMAGEDON
Japan 1983 CD, Volcano Records CPC8 3003
Japan 1983 CD, Canyon C28Y0044
1985 LP, Chord Records Chord 003
Emerson tracks: Theme Of Floi / Toccata & Fugue In D Minor (Bach) / Joe & Michiko / Children Of The Light / Sonny's Skate State / Zamedy Stomp / Challenge Of The Psionics Fighters
Keith Emerson - Keyboards; Jun Aoyama - Drums; Fujimaru Yoshino - Guitars; Rosemary Butler - Vocal

■ MURDEROCK
Italy 1984 LP, Bubble BLULP 1819
Japan 1985 CD, Cinevox Record SLCS-7158
UK 1986 LP, Chord Records Chord 004
Tracks: Murderock / Tonight Is Your Night / Streets To Blame / Not So Innocent / Prelude To Candice / Don't Go In The Shower / Coffee Time / Candice / New York Dash / Tonight Is Not Your Night / The Spillone
Keith Emerson - Keyboards; Tim Nicol & Derek Wilson - Drums; Mike Shepherd - Bass & Lead Guitars; Doreen Chanter - Lead Vocals

■ BEST REVENGE
UK 1985 LP, Chord Records Chord 001
1992 CD, Jimco JICK-89039
CD, Jimco Records CD JIM 0013
Dream Runner / The Runner / Wha'd'ya Mean / Straight Between The Eyes / Orchestral Suite To Best Revenge / Playing For Keeps

■ BEST REVENGE & MURDEROCK
UK CD, Chord Records CDColl:3
Tracks: Dream Runner / The Runner / Wha'd'ya Mean / Straight Between The Eyes /

Orchestral Suite To Best Revenge / Playing For Keeps / Murderock / Tonight Is Your Night / Streets To Blame / Not So Innocent / Prelude To Candice / Don't Go In The Shower / Coffee Time / Candice / New York Dash / Tonight Is Not Your Night / The Spillone

■ LA CHIESA (THE CHURCH)
Italy 1989 LP, Cinevox MDF 33.192 LP
Japan 1997 CD, Cinevox SP/CR-20013
4 tracks by Keith Emerson: The Church (Main Title Theme) / Prelude 24 From The Well Tempered Clavier (Bach) / The Possession / The Church Revisited
Keith Emerson - Keyboards

■ THE CHRISTMAS ALBUM
1989 LP, Emerson Records Keith LP1
1989 MC, Emerson Records Keith MC1
1995 CD, Amp Records AMP-CD018
1995 CD, Emersongs SMB1997KE
Tracks: Variations On O Little Town Of Bethlehem / We Three Kings / Snowman's Land / Aria From Bach's Christmas Oratorio / Captain Starship Christmas / I Saw Three Ships / Petites Litanies De Jesus / It Came Upon A Midnight Clear / Silent Night
Keith Emerson - Keyboards; Frank Scully - Drums; Les Moir - Bass
THE CHRISTMAS ALBUM
USA 1999 CD, Gunslinger Records
Tracks: Troika / Variations On O Little Town Of Bethlehem / We Three Kings / Snowman's Land / Captain Starship Christmas / Aria From Bach's Christmas Oratorio / I Saw Three Ships / Glorietta Part 1 / Glorietta Part 2 / Petites Litanies De Jesus / It Came Upon A Midnight Clear / Silent Night

■ CREAM OF EMERSON SOUP
Original concept for what became Changing States album (see below)

■ CHANGING STATES
UK 1995 CD, Amp Records AMP-CD 026
Tracks: Shelter From The Rain / Another Frontier / Ballade / The Band Keeps Playing / Summertime / The Church / Interlude / Montagues & Capulets / Abaddon's Bolero (with orchestra) / The Band Keeps Playing (aftershock mix)
Keith Emerson - Keyboards; Marc Bonilla - Guitar; Gary Cirimelli - Vocals; Kevin Gilbert - Bass & Drums; Tim Pierce - Guitar; Jerry Watts - Bass; London Philharmonic on Abaddon's Bolero led by John Mayer

■ IRON MAN VOLUME 1
USA 2001 CD, NetEvent
Tracks: Iron Man Main Title Theme / And The Sea Shall Give Up It's Dead / I Am Ultimo The Deliverer / Data In, Chaos Out / Silence My Companion, Death My Destination / Iron Man Theme (alternate)

■ EMERSON PLAYS EMERSON
UK 2002 CD, EMI 7243 5 57301 2 1
Tracks: Vagrant / Creole Dance / Solitudinous / Broken Bough / A Cajun Alley / Prelude To Candice / A Blade Of Grass / Outgoing Tide /

Summertime / Interlude / Roll'n'Jelly / B&W
Blues / For Kevin / The Dreamer / Hammer It Out
/ Ballad For A Common Man / Barrelhouse
Shakedown / Nilu's Dream / Soulscapes / Close
To Home / Honky Tonk Train Blues / Medley:
Nicola / Silver Shoes / I'll See You In My Dreams
Keith Emerson - Keyboards; with Various Artists
including 1976 duet with *Oscar Peterson* on
Honky Tonk Train Blues

COMPILATION ALBUMS

■ **THE BEST OF KEITH EMERSON**
1985 LP, Chord Records ESP1

■ **THE EMERSON COLLECTION**
1986 CD, Chord Records CD Coll 1
Tracks: Orchestral Suite To Best Revenge /
Bach Before The Mast / Hello Sailor / Salt Cay /
Prelude To Candice / Candice / Nighthawks /
Inferno (Main Title Theme) / Mater Tenebrarum /
Starship / Chic Charni / The Dreamer / Playing
For Keeps

■ **BEST WORKS COLLECTION**
Japan 1992 CD, Jimco JICK-89169
Tracks: Inferno (Main Title Theme) / Hello Sailor /
Cigarettes Ices etc / Prelude 24 (Bach) / Playing
For Keeps / Wha'd'ya Mean / Candice / Petites
Litanies De Jesus / Taxi Ride / The Church (Main
Title Theme) / Variations On O Little Town Of
Bethlehem / Dream Runner / Elisa's Story /
Green Ice

■ **CHORD SAMPLER**
LP, Chord Records 1.022.051
Tracks: Intro-Juicing / Big Horn Breakdown /
Chic Charni / Not So Innocent / Candice / Love
Theme From Best Revenge / Playing For Keeps /
Joe & Michiko / Inferno (Main Title Theme) /
Mater Tenebrarum / Children Of The Light

MISCELLANEOUS (selected)

■ **EARTH NEWS**
USA 1981 LP, Radio Show
Interview for the promotion of Nighthawks

■ **JIM LADD INTERVIEW**
USA 1981 LP, Radio Show
Interview for the promotion of Nighthawks

■ **PSYCHEDELIC PSNACK**
USA 1987 LP, Radio Show, Westwood One PP87-34
Brief Emerson interviews + Trilogy track

■ **ROLLING STONE CONTINUOUS HISTORY OF
ROCK & ROLL**
USA 1983 2LP, Radio Show, Volume 2, No.89

■ **SOLID GOLD SCRAPBOOK**
USA 1987 LP, Radio Show
With Emerson interview

■ **THE ROCK CHRONICLES**
USA 1986 2LP, Radio Show, Westwood One 86-31
Brief clip of Keith + Touch And Go track

SESSION APPEARANCES (selected)

■ **ROD STEWART - An Old Raincoat Won't
Ever Let You Down**
UK 1969 LP, Vertigo V04
ROD STEWART - The Rod Stewart Album
1990 LP, Mercury 830 572
1990 MC, Mercury 830572-4
1990/98 CD, Mercury 830572/830572-2
1998 CD, Mercury 558058
ROD STEWART - 1964-1969
LP, Get Back 578
2000 CD, Pilot 44
2001 CD, New Millennium 94000
Keith Emerson - Keyboards on I Wouldn't Ever
Change A Thing

■ **PETER HAMMILL - And Close As This**
1986 CD, Virgin CDV 2409 CD
Keith Emerson - Keyboards on and co-writer
of Empire Of Delight

■ **GIOVANNI JOVANOTTI - Jovanotti**
Italy 1990 CD, YO IBZ 467557 2 CD
Italy 1994 CD, Tristar 80821
Keith Emerson - Keyboards on Giovane Sempre /
Diritti E Doveri / Sceriffo O Bandito

■ **MARC BONILLA - E.E.Ticket**
USA 1991 CD, Reprise 9 26725-2 CD
Keith Emerson - Keyboards on White Noise

■ **TEMPEST - Turn Of The Wheel**
1996 CD, Magna Carta MA-9007-2
Keith Emerson - Keyboards on The Barrow Man

■ **GLENN HUGHES - The Way It Is**
Germany 1999 CD, Steamhammer SPV 085-21032
1999 CD, Shrapnel 1130
1999 CD, Steamhammer SPV 085-21032 CD
Keith Emerson - Keyboards on Stoned In The
Temple / Don't Look Away

■ **MARTIN LUTHER LENNON - Escape To
Paradox Island**
1999 CD, Not Lame NL-047
UK 2000 CD, Castle Music WENCD 208
Keith Emerson - Synth Solo on Somebody Knows
Everything

VARIOUS ARTISTS COMPIL. (selected)

■ **THE BEST OF THE KORG 01/W**
USA 1992 CD, Korg CD 01/W
Keith Emerson - Keyboards on Katoh-San

■ **DEMONSTRATION TEST CD**
CD, Gateway 4620
Keith Emerson - Piano on one untitled track

■ **THE FAMOUS CHARISMA BOX**
1993 4CD, Virgin 39084
Keith Emerson - Keyboards on Freedom Jazz Dance

■ **GOBLIN, Volume 4**
1999 CD, DRG 32934
Emerson tracks: The Church (Main Theme) /
The Possession / The Church Revisited

- **GUITAR'S PRACTICING MUSICIANS, Volume 2**
  MC, Guitar Recordings 88561-5037-4
  CD, Guitar Recordings 88561-5037-2
  Keith Emerson - Keyboards on Marc Bonilla track
  White Noise

- **THE MANHATTAN COLLECTION**
  1988 CD, Chord Records CD 24001
  Emerson tracks: The Dreamer / Prelude To
  Candice / Hello Sailor / Inferno (Main Title Theme)
  Keith Emerson - Keyboards

- **MUSIC FOR THE 3rd MILLENNIUM**
  UK 1999 CD, AMP-CD0039
  Keith Emerson - Keyboards on Katoh-San

- **MUSIC FROM FREE CREEK**
  1973 LP, Charisma CADS 101
  CD, SL-127
  Keith Emerson - Keyboards on Freedom Jazz
  Dance / Mother Nature's Son / On The Rebound
  with *Various Artists*

- **ROCK AID ARMENIA - The Earthquake Album**
  1990 CD, Life Aid Records AID CD001
  1996 CD, Tring International ANT010
  Keith Emerson - Keyboards on Smoke On The
  Water, with *Various Artists*

- ● **ROCK AID ARMENIA**
  SMOKE ON THE WATER / Paranoid
  UK 1989 7" Single, Life Aid Records Armen 001
  1989 7" Single, Eml Armen 001
  1989 12" Single, Eml Arment 001
  Keith Emerson - Keyboards on Smoke On The
  Water, with *Various Artists*

- **ROCK CLASSICS - THE EARTHQUAKE ALBUM**
  1995 CD, Tring International JHD142
  Keith Emerson - Keyboards

- **SONGS FOR A MODERN CHURCH**
  UK 1983 LP, Charisma CAS 1159 LP
  Keith Emerson - Keyboards on My Name Is Rain

- **STALLONE - MUSIC FROM THE FILMS OF
  SYLVESTER STALLONE**
  USA 1993 CD, SILVA SSD 1032
  Emerson track: Nighthawks - Main Theme

- **STEINWAY TO HEAVEN**
  1996 CD, Magna Carta MA-9011-2
  Keith Emerson - Steinway Piano

- **TO CRY YOU A SONG - A COLLECTION OF
  TULL TALES**
  USA 1996 CD, Magna Carta MA-9009-2
  Jethro Tull tribute album
  Keith Emerson - Keyboards on Living In The Past

AS A MEMBER OF OTHER BANDS

GARY FARR & THE T-BONES

*Gary Farr - Vocals; David 'Cyrano' Langston - Guitar;
Keith Emerson - Keyboards; Lee Jackson - Bass;
Alan Turner - Drums*

SINGLE

- ● **IF I HAD A TICKET**
  1966 7" Single, CBS 202394
  *With Kenneth Washington - Vocals;
  Chris Barber - Trombone*

THE V.I.P.S

*Mike Harrison - Vocals & Harmonica;
Luther Grosvenor - Guitar; Keith Emerson - Keyboards;
Mike Kellie - Drums*

EP

- ● **STAGGER LEE** / Rosemarie / Late Night Blues
  EP 1967 7" EP, Fontana 460 219 ME

ALBUMS

- **KEITH EMERSON WITH THE V.I.P.S**
  Switzerland 1998 CD, RCD 003
  Keith Emerson - Keyboards

- **THE V.I.P.S**
  Australia 2LP, Funtona V 8500

- **THE V.I.P.S - LOST & FOUND**
  1989 CD, Document Records DR035 CD

EMERSON, LAKE & PALMER

*Keith Emerson - Keyboards;
Greg Lake - Bass, Guitars & Vocals;
Carl Palmer - Drums & Percussion*

SINGLES & EPS

- ● **LUCKY MAN** / From The Beginning
  7" Single, Atlantic OS 13153
  LUCKY MAN / Knife Edge
  1971 7" Single, Cotillion 45-44106
  1971 7" Single, Island 6014 0411971
  7" Single, Island S 10203-AT
  7" Single, Manticore 13961 AT
  Spain 1971 7" Single, Island A10 203-A
  1972 7" Single, Cotillion COT 44106
  1971 7" Single, Cotillion 45-44106
  Portugal 7" Single, Island 6014 041
  Japan 1971 7" Single, Atlantic P-1033 A
  Canada 1971 7" Single, Cotillion COT 44106
  Italy 1971 7" Single, Island 6014 041
  Sweden 1971 7" Single, Island 6014 041
  Belgium 1971 7" Single, Island 6014 41
  France 1971 7" Single, Island 6014041 Serie Parade
  Germany 1971 7" Single, Island 6016 041
  France 1971 7" Single Juke Box Promo,
  Philips 6832996
  Poland 7" Single
  LUCKY MAN / Lucky Man
  1971 7" Single Promo, Cotillion 45-44106

LUCKY MAN (3.33) / Lucky Man (3.33)
USA 1971 7" Single, Cotillion 44106 (blue label)
USA 1971 7" Single, Cotillion 45-44106 (white label)
LUCKY MAN (4.36) / Lucky Man (3.33)
USA 1971 7" Single, Cotillion 45-44106 mono
USA 1971 7" Single, Cotillion 45-44106 stereo
LUCKY MAN / Look At Yourself - *Uriah Heep*
Spain 1971 7" Single Promo, Island 001-A

● **TAKE A PEBBLE** / Lucky Man
USA 1971 7" Single Promo, Cotillion PR-176
TAKE A PEBBLE / Lucky Man (Live)
USA 1972 7" Single Promo, Atco Sampler PR 176

● **STONES OF YEARS** / Stones Of Years
1971 7" Single, Cotillion 45-44131
USA 1971 7" Single Promo, Atlantic 44131
New Zealand 1971 7" Single, Atlantic ATL 81
Japan 1971 7" Single Promo, Atlantic P 1087 A
USA 1971 7" Single, Cotillion 44131
USA 1971 7" Single, Cotillion 44141
Argentina 1973 7" Single Promo, Music Hall 40.002

● **NUTROCKER** / The Great Gates Of Kiev
Japan 1972 7" Single, Atlantic P 1128-A
1972 7" Single, Atlantic P-119-A
New Zealand 1972 7" Single, Atlantic ATL 96
USA 1972 7" Single, Cotillion45-44151
Canada 1972 7" Single, Cotillion COT 44151
Argentina 1972 7" Single Promo, Atlantic 216
NUTROCKER / Nutrocker
1972 7" Single, Cotillion 45-44151
USA 1971 7" Single Promo, Cotillion 45-44151

● **EXCERPTS FROM TRILOGY**
Japan 1973 7" EP Promo, Atlantic PS-1003-2

● **FROM THE BEGINNING** / Living Sin
1972 7" Single, Cotillion 45-44158
Canada 1972 7" Single, Cotillion COT 44158
New Zealand 1972 7" Single, Atlantic ATL111 mono
Japan 1972 7" Single, Atlantic P 1155-A
Argentina 1973 7" Single Promo, Music Hall 40.020
FROM THE BEGINNING / From The Beginning
USA 1972 7" Single Promo, Cotillion 45-44158
USA 1972 7" Single, Atlantic 44158 mono

● **HOEDOWN** / Living Sin
France 1972 7" Single, Island 6387 078
France 1972 7" Single Promo, Island 6837 078

● **BRAIN SALAD SURGERY** / Excerpts From Brain
Salad Surgery
1973 7" Single Flexi-disc, Lyntone LYN 2762
Free with New Musical Express
BRAIN SALAD SURGERY / Still...You Turn Me On
1974 7" Single Promo, Manticore MC-2003-PR
BRAIN SALAD SURGERY / Brain Salad Surgery
UK 1997 7" Single, Castle ORRLP02

● **JERUSALEM** / Jerusalem
USA 1973 7" Single Test Pressing, Atlantic MC2003
JERUSALEM / When The Apple Blossoms
Bloom In The Windmills Of Your Mind I'll Be
Your Valentine
UK 1973 7" Single, Manticore K13503
Spain 1973 7" Single, Manticore 13.072-A
Portugal 1973 7" Single, Manticore 13072
Germany 1973 7" Single, Manticore 13072 AT
Holland 1973 7" Single, Manticore 13072 AT

France 1973 7" Single, Manticore K13503
USA 1973 7" Single, Manticore K13503
UK 1973 7" Single Demo, Manticore K13503
Italy 1973 7" Single, Manticore MAN 5402
Italy 1973 7" Single Juke Box Promo,
Manticore MAN 5402

● **EXCERPTS FROM WORKS Volume 1**
Germany 1977 7" Single, Ariola 17915 TXT

● **FANFARE FOR THE COMMON MAN** /
Brain Salad Surgery
UK 1977 7" Single, Atlantic K10946
1977 7" Single, Atlantic K10946
1977 7" Single, Atlantic K10946 (silver label)
France 1977 7" Single, Atlantic K10946
Holland 1977 7" Single, Ariola 17977 AT
Canada 1977 7" Single, Atlantic
USA 1977 7" Single, Atlantic 398
USA 1977 7" Single, Atlantic 3398
1977 7" Single, Atlantic 45 3398
1977 7" Single, Atlantic P 189 A
Japan 1977 7" Single Promo, Atlantic P 189 A
FANFARE FOR THE COMMON MAN / Living Sin
1977 7" Single, Manticore 5408
FANFARE FOR THE COMMON MAN / Piano
Concerto No.1
1977 12" Single Promo, Atlantic PR 277
FANFARE FOR THE COMMON MAN (LP version)
/ Fanfare For The Common Man (7" version)
USA 1977 7" Single Promo, Atlantic 3398
FANFARE FOR THE COMMON MAN (LP version)
/ Fanfare For The Common Man (7" version) /
Brain Salad Surgery
UK 1977 12" Single, Atlantic K10946 T
FANFARE FOR THE COMMON MAN /
Peter Gunn / Knife Edge
Holland 1980 12" Single, Atlantic ATL 2022
FANFARE FOR THE COMMON MAN (7" version)
/ Hoedown (Live) / Fanfare For The Common Man
(LP version)
UK 2002 CD Single, Castle CMNX520

● **TIGER IN A SPOTLIGHT** / So Far To Fall
Germany 1977 7" Single, Ariola 11776 AT
USA 1977 7" Single, Atlantic 3641
TIGER IN A SPOTLIGHT / Tiger In A Spotlight
1977 7" Single Promo, Atlantic 3461

● **WATCHING OVER YOU** / Barrelhouse Shakedown
Argentina 1978 7" Single, Atlantic 10052

● **ALL I WANT IS YOU** / All I Want Is You
1978 7" Single Promo, Atlantic 3555
ALL I WANT IS YOU / Tiger In A Spotlight
UK 1977 7" Single, Atlantic K11225
1978 7" Single, Atlantic AT3555
Japan 1978 7" Single, Atlantic P-362A

● **CANARIO** / All I Want Is You
1978 7" Single, Ariola 100 238 100

● **PETER GUNN** / Knife Edge
1979 7" Single, Ariola 100 824
1979 7" Single, Ariola 100 824-100
1979 7" Single, Ariola A 101103
1979 7" Single, Ariola S 100 824
PETER GUNN / Tiger In A Spotlight
1979 7" Single Promo, Atlantic AT 3641
1979 7" Single, Atlantic ST-A-37822 SP

Canada 1979 7" Single, Atlantic AT 3641
PETER GUNN / Barrelhouse Shakedown
USA 1979 7" Single Promo, Atlantic 3641
PETER GUNN / Knife Edge
Holland 1979 7" Single, Atlantic 11413
Belgium 1979 7" Single, Atlantic ATL 11416
Holland 1979 7" Single, Atlantic ATL 11416
UK 1979 7" Single, Atlantic K11416
PETER GUNN / Hoedown
Bolivia 1981 7" Single, Ariola ASS-1124

● **TOCCATA**
Russia 1980 7" Single, Amateur Art
(blue flexi-disc)

● **BLACK MOON** / Black Moon (album version)
UK 1992 7" Single, Victory LON 320
BLACK MOON / A Blade Of Grass
Germany 1992 7" Single, Victory 869 836-7
BLACK MOON / A Blade Of Grass / Black Moon
(album version)
UK 1992 12" Single, Victory LONX 320
Germany 1992 12" Single, Victory 869 737-1
UK 1992 CD Single, Victory LONCD 320
1992 CD Single, Victory 869 737-2
Germany 1992 CD Single, Victory 869 857-2
BLACK MOON / ?
USA 1992 CD Single, Victory CDP 694
1992 CD Single, Victory 0001-2
1992 MC Promo, Victory 383 480 003-4
BLACK MOON / Let's Get Rocked - *Def Leppard*
1992 7" Single, Polygram AS 5000 921

● **EXCERPTS FROM 'BLACK MOON'**
UK 1992 CD Single Promo, Victory ELP-1
Germany 1992 CD Single Promo, Victory ELP-1
Canada 1992 CD Single Promo, Victory PCD 242
Tracks: Black Moon / Paper Blood / Affairs Of The
Heart / Changing States

● **PAPER BLOOD** / Romeo & Juliet
Japan 1992 CD Single, Victory VPCD-42
PAPER BLOOD Radio Edit / Paper Blood
1992 CD Single, Victory CDS-149

● **AFFAIRS OF THE HEART** / Black Moon /
Fanfare For The Common Man
1992 CD Single, Victory CDP 739
USA 1992 CD Single Promo, Victory CDP 739
1992 CD Single, Victory 869 859-2
UK 1992 CD Single, Victory LOCDP 327
AFFAIRS OF THE HEART / Better Days
1992 7" Single, Victory LON 327
UK 1992 MC Single, Victory LONC 327
Germany, Victory 869-857-7
Germany 1992 CD Single, Victory 869 833-2
AFFAIRS OF THE HEART (Limited Edition)
1992 2CD Single, Victory LONCD 327
Germany 1992 2CD Single, Victory 869857-2
Tracks: Affairs Of The Heart / Better Days /
A Blade Of Grass / Black Moon / Affairs Of The
Heart / Black Moon (radio edit) / Fanfare For
The Common Man / Jerusalem
AFFAIRS OF THE HEART / Affairs Of The Heart
USA 1992 MC Single, Victory SAC 544
AFFAIRS OF THE HEART / A Blade Of Grass /
Fanfare For The Common Man / Jerusalem
1992 CD Single, Victory VICP 15019

● **ROMEO & JULIET**

1992 MC Single Promo, Victory

● **FAREWELL TO ARMS**
Germany 1992 CD Single Promo, Victory

● **LUCKY MAN** / Paper Blood / Romeo & Juliet
1992 CD Single, Victory 857 081-2

● **PICTURES AT AN EXHIBITION**
USA 1993 CD Single Promo DSS
Victory/Kore KORE 8401
Victory/Kore VMPR 0002

● **I BELIEVE IN FATHER CHRISTMAS** /
Troika / Humbug / I Believe In Father Christmas /
Nutrocker
USA 1995 CD EP, Rhino R2 72242
I BELIEVE IN FATHER CHRISTMAS /
Jerusalem / When the Apple Blossoms Bloom
In The Windmills Of Your Mind I'll Be Your
Valentine
USA 1993 CD Single, Victory 383 483 004-2
I BELIEVE IN FATHER CHRISTMAS (3 versions)
USA 1993 CD Single, Polygram 373361
1993 CD Single, Victory 855055-2
(including 1975 Single version with orchestra /
Version from Works Volume 2 /
1993 rerecording from Return Of The Manticore)

● **DADDY** / Heart On Ice
USA 1994 CD Single, Victory VMPR 0005

● **GONE TOO SOON** / ?
Japan 1994 CD Single, Victory 857 717-2

ALBUMS

■ **EMERSON LAKE & PALMER**
LP, Atlantic P-10111
1971 LP, Cotillion SD 9040
LP, Island 6339 026
1970 LP, Island ILPS 9132
1970 LP, Cotillion SD 9040
1970 MC, Cotillion AC-9040
USA Reel To Reel Tape, Cotillion M 9040
LP, Manticore K43503
CD, Atlantic 781 519-2
1993 CD, Victory 383 480 016-2
1993 CD, Victory 828 464-2
1999 CD 20-bit remaster (mini-LP sleeve),
Victory VICP-60633
UK 2001 CD, Castle CMRCD165
Tracks: The Barbarian / Take A Pebble / Knife
Edge / The Three Fates (Clotho / Lachesis /
Atropos) / Tank / Lucky Man)

■ **TARKUS**
UK LP, Island ILPS 9155
USA LP, Cotillion SD 9900
Japan LP, Atlantic P-10126
1973 LP, Manticore K43504
1971 8 Track Cartridge, Cotillion A8TC-9900
1971 Reel To Reel Tape, Cotillion M 9900
USA 1993 LP, Mobile Fidelity Sound Labs 1-203
CD, Atlantic 781 529-2
UK CD, Castle ESM CD 341
USA 1994 CD, Mobile Fidelity Sound Labs
Ultradisc UDCD 598
1993 CD, Victory 828 465-2

1999 CD 20-bit remaster (mini-LP sleeve),
Victory VICP-60634
2001 CD, Castle CMRCD166
UK 2002 CD (mini-LP sleeve), Castle CMTCD434
Tracks: Tarkus (Eruption / Stones Of Years /
Iconoclast / Mass / Manticore / The Battlefield /
Aquatarkus) / Jeremy Bender / Bitches Crystal /
The Only Way (Hymn) / Infinite Space
(Conclusion) / A Time And A Place / Are You
Ready Eddy?

■ **PICTURES AT AN EXHIBITION**
USA 1971 LP, Cotillion ELP 666666
UK 1971 LP, Island HELP 1
1971 8 Track Cartridge, Cotillion COT M 86666
1973 LP, Manticore K33501
1973 MC, Manticore K433501
USSR 1981 LP, Melodiya C 90-16383-4
USA 1981 LP, Mobile Fidelity Sound Lab MFSL1-031
1992 CD, Victory 828 466-2
CD, Atlantic 781 521-2
1999 CD 20-bit remaster (mini-LP sleeve),
Victory VICP-60635
UK 2001 CD, Castle CMRCD167 (with bonus
track: Pictures At An Exhibition (1993 version))
Tracks: Promenade / The Gnome / Promenade /
The Sage / The Old Castle / Blues Variations /
Promenade / The Hut Of Baba Yaga / The Curse Of
Baba Yaga / The Great Gates OfKiev / Nutrocker

■ **TRILOGY**
1972 LP, Atlantic K43505
LP, Atlantic 781 522-2
Japan LP, Atlantic P-10113 A
UK 1972 LP, Island ILPS 9186
1972 MC, Cotillion AC-9903
1972 8 Track Cartridge, Cotillion 9903-8
1972 8 Track Cartridge, Cotillion TP 9903
1972 8 Track Cartridge, Peace Tapes
USA 1973 LP, Cotillion SD 9903
USA 1973 LP, Cotillion/Capitol Record Club
SMAS94773
China LP, IANT TD-1138
1973 LP, Manticore K43505
CD, Atlantic 19123-2
UK CD, Castle ESM CD 343
1993 CD, Victory 828 467-2
1999 CD 20-bit remaster (mini-LP sleeve),
Victory VICP-60636
UK 2001 CD, Castle CMRCD200 (with bonus
track: Hoedown (Live))
UK 2002 CD (mini-LP sleeve), Castle CMTCD435
Tracks: The Endless Enigma Part 1 / Fugue /
The Endless Enigma Part 2 / From The Beginning
/ The Sheriff / Trilogy / Living Sin / Abaddon's
Bolero

■ **BRAIN SALAD SURGERY**
1973 LP, Manticore 87 302 IT
1973 8 Track Cartridge, Manticore MAN TP-66669
USA LP, Manticore LP 66669
USA MC, Manticore MC 66669
Japan LP, P-1-10114
1973 MC, Atlantic CS 19124
1973 MC, Manticore CMC-66669
LP, Manticore K53501
CD, Atlantic 781 523-2
CD, Manticore 258174
1993 CD, Victory 828 468-2
1996 CD, Rhino R2 72459

UK 1997 LP, Castle ORRLP002 Ltd. Ed. of 5000
UK CD, Castle ESM CD 344
1999 CD 20-bit remaster (mini-LP sleeve),
Victory VICP-80637
2000 DVD-Audio, Rhino R9 75980
UK 2001 CD, Castle CMRCD201 (with bonus
tracks: Brain Salad Surgery / When The Apple
Blossoms Bloom In The Windmills Of Your Mind
I'll Be Your Valentine / Excerpts From Brain Salad
Surgery flexi-disc (free with NME in 1973))
2002 CD (mini-LP sleeve), Castle CMTCD433
Tracks: Jerusalem / Toccata / Still...You Turn Me
On / Benny The Bouncer / Karn Evil 9 (lst
Impression / 2nd Impression / 3rd Impression)

■ **WELCOME BACK MY FRIENDS TO
THE SHOW THAT NEVER ENDS ~ LADIES
AND GENTLEMEN**
1974 3LP, Manticore 88 147 XT
1974 3LP, Manticore MAN TP 3-200
1974 3LP, Manticore MC 3-200
2CD, Victory VICP-60638-39
UK 2CD, Castle ESD CD 359
UK 2001 2CD, Castle CMDDD202
Tracks: Hoedown / Jerusalem / Toccata / Tarkus
(includes Epitaph) / Take A Pebble (includes
Still...You Turn Me On / Lucky Man) / Piano
Improvisations (includes Fugue / Little Rock
Getaway) / Take A Pebble (conclusion) / Jeremy
Bender - The Sheriff (medley) / Karn Evil 9 (lst
Impression / 2nd Impression / 3rd Impression)

■ **WORKS - Edited Highlights**
1977 LP Promo, Atlantic PR271

■ **WORKS Volume 1**
1977 2LP, Atlantic SD 2-7000
UK 2LP, Atlantic K80009
Japan 2LP, Atlantic P-6311-2A
USA 2LP, SD 2-7000
1977 8 Track Cartridge, Atlantic TP 2-7
1977 8 Track Cartridge, Atlantic TP 2-7000
1999 CD 20-bit remaster (mini-LP sleeve),
Victory VICP-60640-41
2CD, Victory 828 470-2
UK 2001 2CD, Castle CMDDD224 (with live
bonus tracks: Tank / The Enemy God Dances
With The Black Spirits / Nutrocker)
Keith Emerson tracks: Piano Concerto No.1 (1st
Movement: Allegro Giojoso / 2nd Movement:
Andante Molto Cantabile / 3rd Movement:
Toccata Con Fuoco)
Greg Lake tracks: Lend Your Love To Me Tonight /
C'est La Vie / Hallowed Be Thy Name / Nobody
Loves You Like I Do / Closer To Believing
Carl Palmer tracks: The Enemy God Dances With
The Black Spirits / L.A. Nights / New Orleans /
Two Part Invention In D Minor / Food For Your
Soul / Tank
ELP tracks: Fanfare For The Common Man / Pirates

■ **WORKS Volume 2**
UK 1978 LP, Atlantic K50422
Japan 1978 LP, Atlantic P-6403
USA 1978 LP, SD 19147
1978 8 Track Cartridge, Atlantic TP 19147
CD, Atlantic 781 538-2
1993 CD, Victory 828 473-2
1999 CD 20-bit remaster (mini-LP sleeve),
Victory VICP-60642

UK 2001 CD, Castle CMRCD225 (with bonus live tracks: Tiger In A Spotlight / Watching Over You / Show Me The Way To Go Home)
Tracks: Tiger In A Spotlight / When The Apple Blossoms Bloom In The Windmills Of Your Mind I'll Be Your Valentine / Bullfrog / Brain Salad Surgery / Barrelhouse Shakedown / Watching Over You / So Far to Fall / Maple Leaf Rag / I Believe In Father Christmas / Close But Not Touching / Honky Tonk Train Blues / Show Me The Way To Go Home

■ LOVE BEACH
1978 LP, Atlantic SD 19211
USA LP, SD 19211
Germany LP, Ariola 200 249-320
1978 8 Track Cartridge, Atlantic TP 10211
UK CD, Castle ESM CD 363
1993 CD, Victory 828 469-2
1999 CD 20-bit remaster (mini-LP sleeve), Victory VICP-60643
UK 2001 CD, Castle CMRCD226 (with bonus tracks: Canario / Taste Of My Love / Letters From The Front (all 1978 rehearsals))
Tracks: All I Want Is You / Love Beach / Taste Of My Love / The Gambler / For You / Canario / Memoirs Of An Officer And A Gentleman (Prologue / The Education Of A Gentleman / Love At First Sight / Letters From The Front / Honourable Company (A March))

■ IN CONCERT
UK 1979 LP, Atlantic K50652
USA 1979 LP, SD 19255
1979 MC, Atlantic K450652
1979 8 Track Cartridge, Atlantic TP 19255
USA CD, Atlantic CD19255
1999 CD 20-bit remaster (mini-LP sleeve), Victory VICP-60644
Tracks: Introductory Fanfare / Peter Gunn / Tiger In A Spotlight / C'est La Vie / The Enemy God / Knife Edge / Piano Concerto No.1 (3rd Movement: Toccata Con Fuoco) / Pictures At An Exhibition

■ WORKS LIVE
UK 1993 CD, Castle ESD CD 362
1993 CD, Victory 828 477-2
UK 2001 CD, Castle CMDDD229
Tracks: Introductory Fanfare / Peter Gunn / Tiger In A Spotlight / C'est La Vie / The Enemy God Dances With The Black Spirits / Knife Edge / Piano Concerto No.1 (3rd Movement: Toccata Con Fuoco) / Pictures At An Exhibition / Watching Over You / Maple Leaf Rag / Fanfare For The Common Man / Show Me The Way To Go Home / Abaddon's Bolero / Closer To Believing / Tank

■ BLACK MOON
LP, Victory 828-318-1,
1992 MC, Victory 383 480 003-4
MC, Victory 828-318-4
1992 CD, Rhino R2 72235
1992 CD, Victory VICP-60645
1992 CD, Victory 828-318-2
Japan CD, VICP-5164 (with bonus track: A Blade Of Grass)
UK 2001 CD, Castle CMRCD227 (with bonus tracks: Black Moon (single edit) / Affairs Of The Heart (edit) / Paper Blood (edit) / Romeo & Juliet (edit))

Tracks: Black Moon / Paper Blood / Affairs Of The Heart / Romeo & Juliet / Farewell To Arms / Changing States / Burning Bridges / Close To Home / Better Days / Footprints In The Snow

■ LIVE AT THE ROYAL ALBERT HALL
UK 1992 CD, Castle ESM CD 504
1993 CD, Victory 383-480-011-2
1993 CD, Victory 828 393-2
UK 2001 CD, Castle CMRCD228
Tracks: Karn Evil 9 (First Impression Part 2) / Tarkus / Knife Edge / Paper Blood / Romeo & Juliet / Creole Dance / Still...You Turn Me On / Lucky Man / Black Moon / Fanfare For The Common Man / America / Rondo

■ IN THE HOT SEAT
1994 CD, Victory 828 554-2
Japan 1994 CD, Victory VICP-60646
1994 MC, Victory 383 480 034-4
Tracks: Hand Of Truth / Daddy / One By One / Heart On Ice / Thin Line / Man In The Long Black Coat / Change / Give Me A Reason To Stay / Gone Too Soon / Street War / Bonus track: Pictures At An Exhibition (1993 version)

■ LIVE IN POLAND
1997 CD, Manticore Prog CD 0060
2000 CD, Plastic Head PROGCD6
Tracks: Karn Evil 9 (First Impression Part 2) / Touch And Go / From The Beginning / Knife Edge / Bitches Crystal / Piano Solo / Take A Pebble / Lucky Man / Tarkus / Pictures At An Exhibition / Fanfare For The Common Man

■ LIVE AT THE ISLE OF WIGHT FESTIVAL
1997 CD, Manticore M-CD101
UK 2002 CD, Sanctuary CMCRD458
Tracks: The Barbarian / Take A Pebble / Pictures At An Exhibition / Rondo / Nutrocker / Interview

COMPILATION ALBUMS

■ THE BEST OF EMERSON LAKE & PALMER
1980 LP, Atlantic K50757
1980 8 Track, Atlantic S153358
USA CD, Atlantic 19283-2
Tracks: Hoedown / Lucky Man / Karn Evil 9 (First Impression Part 2) / Jerusalem / Peter Gunn / Fanfare For The Common Man / Still...You Turn Me On / Tiger In A Spotlight

■ THE BEST OF EMERSON LAKE & PALMER
UK 1995 CD, Castle ESS CD 296
USA 1994 CD, Victory 383 480 036-2
Tracks: From The Beginning / Jerusalem / Still... You Turn Me On / Fanfare For The Common Man / Knife Edge / Tarkus / Karn Evil 9 / C'est La Vie / Hoedown / Trilogy / Honky Tonk Train Blues / Black Moon / Lucky Man / I Believe In Father Christmas

■ THE ATLANTIC YEARS
USA 1992 2CD, Atlantic 7567-82403-2
Tracks: CD1: Knife Edge / Take A Pebble / Lucky Man / Tank / Tarkus / Pictures At An Exhibition / The Endless Enigma
CD2: From The Beginning / Karn Evil 9 / Jerusalem / Still...You Turn Me On / Toccata /

Fanfare For The Common Man / Pirates /
I Believe In Father Christmas / Honky Tonk Train
Blues / Canario

■ **THE ATLANTIC YEARS COLLECTION**
USA 1992 CD Promo 6 track Sampler,
Atlantic PRCD 4599-2
Tracks: Lucky Man / From The Beginning /
Karn Evil 9 (1st Impression Part 2) /
Jerusalem / Still...You Turn Me On / I Believe In
Father Christmas

■ **THE RETURN OF THE MANTICORE**
1993 4CD Box Set, Victory 828 459-2
UK 1996 4CD Slimline Box Set, Castle ESFCD421
Tracks: CD1: Touch And Go / Hang On To A
Dream / 21st Century Schizoid Man / Fire /
Pictures At An Exhibition / I Believe In Father
Christmas (first 6 tracks new recordings by ELP) /
Introductory Fanfare / Peter Gunn / Tiger In A
Spotlight / Toccata / Trilogy / Tank / Lucky Man
CD2: Tarkus / From The Beginning / Take A Pebble
(Live) / Knife Edge / Paper Blood / Hoedown /
Rondo (Live)*
CD3: The Barbarian / Still...You Turn Me On /
The Endless Enigma / C'est La Vie / The Enemy God
Dances With The Black Spirits / Bo Diddley* /
Bitches Crystal / A Time And A Place / Living Sin
/ Karn Evil 9 / Honky Tonk Train Blues
CD4: Jerusalem / Fanfare For The Common Man /
Black Moon / Watching Over You / Piano Concerto
No.1 (3rd Movement: Toccata Con Fuoco) /
For You / Prelude And Fugue* / Memoirs Of An
Officer And A Gentleman / Pirates / Affairs Of
The Heart
*Previously unreleased

■ **THE RETURN OF THE MANTICORE**
1993 CD 12 track Promo, Victory SACD 757
Tracks: I Believe In Father Christmas / Touch And
Go / Hang On To A Dream / 21st Century
Schizoid Man / Fire / Pictures At An Exhibition
(first 6 tracks were new recordings by ELP) /
Karn Evil 9 / From The Beginning / Jerusalem /
Still...You Turn Me On / Lucky Man / Fanfare For
The Common Man

■ **GREG LAKE – FROM THE BEGINNING**
1997 2CD, Essential ESDCD552
ELP tracks: Knife Edge / Lucky Man / From The
Beginning / Take A Pebble / Still...You Turn Me
On / Jerusalem / Karn Evil 9 / I Believe In Father
Christmas / C'est La Vie / Closer To Believing /
Watching Over You / Black Moon / Paper Blood /
Affairs Of The Heart / Daddy / Heart Of Ice
Emerson Lake & Powell tracks: Lay Down Your
Guns / Touch And Go

■ **THREE CLASSIC ALBUMS:**
EMERSON, LAKE & PALMER / TARKUS /
PICTURES AT AN EXHIBITION
UK 1998 3CD Box Set, Essential ESMBX303

■ **THEN & NOW**
1998 2CD, Eagle EDGCD040
Tracks: 1974: Toccata / Take A Pebble / Karn Evil 9
1997-98: A Time And A Place / Piano Concerto
No.1 / From The Beginning / Karn Evil 9 / Tiger In
A Spotlight / Hoedown / Touch And Go / Knife
Edge / Bitches Crystal / Honky Tonk Train Blues /

Lucky Man / Fanfare For The Common Man /
Rondo / 21st Century Schizoid Man / America

■ **THEN & NOW – BACKSTAGE PASS**
USA 1998 CD Promo, Eagle CD PRO1001
Tracks: 1974: Karn Evil 9 / Take A Pebble
1997-98: Fanfare For The Common Man / Rondo
/ 21st Century Schizoid Man / Karn Evil 9

■ **EXTENDED VERSIONS**
USA 2000 CD, BMG 75517456162
Tracks: Peter Gunn Theme / Tiger In A Spotlight /
The Enemy God Dances With The Black Spirits /
Still...You Turn Me On / Lucky Man / Watching
Over You / Fanfare For The Common Man /
Hoedown / Piano Improvisation / Maple Leaf Rag

■ **FANFARE FOR THE COMMON MAN**
UK 2001 2CD, Sanctuary CMEDD110
Tracks: CD1: The Barbarian / Take A Pebble /
Knife Edge / Lucky Man / Tarkus / Jeremy Bender
/ Nutrocker / Living Sin / The Endless Enigma
CD2: From The Beginning / Hoedown / Trilogy /
Jerusalem / Still...You Turn Me On /
Karn Evil 9 / Fanfare For The Common Man /
C'est La Vie / Pirates / Brain Salad Surgery /
Honky Tonk Train Blues / Love Beach /
Black Moon / Affairs Of The Heart

■ **THE VERY BEST OF EMERSON LAKE & PALMER**
US 2001 CD, Wea/Rhino 3R279777
Tracks: Lucky Man / Knife Edge / From The
Beginning / Trilogy / Jerusalem / Toccata /
Karn Evil 9 (1st Impression Part 2) / Still...You
Turn Me On / Pirates / Fanfare For The Common
Man / C'est La Vie (Live) / Peter Gunn (Live) /
The Hut Of Baba Yaga (Live) / The Great Gates
Of Kiev (Live)

■ **CARL PALMER – DO YA WANNA PLAY, CARL?**
– ANTHOLOGY
UK 2001 2CD, Castle Music CMEDD163
ELP tracks: Concerto For Percussion* / The Enemy
God Dances With The Black Spirits /
Pancha Suite* / Bullfrog / Toccata / Close But
Not Touching / L.A. Nights / Canario / Tank /
Bach Two Part Invention In D Minor / Fanfare For
The Common Man / March Militaire*
*Previously unreleased
'3' tracks: Desde La Vida / Eight Miles High

■ **THE ORIGINAL BOOTLEG SERIES FROM THE**
MANTICORE VAULTS
UK 2001 7CD Box Set, Castle CMXBX309
VOLUME ONE, SET 1:
'Stomping Encore' Gaelic Park, New York 1.9.71
'The Stratosphere vs The Spectre'
UK 2001 2CD, Castle CMXBX309/CMDDD311
Tracks: CD1: The Barbarian / Take A Pebble /
Tarkus
CD2: Knife Edge / Rondo / Piano Interlude /
Hoedown
VOLUME ONE, SET 2:
Louisville Town Hall, Kentucky 21.4.72
'The Irridescent Concubine'
UK 2001 2CD, Castle CMXBX309/CMDDD313
Tracks: CD1: Hoedown / Tarkus / Take A Pebble /
Lucky Man / Piano Improvisations
CD2: Abaddon's Bolero / Pictures At An Exhibition
/ Nutrocker / Rondo

VOLUME ONE, SET 3:
Long Beach Arena, California 28.7.72
'Celestial Doggie: The Lobster Quadrille'
UK 2001 2CD, Castle CMXBX309/CMDDD312
Tracks: CD1: Tarkus / The Endless Enigma /
The Sheriff / Take A Pebble
CD2: Take A Pebble / Pictures At An Exhibition /
Hoedown / Rondo
VOLUME ONE, SET 4:
Saratoga Performing Arts Center, NY 13.8.72
'Iconoclastic Madness'
UK 2001 CD, Castle CMXBX309/CMRCD314
Tracks: Hoedown / Tarkus / The Endless Enigma /
The Sheriff / Take A Pebble / Pictures At An
Exhibition

■ **THE ORIGINAL BOOTLEG SERIES FROM THE
MANTICORE VAULTS**
UK 2001 8CD Box Set, Castle CMXBX330
VOLUME TWO, SET 1:
Hammersmith Odeon, London 26.11.72
'A Right Cordial Shocker'
UK 2001 2CD, Castle CMXBX330/CMDDD310
Tracks: CD1: Hoedown / Tarkus / The Endless
Enigma / At The Sign Of The Swinging Cymbal /
The Sheriff / Take A Pebble / Lucky Man
CD2: Piano Improvisations / Pictures At An
Exhibition / Nutrocker
VOLUME TWO, SET 2:
Henry Lewit Arena, Wichita 26.3.74
'Waiting For The Corduroy Purpose'
UK 2001 2CD, Castle CMXBX330/CMDDD315
CD1: Hoedown / Jerusalem / Toccata / Tarkus /
Benny The Bouncer / Jeremy Bender / Take A
Pebble / Still...You Turn Me On / Lucky Man
CD2: Piano Improvisations / Take A Pebble /
Karn Evil 9
VOLUME TWO, SET 3:
Rich Stadium, Buffalo 26.7.74
'My Darling Nemesis'
UK 2001 2CD, Castle CMXBX330/CMDDD316
Tracks: CD1: Hoedown / Jerusalem / Toccata /
Tarkus / Take A Pebble / Still...You Turn Me On /
Lucky Man / Piano Improvisation
CD2: Take A Pebble / Karn Evil 9 / Pictures At An
Exhibition
VOLUME TWO, SET 4:
New Haven Civic Centre, New Haven
'Strangely Beneficient'
UK 2001 2CD, Castle CMXBX330/CMDDD317
Tracks: CD1: Peter Gunn / Hoedown / Tarkus /
Take A Pebble / Piano Concerto No.1 /
Maple Leaf Rag / Take A Pebble / C'est La Vie /
Lucky Man
CD2: Karn Evil 9 / Tiger In A Spotlight /
Watching Over You / Nutrocker / Pirates /
Fanfare For The Common Man

■ **THE ORIGINAL BOOTLEG SERIES FROM THE
MANTICORE VAULTS**
UK 2002 5CD Box Set, Castle CMXBX524
VOLUME THREE, SET 1:
Anaheim Convention Centre, California 10.2.74
Wheeling Colosseum ?.?.77
UK 2001 1CD, Castle CMXBX524/1
Tracks: Hoedown / Tiger In A Spotlight / C'est La
Vie / Still...You Turn Me On / Tank / The Enemy
God / Karn Evil 9 / Fanfare For The Common Man
/ Take A Pebble / Pictures At An Exhibition
VOLUME THREE, SET 2:

Royal Albert Hall, London 2.10.92
UK 2001 2CD, Castle CMXBX524/2 & 3
Tracks: CD1: Tarkus / Knife Edge / Paper Blood /
Black Moon / Close To Home / Creole Dance /
From The Beginning / Still...You Turn Me On /
Lucky Man
CD2: Honky Tonk Train Blues / Romeo & Juliet /
Pirates / Pictures At An Exhibition / Fanfare For
The Common Man
VOLUME THREE, SET 3:
Wiltern Theatre, Los Angeles 3.93
UK 2001 2CD, Castle CMXBX524/4 & 5
Tracks: CD1: Karn Evil 9 (First Impression Part 2)
/ Tarkus / Knife Edge / Paper Blood / Black Moon
/ Close To Home / Creole Dance / Still...You Turn
Me On / C'est La Vie / Lucky Man / Honky Tonk
Train Blues / Touch And Go / Pirates
CD2: Hoedown / Pictures At An Exhibition
(including Carl Palmer Solo) / Fanfare For The
Common Man

■ **THE BEST OF THE BOOTLEGS**
UK 2002 2CD, Castle CMDDD442
Tracks: Hoedown (13.8.72 Saratoga Springs) /
Knife Edge (1.9.71 Gaelic Park, NY) / Pictures At
An Exhibition (28.6.72 Long Beach Arena) /
Take A Pebble / Lucky Man (28.6.72 Long Beach
Arena) / Tarkus (21.4.72 Louisville Town Hall) /
The Endless Enigma (13.8.72 Saratoga) /
Nutrocker (21.4.72 Louisville Town Hall) /
Jerusalem (26.3.74 Henry Lewit Arena) /
Pirates (30.11.77 Civic Centre, New Haven) /
Karn Evil 9 (1st Impression) (26.3.74 Henry Lewit
Arena) / Still...You Turn Me On (26.7.74 Rich
Stadium, Buffalo) / Barbarian (1.9.71 Gaelic Park,
NY) / C'est La Vie (30.11.77 Civic Centre, New
Haven) / Fanfare For The Common People
(30.11.77)

■ **OUTSTANDING COLLECTION**
UK 2002 2CD, Essential CMDDD447

MISCELLANEOUS (selected)

● **ROCK 'N' ROLL YOUR EYES**
USA 7" Single, April Fool's Films
Rock 'n' Roll Your Eyes was the US title for the
Pictures At An Exhibition movie (filmed 12.70)

■ **BRITISH PROGRESSIVE BANDS**
USA 1986 LP, Radio Show, short interview with
Greg Lake with track Karn Evil 9

■ **CALIFORNIA JAM**
1974 LP, HHCER 113

■ **CLASSIC ROCK**
USA 1994 CD, Rebound 314 520 227-2
Tracks: Promenade / The Hut Of Baba Yaga /
The Curse Of Baba Yaga / The Great Gates Of Kiev
/ Fanfare For The Common Man / Hoedown /
Jerusalem / Toccata / Lucky Man

■ **CLASSIC ROCK TRAXX**
1999 CD, St. Clair
ELP track: Lucky Man

■ **CLASSICS FROM PROGRESSIVE ROCK Volume 1**
CD, POCL-4157

■ **EMERSON LAKE & PALMER**
Germany 1980 LP, Amiga 8 55 724
Tracks: Love Beach / Fanfare For The Common
Man / Maple Leaf Rag / L.A. Nights / The Barbarian
■ **EMERSON LAKE & PALMER**
Spain 1982 4LP Box Set, Eurodisc XF301883/4/5/6
Box set of first 4 LPs: Emerson, Lake & Palmer /
Tarkus / Pictures At An Exhibition / Trilogy

■ **IN CONCERT**
UK 2002 2CD, King Biscuit 70710880252
Tracks: CD1: Peter Gunn / Tiger In A Spotlight /
C'est La Vie / Piano Improvisation / Maple Leaf
Rag / Drum Solo / The Enemy God Dances With
The Black Spirits / Watching Over You / Pirates /
Fanfare For The Common Man / Hoedown /
Still...You Turn Me On / Lucky Man / Piano
Improvisation
CD2: Karn Evil 9 / Interactive CD-R content

■ **IN THE STUDIO – BRAIN SALAD SURGERY**
USA 1996 CD, Radio Show, 441 (2.12.96)

■ **IN THE STUDIO – TRILOGY 25th ANNIVERSARY**
USA 1997 CD, Radio Show, 473 (14.7.97)
Interviews + tracks: Lucky Man / Take A Pebble /
From The Beginning / Endless Enigma / Fugue /
The Sheriff / Hoedown

■ **JIM LADD INTERVIEW**
USA LP, Radio Show, Series 37, Show No.9

■ **KING BISCUIT – CLASSIC HITS LIVE**
1997 CD, King Biscuit 88025-2

■ **KING BISCUIT FLOWER HOUR**
USA 1993 CD, Radio Show - Broadcast
27.9.93 and 3.10.93
Tracks: Hoedown / Still...You Turn Me On /
Lucky Man / Karn Evil 9

■ **LEGENDS OF ROCK**
USA 1988 2LP, Radio Show, NBC Entertainment

■ **LIVE**
1971 LP, N504

■ **LIVE IN ITALY AT PALASPORT**
1972 LP Vinyl Acetate

■ **LUCKY MAN AND OTHER HITS**
USA 1997 CD, Flashback R2 72922
Tracks: Lucky Man / C'est La Vie / Paper Blood /
Still...You Turn Me On / From The Beginning /
Karn Evil 9 / Fanfare For The Common Man

■ **MUSICAL BIOGRAPHIES – With Alison Steele**
USA 2LP, Radio Show

■ **OFF THE RECORD – With Mary Turner**
USA 1986 2LP Promo, Radio Show,
Westwood One W 88-21
Interview + tracks: Peter Gunn / The Miracle /
Lay Down Your Guns / Love Blind / Tank /
The Score / Learning To Fly / Lucky Man /
Karn Evil 9 / Still...You Turn Me On /
Hoedown / Fanfare For The Common Man / Mars

■ **ON TOUR WITH EMERSON LAKE & PALMER**
USA 1977 LP Promo, Radio Show, Atlantic PR281

■ **PIONEERS IN MUSIC**
USA 1986 2LP, Radio Show
History of ELP with The Nice track: America /
ELP tracks: Lucky Man / Bitches Crystal /
Nutrocker / From The Beginning / Hoedown /
Karn Evil 9

■ **PSYCHEDELIC PSNACK**
USA 1987 LP, Radio Show, Westwood One PP87-11
Carl Palmer Interview with Lucky Man track

■ **RETRO ROCK**
USA 1981 LP, Radio Show, Clayton Webster Corp.

■ **ROCKING NOW AND THEN**
USA 1987 LP, Radio Show
Tracks: Hoedown / Still...You Turn Me On /
Lucky Man / Touch And Go

■ **ROCK AROUND THE WORLD**
USA 1977 LP, Radio Show No.163
Interview + Music from Works Volume 1 plus
America by The Nice

■ **ROLLING STONE CONTINUOUS HISTORY OF ROCK & ROLL**
USA 1981 LP, Radio Show, RSMP-82-45
Includes Eddy Offord (ELP engineer) talking
about ELP and the recording of Pictures At An
Exhibition and Are You Ready Eddy?

■ **THE SHOW THAT NEVER ENDS**
UK 2001 2CD, Snapper Music SMD CD 370
Tracks: CD1: A Time And A Place / Piano
Concerto No.1 (3rd Movement: Toccata Con
Fuoco) / From The Beginning / Karn Evil 9
(First Impression Part 2) / Tiger In A Spotlight /
Hoedown / Touch And Go / Knife Edge /
Bitches Crystal
CD2: Honky Tonk Train Blues / Take A Pebble /
Lucky Man / Fanfare For The Common Man /
Rondo / 21st Century Schizoid Man / America

■ **TOUR OF THE AMERICAS – Part Three**
LP, An Aftermath Record

■ **TOUR SPECIAL**
USA LP, Radio Show, Westwood One
Tracks: Mars / Love Blind / Peter Gunn / Lay
Down Your Guns / The Score / Learning To Fly /
Hoedown / Fanfare For The Common Man / Tank
/ Are You Ready Eddy? / Still...You Turn Me On /
Karn Evil 9 / Lucky Man / Touch And Go

■ **UP CLOSE**
USA 1992 CD, Radio Show, Neer Perfect
Productions 9213

■ **WELCOME BACK... THE ELP STORY**
USA 1997 CD Promo, Radio Show,
Manticore M-CD102 PRO
Interviews + tracks: Touch And Go / Karn Evil 9
(1st Impression Part 2) / Lucky Man / Hoedown

—— **VARIOUS ARTISTS COMPIL.** (selected) ——

■ **ATLANTIC ROCK & ROLL BOX**
1991 CD, Atlantic 82306
ELP track: Karn Evil 9 (1st Impression Part 2)

■ BABY BOOMER CLASSICS - THE
PROGRESSIVE SEVENTIES
1993 MC, JCI OPCS-1632
1995 CD, JCI 3305
ELP track: Karn Evil 9 (1st Impression)

■ BY INVITATION ONLY
1976 2LP, Atlantic K60112
ELP track: Karn Evil 9 (1st Impression)

■ CLASSIC CUTS - WHERE LEGENDS LIVE
2000 CD, Classic Rock CR 20.11.00

■ CLASSIC ROCK - WHERE LEGENDS LIVE
SUMMER SPECIAL
2002 CD, ROC41/06/02 CMZCM477

■ EL PEA
1971 2LP, Island IDLP1
ELP track: Knife Edge

■ HARD ROCK ESSENTIALS - THE 70'S
1994 CD, Rebound 314 520 278-2

■ JOURNEY TO THE EDGE
1994 CD, MCI Music MUSCD 018

■ KING BISCUIT FLOWER HOUR RECORDS
PRESENTS EMERSON LAKE & PALMER
USA CD Promo, King Biscuit KBJC-09
ELP track: Lucky Man

■ LE CONCERT DU SIÈCLE
2001 CD, Import 15106
ELP track: Fanfare For The Common Man

■ LEGENDS OF ROCK - The Progressive Rockers
1999 CD, Pet Rock Records PET-CD-60045
ELP track: Tiger In A Spotlight

■ LEGENDS OF ROCK - British Rock Invasion
CD, Pet Rock Records PET-CD-60046
ELP track: Lucky Man

■ MAR Y SOL, PUERTO RICO POP FESTIVAL
1972 2LP, ATCO SD2-705
1972 2LP, Atlantic K60029
ELP tracks: Take A Pebble / Lucky Man

● EXCERPTS FROM MAR Y SOL, PUERTO RICO
POP FESTIVAL
1972 7" Single Promo, Atlantic PR-176

■ ROCK THE PLANET - '70s SUPER GROUPS
1995 CD, Rock The Planet RPD - 4019

■ ROCKIN' AROUND THE CHRISTMAS TREE
1994 CD, PSM 314 520 235-2
ELP track: I Believe In Father Christmas

■ SPIRIT OF THE AGE
1997 CD, Renaissance RENCD 118
ELP track: Brain Salad Surgery

■ SUPERHITS OF ROCK - 1965-1979
1996 4CD, L&D Records LBSCD 009/3
ELP track: Fanfare For The Common Man

■ SUPERNATURAL FAIRY TALES SAMPLER
1996 CD Promo, Rhino PRCD 7195

■ SUPERNATURAL FAIRY TALES: THE
PROGRESSIVE ROCK ERA
1996 4CD, Rhino R 2 72451
ELP tracks: Knife Edge / Karn Evil 9 (1st
Impression)

■ THE BEST OF BRITISH ROCK
1999 CD, Center Stage 5215
ELP tracks: Peter Gunn / Tiger In A Spotlight

■ THE BEST OF PROGRESSIVE ROCK
1999 CD, Center Stage 5216
ELP track: Tiger In A Spotlight

DVDS, VIDEOS, ETC

➤ ISLE OF WIGHT FESTIVAL 1970 -
MESSAGE TO LOVE
UK 1995 Video, Pearson PNV1005
UK 2000 DVD, Castle CMP1001
ELP section: The Great Gates Of Kiev / Rondo
13 minutes approx.

➤ PICTURES AT AN EXHIBITION
Lyceum, London 9.12.70
Two video versions have been released, one 40
mins. (with Pictures At An Exhibition only), the
other 90 mins. (which includes The Barbarian /
Take A Pebble / Knife Edge / Rondo)
USA Theatre release as 'Rock 'n' Roll Your Eyes'
Video, Polygram 630 332 3
1990 Laser Disc, Victory VPLR-70116
Video, D2 Vision DTV481
1999 DVD, D2 Vision Ltd DVDP001 (double
sided disc: 1 side DVD + 1 side audio soundtrack)
1999 DVD/CD, D2 Vision Ltd DVDP002
(2 disc set: 1DVD + 1CD audio soundtrack)

➤ BEAT CLUB - BEST OF '73
2001 Germany DVD
ELP performance: Knife Edge
Footage also exists of Take A Pebble from same
show, recorded circa Nov/Dec 1970

➤ THE MANTICORE SPECIAL
1973 Video, Manticore M-V1001
1 hour documentary with 'behind the scenes'
and concert footage

➤ LIVE '77
1977 Video, Hendring HEN 2 005 G
Montreal, 26.8.77

➤ WORKS ORCHESTRAL TOUR - Olympic Stadium
Montreal 1977
1977 Video, Manticore M-V1002
87 minutes, with full symphony orchestra

➤ LIVE AT THE ROYAL ALBERT HALL
UK 1992 Video, Castle BMO 015
USA DVD, Image Entertainment ID9699CLDVD
Tracks: Introduction / Welcome Back / Tarkus /
Knife Edge / Paper Blood / Creole Dance /
From The Beginning / Lucky Man /
Honky Tonk Train Blues / Romeo & Juliet /
Pirates / Pictures At An Exhibition /
Fanfare For The Common Man / America /
Rondo / End Credits

➤ **WELCOME BACK**
1992 Video
1992 Laser Disc, Victory VILP-49
USA DVD, Image Entertainment ID9700CLDVD
85 minutes
Tracks: Romeo & Juliet / Karn Evil 9 / Pictures At
An Exhibition / Paper Blood / Honky Tonk Train
Blues / Creole Dance / Close To Home / Pirates /
C'est La Vie / Tiger In A Spotlight / Watching
Over You / Lucky Man / Changing States /
Hoedown / Black Moon / Drum Solo / Maple Leaf
Rag / Fanfare For The Common Man / Tarkus

➤ **ROCK FAMILY TREES**
1998 Video, BBC2 Progressive Rock documentary
featuring ELP & Yes

**Though not thought to be commercially
available, other 'Official' ELP footage
is known to exist including the following:**

➤ **ROCK OF THE SEVENTIES**
1970/71, 60 minutes
ELP tracks: The Barbarian / Take A Pebble /
Nutrocker / Rondo

➤ **SUPERGROUPS IN CONCERT**
1971 Dusseldorf, Germany
ELP track: Rondo

➤ **KARAKEUN STADIUM, TOKYO**
22.7.72, 70 minutes

➤ **CALIFORNIA JAM – ONTARIO SPEEDWAY**
6.4.74, ABC, 60 minutes
Includes Keith's famous 'rotating piano'
during Chopin's 'Rotating Symphony'!

➤ **BBC OLD GREY WHISTLE TEST**
Montreal and Memphis 1977/78, 45 minutes

➤ **MUNICH, GERMANY**
1997, 67 minutes, satellite TV broadcast

EMERSON, LAKE & POWELL

*Keith Emerson - Keyboards; Greg Lake - Bass;
Guitars & Vocals; Cozy Powell - Drums & Percussion*

SINGLES

● **LAY DOWN YOUR GUNS** / Step Aside
1986 7" Single, Polydor PDS 2299
USA 1986 7" Single, Polydor 885-277
USA 1986 12" Single Promo, Polydor PRO 441-1
LAY DOWN YOUR GUNS / Lay Down Your Guns
1986 7" Single DJ Promo, Polydor 885-277-7
Canada 1986 12" Promo, Polydor PRODJP199

● **LEARNING TO FLY** / Lay Down Your Guns
UK 1986 7" Single Promo, Polydor

● **THE SCORE** / The Score
1986 12" Single Promo, Polydor PRO 432-1

● **TOUCH AND GO** / Learning To Fly

1986 7" Single, Polydor 885-101-7
1986 7" Single, Polydor PDS 2295
France 1986 7" Single, Polydor 885101-7
1986 7" Single, Polygram POSP 804
Japan 1986 12" Single, Polydor 13MM 7035
TOUCH AND GO / Learning To Fly /
The Loco-motion
1986 12" Single, Polydor POSPX 804
TOUCH AND GO / Touch And Go
USA 1986 7" Single, Polydor 885101
1986 7" Single Promo, Polydor 885 101-7 DJ
1986 12" Single Promo, Polydor PRO 421-1

ALBUM

■ **EMERSON, LAKE & POWELL**
UK 1986 LP, Polydor POLD 5191
1986 MC, Polydor 829 297-4 Y-1
USA 1986 CD, Polygram 829 297-2
Russia 1988 LP, Melodiya C60 26463 008
USA 1992 CD, Polygram 829 297-2 (with bonus
tracks: The Loco-motion / Vacant Possession)
Tracks: The Score / Learning To Fly / The Miracle /
Touch And Go / Love Blind / Step Aside / Lay
Down Your Guns / Mars (The Bringer Of War)

MISCELLANEOUS

■ **IN CONCERT**
USA 1986 2LP, Radio Show, Westwood One 86-22
Tracks: The Score / Touch And Go / Knife Edge /
Still...You Turn Me On / Learning To Fly / Pirates /
From The Beginning / Lucky Man / Fanfare For
The Common Man / Karn Evil 9

3

*Keith Emerson - Keyboards;
Robert Berry - Bass, Guitars & Vocals;
Carl Palmer - Drums & Percussion*

SINGLES

● **TALKIN 'BOUT** / Desde La Vida
1988 7" Single, Geffen 7-27988
Germany 1988 7" Single, Geffen 927 988-7
USA 1988 MC, Geffen
USA 1988 12" Single, Geffen 920 934-0
Germany 1988 12" Single, Geffen 920 934-0

ALBUM

■ **TO THE POWER OF 3**
1988 LP, Geffen 924-181-1
1988 MC, Geffen 924-181-4
1988 CD, Geffen 924-181-2
1998 CD, Geffen Goldline
UK 2001 CD, Manticore Vaults MANTVP110CD
Japan 2002 CD, (mini-LP sleeve)
Tracks: Talkin 'Bout / Lover To Lover / Chains /
Desde La Vida (La Vida / Frontera / Sangre De
Toro) / Eight Miles High / Runaway / You Do Or
You Don't / On My Way Home

MISCELLANEOUS (selected)

■ **LEGENDS OF ROCK**
USA 1988 2LP, Radio Show, Music and interviews

■ **OFF THE RECORD (With Mary Turner)**
USA 1988 2LP, Radio Show, Westwood One
Interview + Tracks: Eight Miles High / Hoedown /
You Do Or You Don't / Tank / Still...You Turn Me
On / Runaway / Karn Evil 9 / Lover To Lover /
Lucky Man / Desde La Vida / Talkin 'Bout /
On My Way Home

■ **ROCK OVER LONDON**
USA 1988 LP, Radio Show, Music and interviews

P.P. ARNOLD

The Nice played on some unspecified tracks on the
first P.P. Arnold album, The First Lady Of Immediate
(and therefore some unspecified early singles).

SINGLES & EPS (selected)

● **EVERYTHING'S GONNA BE ALRIGHT** / Life Is
But Nothing
1966 7" Single, Immediate IM 040

● **THE FIRST CUT IS THE DEEPEST** / Kings Of Kings
UK 7" Single, Immediate IMS 109
THE FIRST CUT IS THE DEEPEST / Speak To Me
1967 7" Single, Immediate IM 047
7" Single, Immediate IMS 1109
THE FIRST CUT IS THE DEEPEST EP
1967 7" EP, Columbia ESRF 1877
THE FIRST CUT IS THE DEEPEST / The Time
Has Come
1969 7" Single, Immediate IM 079
THE FIRST CUT IS THE DEEPEST / Angel Of
The Morning
1985 7" Single, Old Gold OG 9464

● **THE TIME HAS COME** / If You See What I Mean
1967 7" Single, Immediate IM 055

● **WOULD YOU BELIEVE** / Am I Still Dreaming
1968 7" Single, Immediate 451c 00690002

● **(IF YOU THINK YOU'RE) GROOVY** / Though It
Hurts Me Badly
1968 7" Single, Immediate IM 061

● **ANGEL OF THE MORNING** / Life Is But Nothing
1968 7" Single, Immediate IM 067

● **BURY ME DOWN BY THE RIVER** / Give A Hand,
Take A Hand
1969 7" Single, Polydor 45 56350

● **A LIKELY PLACE OF WORK** / May The Winds Blow
1970 7" Single, Polydor 45 2058061

ALBUMS (selected)

■ **THE FIRST LADY OF IMMEDIATE**
UK 1968 LP, Immediate IMSP11
Germany 1972 LP, OutLine OLLP 5255
Tracks: Everything's Gonna Be Alright / Treat Me
Like A Lady / Would You Believe / Life Is But
Nothing / Speak To Me / The Time Has Come /
(If You Think You're) Groovy / Something
Beautiful Happened / Born To Be Together /
Am I Still Dreaming / Though It Hurts Me Badly /
The First Cut Is The Deepest

■ **KAFUNTA**
UK 1968 LP, Immediate IMSP17
Germany 1972 LP, OutLine OLLP 5225
Tracks: To Love Somebody / Angel Of The Morning
/ Eleanor Rigby / God Only Knows / Yesterday /
It'll Never Happen Again / As Tears Go By /
Letter To Bill / Dreaming / Welcome Home

COMPILATION ALBUMS (selected)

■ **FIRST CUT**
Germany 1972 LP, Line OLLP 52255

■ **GREATEST HITS**
1978 LP, Immediate IML 2006
Tracks: The First Cut Is The Deepest / Dreaming /
Would You Believe / To Love Somebody /
Born To Be Together / Eleanor Rigby / Angel Of
The Morning / As Tears Go By / Am I Still
Dreaming / Though It Hurts Me Badly / Speak To
Me / (If You Think You're) Groovy

■ **ANGEL**
1986 LP, Castle Showcase SHLP 157

■ **THE P.P. ARNOLD COLLECTION**
1988 CD, Line IDCD 9.00611 OCD
Compilation of albums The First Lady Of
Immediate and Kafunta

■ **THE BEST OF P.P. ARNOLD**
1988 CD, See For Miles SEECD 235
Tracks: (If You Think You're) Groovy / Something
Beautiful Happened / Born To Be Together /
Am I Still Dreaming / The First Cut Is The Deepest
/ Everything's Gonna' Be Alright / Treat Me Like
A Lady / Would You Believe / Speak To Me /
God Only Knows / Eleanor Rigby / Yesterday /
Angel Of The Morning / It'll Never Happen Again
/ As Tears Go By / To Love Somebody /
Dreaming / If You See What I Mean /
Though It Hurts Me Badly / Welcome Home /
Life Is But Nothing / The Time Has Come

■ **COLLECTION**
1991, Sony

■ **BEST OF P.P. ARNOLD**
1993 CD, Immediate/Charly CSL 6035
1999, Repertoire (Edel)

■ **THE FIRST CUT**
UK 1998 CD, Castle CCS CD 819
Tracks: (If You Think You're) Groovy / Something
Beautiful Happened / Born To Be Together /
Am I Still Dreaming / Though It Hurts Me Badly /
The First Cut Is The Deepest / Everything's Gonna'
Be Alright / Treat Me Like A Lady / Would You
Believe / Life Is But Nothing / Speak To Me /

The Time Has Come / Letter To Bill / Kafunta One
/ God Only Knows / Eleanor Rigby / Yesterday /
Angel Of The Morning / It'll Never Happen Again
/ As Tears Go By / To Love Somebody / Dreaming
/ Welcome Home

SESSION APPEARANCES (selected)

● CHRIS FARLOWE – Reach Out
1966, Immediate
P.P. Arnold – Backing Vocals

● IKE & TINA TURNER – River Deep, Mountain High
1966 7" Single, A&M
P.P. Arnold – Backing Vocals

● SMALL FACES – Itchycoo Park
1967 7" Single, Immediate
SMALL FACES – Tin Soldier
1967 7" Single, Immediate
P.P. Arnold – Backing Vocals

■ SMALL FACES – There Are But Four Small Faces
1968 LP, Immediate
P.P. Arnold – Backing Vocals

■ JESUS CHRIST SUPERSTAR – Original Cast Rec.
1970 LP, MCA
P.P. Arnold – Vocals

■ ASHTON, GARDNER & DYKE – The Worst Of...
1971 LP, Capitol EST 563
P.P. Arnold – Backing Vocals

■ DR JOHN – The Sun, Moon & Herbs
1971 LP, Atlantic 2400 161
CD Atlantic 7567 80440-2
P.P. Arnold – Backing Vocals

■ GRAHAM NASH – Songs For Beginners
1971 LP, Atlantic 2401 011
P.P. Arnold – Backing Vocals

■ HUMBLE PIE – Rock On
1971 LP, A&M AMLS 2013
P.P. Arnold – Backing Vocals

■ NICK DRAKE – Bryter Layter
1971 LP, Island ILPS 9134
P.P. Arnold – Backing Vocals

■ SKY – Don't Hold Back
1971 LP, RCA SF8168
P.P. Arnold – Backing Vocals

■ OCEAN COLOUR SCENE – Marchin' Already
1997 CD, MCA MCD60048
P.P. Arnold – Backing Vocals

■ OASIS – Standing On The Shoulder Of Giants
2000 CD, Big Brother RKIDCD002
P.P. Arnold – Backing Vocals

VARIOUS ARTISTS COMPIL. (selected)

■ THE IMMEDIATE STORY
1980, Virgin V2165
P.P. Arnold Track: The First Cut Is The Deepest

■ IMMEDIATE As & Bs: THE SINGLES
1981, US Compleat

■ THE IMMEDIATE SINGLES STORY
USA 2LP, Compleat-672007 1

■ THE IMMEDIATE COLLECTION
UK 1995 CD, Charly SUMCD 4036
P.P. Arnold Tracks: Angel Of The Morning /
The First Cut Is The Deepest

■ BLITZ OF HITZ
Germany 2000 2CD, Charly CDBOOK 101
P.P. Arnold Tracks: The First Cut Is The Deepest /
Angel Of The Morning / Speak To Me / Life Is
But Nothing

■ THE IMMEDIATE SINGLES STORY, Vol.1
2000 2CD, Charly CDBOOK101
P.P. Arnold Tracks: The First Cut Is The Deepest /
Angel Of The Morning / Speak To Me / Life Is But
Nothing
THE IMMEDIATE SINGLES STORY, Vol.2
2000 2CD , Charly CDBOOK102
P.P. Arnold Tracks: Everything's Gonna Be Alright
/ Life Is But Nothing

■ THE IMMEDIATE SINGLES COLLECTION
2000 6CD Box Set, Sequel NXTCD324
P.P. Arnold Tracks: Everything's Gonna Be Alright
/ Life Is But Nothing / The First Cut Is The
Deepest / Speak To Me / The Time Has Come /
If You See What I Mean / If You Think You're
Groovy / Though It Hurts Me Badly

■ IMMEDIATE PLEASURE
2002 2CD, Castle Pulse CMDDD425
P.P. Arnold Tracks: Angel Of The Morning /
Everything's Gonna Be Alright / The First Cut Is
The Deepest / Come Home Baby (*with Rod
Stewart*) / The Time Has Come

COVER VERSIONS & TRIBUTES (selected)

THE NICE, KEITH EMERSON, ELP

■ MIKE & LINDA COATES – FALL IN LOVE
1996 CD, Barking Dog 2041
ELP cover: C'est La Vie

■ EKSEPTION 5
1972 LP, Philips 6423042
1972 LP, Philips 700002
The Nice cover: For Example
*Rick van der Linden – Keyboards; Michel van Dijk –
Vocals; Cor Dekker – Bass; Dick Remelink – Sax &
Flute; Huib van Kampen – Sax & Guitar; Rein van
den Broek – Trumpet; Peter de Leeuwe – Drums*

■ ENCORES, LEGENDS & PARADOX
USA 1999 CD, Magna Carta MA-9026-2
ELP covers: Tarkus / Black Moon (instrumental
section) / Abaddon's Bolero
*Artists include John Wetton – Vocals; Marc Bonilla
– Guitar; Glenn Hughes – Vocals; Simon Phillips –
Drums; Robert Berry – Vocals & Bass*

■ **FANFARE FOR THE PIRATES – TRIBUTE TO ELP**
Italy 1998 3CD, Mellow MMP 343 ABC
ELP covers: CD1: Tarkus / Knife Edge /
Jerusalem / The Barbarian / Pirates / Fanfare For
The Common Man / Still...You Turn Me On /
Lucky Man
Performed by: Works 3; House Of Usher; Lukala &
Friends; Synthetic Block; Trama; Noddy's Puncture;
Mary Newsletter; Nostalgia
CD2: Canario / Tarkus / The Infection Of Karn Evil
9.3 With A Lucky Man Intro / Love At First Sight
/ From The Beginning / Rondo / Promenade /
Romeo & Juliet / Karn Evil 9 / The Sheriff
Performed by: Luz Escondida; Lorien; Matrix
Mind; Page; Letrickramer; Myros; Maria Tortorici;
Zauber; Trilogy; Eclipse
CD3: Take A Pebble / Dedicato / The Sage /
Infinite Space / Tank / The Fourth Fate /
The Endless Enigma Part 1 / C'est La Vie /
Abaddon's Bolero / Living Sin
Performed by: Algebra; Sequenza Principale;
Prowlers; Ed Macan's Hermetic Science;
Phil Beane; Ken Taylor; Rivendell; TNR; Osvaldo
Giordano; Divae

■ **JOHN GRINDELL – ALIVE AGAIN**
UK 1996 CD, JGCDD1
UK 1996 MC, JGMCC1
ELP covers: Karn Evil 9 (First Impression Part 2) /
Eruption / Black Moon (instrumental section) /
Abaddon's Bolero
John Grindell - Keyboards

■ **GREG LAKE**
KING BISCUIT PRESENTS... LIVE
USA 1996 CD, Imports 880102
1998 CD, King Biscuit KBFHCD018
ELP covers: Medley: Fanfare For The Common
Man - Karn Evil 9 / Lucky Man
Greg Lake - Guitar, Bass & Vocals;
Various band members

■ **LEGENDS OF ROCK – Classic Rock Heroes**
CD, Pet Rock Records PET-CD-60050
ELP cover: Lucky Man
Greg Lake - Guitar & Vocals (+ Band?)

■ **ED MACAN'S HERMETIC SCIENCE**
USA 1986 MC, HTW 001-006
ELP covers: Eruption / Battlefield
ED MACAN'S HERMETIC SCIENCE
USA 1997 CD, Magnetic Oblivion 1-MERM1-97
ELP cover: Infinite Space (Conclusion)
Ed Macan - Marimba; Donald Sweeney - Bass;
Michael Morris - Drums
ED MACAN'S HERMETIC SCIENCE –
PROPHESIES
USA 1999 CD, Magnetic Oblivion 2-MERM2-99
ELP track: Tarkus
Ed Macan - Solo Piano

■ **NODDY'S PUNCTURE – WARTS AND ALL**
UK 2000 CD, NPCD01
ELP covers: Peter Gunn / Affairs of the Heart /
Lucky Man / Fanfare For The Common Man /
Hoedown / Nutrocker / Honky Tonk Train Blues
Tom Szakaly - Keyboards;
Tony Gunderson - Bass; Guitar & Vocals;
Lez Piszkalo - Drums & Percussion

➤ **NODDY'S PUNCTURE – CHIDDINGLY**
UK 2002 2VCD
Live footage of UK ELP tribute band
The Nice & ELP covers: Peter Gunn / Jerusalem /
Romeo & Juliet / Touch And Go / C'est La Vie /
Lucky Man / Medley (Tarkus / America / Rondo) /
Hoedown (includes 'Ribbon Controller assault') /
Fanfare For The Common Man (including The Old
Castle / Blues Variation / The Hut Of Baba Yaga /
'Hammond abuse') / Medley (Nutrocker /
Honky Tonk Train Blues)
(with 3 Bonus videos from earlier NP line-ups:
The Score / Learning To Fly / Medley (Show Me
The Way To Go Home / Tiger In A Spotlight))
Tom Szakaly - Keyboards; Bernd Wippich - Bass,
Guitar & Vocals; Lez Piszkalo - Drums & Percussion
NODDY'S PUNCTURE – THE LIMELIGHT CLUB
UK 2002 VCD
Live footage of UK ELP tribute band
Peter Gunn / Romeo & Juliet / Touch And Go /
The Score / Affairs Of The Heart / From The
Beginning / Hoedown (including 'Ribbon
Controller assault') / Medley (Karn Evil 9 / Tarkus
/ America / Rondo) / Fanfare For The Common
Man (including The Old Castle / Blues Variation /
The Hut Of Baba Yaga / 'Hammond abuse') /
Medley (Nutrocker / Honky Tonk Train Blues) /
Lucky Man
Tom Szakaly - Keyboards; Tony Gunderson - Bass,
Guitar & Vocals; Lez Piszkalo - Drums & Percussion

■ **CARL PALMER – WORKING LIVE**
2002 CD
ELP covers include: Toccata / Tank / Hoedown
/ The Barbarian / The Enemy God Dances With
The Black Spirits / Fanfare For The Common Man
/ Bullfrog / Canario / L.A. Nights / Tarkus
Carl Palmer - Drums & Percussion;
Shaun Baxter - Guitar; Dave Marks - Bass

■ **TOP OF THE POPS, Volume 60**
1977 LP, Pickwick SHM 990
ELP cover: Fanfare For The Common Man
The Top Of The Pops Orchestra

■ **TRIBUTE TO THE TITANS**
USA 1999 CD, Magna Carta MA-9032-2
ELP covers: Hoedown / Knife Edge
Glenn Hughes - Vocals; Robert Berry - Bass;
Jerry Goodman - Violin; Jordan Rudess & Erik
Norlander - Keyboards; Marc Bonilla - Guitar;
Simon Phillips - Drums

■ **WORKS III – REWORKS**
UK 1998 CD, JGCDD5
ELP covers: Pirates / Black Moon / Hoedown /
Lucky Man / Fanfare For The Common Man /
Touch And Go / Tarkus / Abaddon's Bolero
John Grindell - Keyboards; Laurence Ellis - Bass
& Vocals; Frank Askew - Drums

■ **THRILLERS!**
1997 CD, Silva 5011
Keith Emerson cover: Nighthawks (Main Theme)
The London Screen Orchestra

■ **2 MANY DJS – AS HEARD ON RADIO**
SOULWAX Part 2
Belgium 2002 CD, CD-Wax 941.0065.020

BBC SESSIONS

22nd OCT 1967 - TOP GEAR

Personnel: Emerson, Jackson, Davison, O'List
Recorded: 19th October 1967

Tracks: Flower King Of Flies / Azrial (Angel Of Death) / Sombrero Sam / Tantalising Maggie / Rondo / The Thoughts Of Emerlist Davjack

28th JAN 1968 - TOP GEAR

Personnel: Emerson, Jackson, Davison, O'List
Recorded: 17th January 1968

Tracks: Daddy Where Did I Come From / For No One / La Aresa Dia Conte / She Belongs To Me

16th JUN 1968 - TOP GEAR

Personnel: Emerson, Jackson, Davison, O'List
Recorded: 10th June 1968

Tracks: Get To You / The Diamond Hard Blue Apples Of The Moon / Brandenburger / Little Arabella / Sorcery

4th AUG 1968 - STUART HENRY

Personnel: Emerson, Jackson, Davison, O'List
Recorded: 29th July 1968

Tracks: Little Arabella / Rondo / Flower King Of Flies

25th AUG 1968 –TOP GEAR

Personnel: Emerson, Jackson, Davison, O'List
Recorded: 6th August 1968

Tracks: America (America/2nd Amend.) / Lumpy Gravy / Aries The Fire Fighter / Ars Longa Vita Brevis

29th AUG 1968 –POP NORTH

Personnel: Emerson, Jackson, Davison, O'List
Recorded: 26th August 1968

Tracks: Hang On To A Dream / Little Arabella / America (America/2nd Amend.)

1st DEC 1968 - TOP GEAR

Personnel: Emerson, Jackson, Davison
Recorded: 26th November 1968

Tracks: Happy Freuds / Brandenburger / Hang On To A Dream / Intermezzo 'Karelia Suite' / Handel's Water Music

20th APR 1969 - TOP GEAR

Personnel: Emerson, Jackson, Davison
Recorded: 4th March 1969
*The band received an extra £50 for playing this!

Tracks: I'm One Of Those People That My Father Tells My Sister Not To Go Out With / Azrael Revisited / Diary Of An Empty Day / Blues For The Prairies / Top Gear Theme*

8th JUN 1969 - TOP GEAR

Personnel: Emerson, Jackson, Davison
Recorded: 2nd June 1969

Tracks: Get To You / Country Pie / For Example / St. Thomas (with Roy Harper)

6th APR 1970

Personnel: Emerson, Jackson, Davison
Recorded: 25th March 1970

Tracks: Country Pie / Five Bridges Suite / Pathetique (Tchaikovsky's 6th Symphony, 3rd Movement) / My Back Pages

LIST OF GIGS

With special thanks to: David Terralavoro, Michael A. Tusa, Paolo Rigoli, John Hellier and Barry Green

1967

P.P. ARNOLD & THE NICE

MAY
29 Cellar Club, Kingston, London

JUNE
3   Cooks Ferry Inn, Edmonton, London
6   Embassy Club, Northampton
11 Refectory, Golders Green, London
12 Wykeham Hall, Romford
16 Manor House, London

JULY
1   Manor House, London
2   Ram Jam Club, Brixton, London
7   White Hart, Acton, London
23 Blenheim Place, Oxford
    (with Jeff Beck Group with
    Rod Stewart, Manfred Mann)
29 'Saturday Club' Radio Show

AUGUST
13 7th National Jazz & Blues
    Festival, Windsor
    (with Cream, the debut gig
    of Fleetwood Mac)
16 White Hart, Acton, London
23 The Flamingo, London
28 The Flamingo, London
    (last gig with P.P. Arnold,
    first gig with Brian Davison)

THE NICE

SEPTEMBER
1   Big C, Farnborough
    (The first show The Nice
    played as a fully-fledged
    band)
21 Klooks Kleek, London

OCTOBER
2   Marquee, London
16 Marquee, London
19 BBC Session (see Page 200)
23 Palace Theatre, Manchester
24 Marquee, London
    (supporting Jimi Hendrix)
27 Middle Earth, London

NOVEMBER
6   Marquee, London
12 Saville Theatre, London
13 Marquee, London
Jimi Hendrix, Pink Floyd, etc.
Package Tour (all two shows
up until Dec 5th):
14 Royal Albert Hall, London
15 Winter Gardens,
    Bournemouth
17 City Hall, Sheffield
18 Empire, Liverpool
19 Coventry Theatre, Coventry
22 Guild Hall, Portsmouth
23 Sophia Gardens, Cardiff
24 Colston Hall, Bristol
25 Opera House, Blackpool
27 Marquee, London (not part
    of Hendrix tour)

DECEMBER
1   Town Hall, Chatham
2   Dome, Brighton
3   Theatre Royal, Nottingham
4   City Hall, Newcastle upon
    Tyne
5   Green Playhouse, Glasgow
Scandinavian Tour:
?   Included Gothenberg
    (venues/dates unconfirmed)
18 Marquee, London
27 Top Rank, Brighton

1968

JANUARY
1   Marquee, London
    (with Mabel Greer's Toyshop,
    soon to evolve into Yes)
8   Marquee, London
12 Middle Earth, London
15 Marquee, London
17 BBC Session (see Page 200)
22 Marquee, London
27 Students' Union, Newcastle
    University, Newcastle upon
    Tyne
First United States Tour:
29 Scene Club, New York
30 Scene Club, New York
31 Scene Club, New York

FEBRUARY
1   Scene Club, New York
2   Scene Club, New York
3   Scene Club, New York
4   Scene Club, New York
5   Scene Club, New York
6   Scene Club, New York
7   Scene Club, New York
8   Scene Club, New York

9   Scene Club, New York
10 Scene Club, New York
11 Scene Club, New York
15 Whiskey A Go Go, Los Angeles
16 Whiskey A Go Go, Los Angeles
17 Whiskey A Go Go, Los Angeles
18 Whiskey A Go Go, Los Angeles
22 Fillmore West, San Francisco
    (with The Who, Cannonball
    Adderley, The Vagrants)
23 Winterland, San Francisco
24 Winterland, San Francisco
26 Marquee, London
    (billed as 'Welcome Back
    From The US')

MARCH
4   Marquee, London
9   Arts Festival Rave, University
    Union, Leeds
11 Marquee, London
18 Marquee, London
23 Middle Earth, London
25 Marquee, London

APRIL
1   Marquee, London
11 Marquee, London
23 Klooks Kleek, London
26 Marquee, London

MAY
2   Marquee, London
5   International Pop Festival,
    Rome, Italy
    (with Ten Years After,
    The Move)
7   Falconer Theatre,
    Copenhagen, Denmark
    (with Ten Years After,
    The Fugs)
9   Gothenburg, Sweden
    (with Ten Years After,
    The Fugs)
10 Stockholm, Sweden
    (with Ten Years After,
    The Fugs)
21 Marquee, London

JUNE
4   Klooks Kleek, London
6   Marquee, London
8   City Hall, Newcastle upon
    Tyne
10 BBC Session (see Page 200)
11 Fishmongers Arms, London
20 Marquee, London
26 'Come Back Africa',
    Royal Albert Hall, London
27 Norwich
29 Institute Of Contemporary
    Art, London
    (with Bonzo Dog Doo Dah Band)

30 Middle Earth, London

JULY
4 Marquee, London
11 Marquee, London
12 The Manor House, London
13 The Magic Village, Manchester
16 Klooks Kleek, London
18 Marquee, London
(The Nice broke the Box Office record with this gig!)
27 Hyde Park Free Concert, London
(with Traffic, The Pretty Things, etc.)
29 BBC Session (see Page 200)

AUGUST
2 Metropole Exhibition Hall, Brighton
3 Baldry Goldcrest, London
4 Norwich Industrial Club, Norwich
6 BBC Session (see Page 200)
7 Starlight Rooms, Boston
8 Marquee, London
(now billed as 'Fantastic')
9 Pavillion, Hemel Hempstead
10 8th National Jazz & Blues Festival, Kempton
(with Jeff Beck, Roy Harper joined The Nice for one song)
11 Top Rank, Birmingham
14 Country Club, Hampstead
15 Marquee, London
21 Pier Pavillion, Bournemouth
22 Marquee, London
23 'How It Is' BBC TV Show (see Page 200)
24 Winter Gardens, Weston-Super-Mare
26 BBC Session (see Page 200)
28 Eel Pie Island, London
29 Beat Club TV Show, Bremen, West Germany
30 Hits A Go Go, Switzerland
31 Hits A Go Go, Switzerland

SEPTEMBER
5 Marquee, London
11 Middle Earth, London
14 Mothers, Birmingham
17 Fishmongers Arms, London
19 Marquee, London
(with Yes)
20 California Ballroom, Dunstable
21 Town Hall, Glastonbury
24 Klooks Kleek, London
28 Technical College, Ewell
29 Fairfield Hall, Croydon
(Olympic Appeal)

OCTOBER
1 Ritz, Bournemouth
(date unconfirmed; Davy was sacked at this gig)
3 Toby Jug, Tolworth
(date unconfirmed; first gig

proper as a trio)
4 Brunel University, Uxbridge
9 Country Club, London
11 Hornsey Wood Tavern, London
12 Club 66, Honseleidik, Holland
13 Schiedam, Arkada, Holland
15 Marquee, London
18 Candlelight, Scarborough
19 Students Union, Colchester
21 Paris, TV show
23 Guildhall, Portsmouth
24 Queen Mary's College, London
25 Colston Hall, Bristol
(with Small Faces, Canned Heat)

NOVEMBER
2 Magic Village, Manchester
5 Marquee, London
10 Mothers, Birmingham
11 Rhodes Centre, Bishops Stortford
14 Queens University, Whitla Hall, Belfast (Annual Music Festival) (2 shows)
18 Loyola Hall, London
19 Edward Herbert Building, Loughborough University
21 Red Lion Hotel, Leytonstone, London
26 BBC Session (see Page 200)
? Blues Festival, Zurich, Switzerland
(date unconfirmed)

DECEMBER
5 Red Lion Hotel, Leytonstone, London
10 Kings College, London
12 York University, York
13 Technical College, Nottingham
14 Key Club, Bridgend
15 Mothers, Birmingham
17 Ritz, Bournemouth
19 City Hall, Newcastle upon Tyne
22 Beat Festival, Prague
27 Brighton, Top Rank
28 Boston, Gliderdome

1969

JANUARY
19 Golden Torch, Stoke on Trent
25 Students' Union, Manchester University, Manchester
26 Mothers, Birmingham
27 City Hall, Sheffield
28 Marquee, London

FEBRUARY
1 Starlight Room, Boston
4 Institute Of Contemporary Art, London
(with John Mayer and orchestra)

5 Top Rank Suite, Leicester
6 City Hall, Newcastle upon Tyne
7 The Coatham Hotel, Redcar
8 Leeds University, Leeds
10 College of Commerce, Manchester
11 The Large Room, Guildhall, Cambridge
15 UCL, Gower Street, London (with Deep Purple)
19 Star Club, Hamburg, West Germany
20 Speakeasy, London
21 Marquee, Leeds
23 The Black Prince, Bexley

MARCH
4 BBC Session (see Page 200)
8 Middle Earth, London
14 Fairfield Hall ,Croydon
Second United States Tour:
21-23 Boston Tea Party, Boston (with Jeff Beck)
? Concerts at New York, Chicago, Miami and Agura (dates unconfirmed)

APRIL
9-10 Fillmore East, New York (with Ten Years After, Family)
11-13 Grande Ballroom, Detroit (with The Velvet Underground)
? Toronto (date unconfirmed)

MAY
6-8 Boston Tea Party, Boston
30 'Midnight Court', Lyceum, London (with Steppenwolf)
31 North College, London

JUNE
2 BBC Session (see Page 200)
6 The Factory, Birmingham
8 Mothers, Birmingham
10 Marquee, London
(The Nice's 35th and final appearance at the Marquee)
21 Antwerp Pop Festival, Belgium (with Yes, Colosseum)
22 Fairfield Hall, Croydon
28 Bath Festival, Bath (with Led Zeppelin, Ten Years After)
30 Ossiach Hall, Vienna (with Duncan Browne)

JULY
4 Winter Gardens, Malvern
9 Van Dyke, Plymouth
11 'Midnight Court', Lyceum, London
12 Nottingham Racecourse, Nottingham (with King Crimson, Yes, Status Quo)
13 Mothers, Birmingham
14 Kings Hall, Romford

15 Cherry Tree, Welwyn Garden
City
Tour Of Ireland:
18 Ulster Hall, Belfast
(with Bonzo Dog Doo Dah
Band, Yes)
19 National Boxing Stadium,
Dublin
(with Bonzo Dog Doo Dah
Band, Yes)
20 Football Stadium, Cork
(cancelled) (would have been
with Bonzo Dog Doo Dah
Band, Yes)

AUGUST
10 9th National Jazz, Pop &
Blues Festival, Plumpton
(with Family, King Crimson)
16 Civic Hall, Dunstable
22 Humberside Festival, Burton
Constable Hall, Sproatley
29 Isle Of Wight Festival
(with Bob Dylan, The Who,
etc)

SEPTEMBER
12 Civic Hall, Wolverhampton
13 Rainsbrook, Rugby
19 Van Dyke, Plymouth
22 Kings Hall, Romford
27 Starlight Room, Boston,
England
28 Harrogate Theatre, Harrogate
(with Yes)

OCTOBER
7 Norway, TV show
9 Oslo, Norway
10 City Hall, Newcastle upon
Tyne
(Premiere of 'Five Bridges'
with band only)
11 First German Blues Festival,
Gruga Halle, Essen, West
Germany
(with Deep Purple, Taste, Pink
Floyd)
12 Concertbegouw, Amsterdam
13 Civic Centre, Dunstable
16 Winter Gardens, Malvern
17 Fairfield Hall, Croydon
('Five Bridges' recorded with
orchestra)
(with King Crimson)
18-22 Various venues in Sweden,
Denmark and Belgium
25 Beat Club TV Show, Bremen,
West Germany
26 Festival Actuel, Paris, France
29 State Theatre, Basle,
Switzerland

NOVEMBER
1 Jazz Festival, Prague
5 Concert House, Vienna
7 Bonn, West Germany
9 Lyceum, London
(with John Mayer and The
London City Ensemble,

Rare Bird)
Third United States Tour:
15 Madison Square Garden
(cancelled due to illness of
headliners, The Isley Brothers)
16-19 Unganos, New York
21-22 Grande Ballroom, Detroit
(with Santana, Spooky Tooth)
23 Hawks Nest, Toronto
26 Times Square, Minneapolis
28-29 Birmingham, Michigan
30 Chicago, Illinois

DECEMBER
3 Long Island, New York
4 -6 Boston Tea Party, Boston
(2 shows a night) (with The
Allman Brothers Band)
7 Buffalo, New York
11-14 Fillmore West, San
Francisco
(with King Crimson)
15-17 The Experience, Los
Angeles
19-20 Fillmore East, New York
(with The Byrds, Dion)

1970

JANUARY
17 Rome Festival, Rome, Italy
(Start of 10-day tour of Italy,
France and West Germany)
25 Olympia, Paris, France
26 TV Show, Paris
27 Colston Hall, Bristol
29 City Hall, Sheffield
30 Leeds University, Leeds

FEBRUARY
1 Empire Theatre, Sunderland
(with Yes)
2 Civic Hall, Wolverhampton
3 Free Trade Hall, Manchester
4 Philharmonic, Liverpool
5 Winter Gardens, Bournemouth
6 Winter Gardens, Bournemouth
7 Festival Hall, London
(2 shows) (with Yes)
8 Oxford Polytechnic, Oxford
13-17 'Switched on Symphony',
Los Angeles
(TV show with
Zubin Mehta,
Ray Charles,
Santana, Jethro
Tull, etc)
21 Brussels,
Belgium
24 De Montfort Hall,
Leicester
25 Town Hall,
Birmingham
26 TV show,
Cologne,
West Germany
27 Royal Hall,
Harrogate

28 City Hall, Newcastle
upon Tyne

MARCH
6 Festival Hall, London
(with Royal Philharmonic
Orchestra with Joseph Eger)
11 Usher Hall, Edinburgh
12 Caird Hall, Dundee
13 Playhouse, Glasgow
14 Public Hall, Preston
16 Civic Hall, Dunstable
18 Guildhall, Southampton
22 Fairfield Hall, Croydon
(2 shows)
25 BBC Session (see Page 200)
28 Ernst Merk Halle, Hamburg,
West Germany
30 Sportspalast, Peace Festival,
Berlin, West Germany
(with Deep Purple)
(The Nice's last gig, or so it
seemed...)

1999

MARCH
6 Worthing
(Private function for Keith
Emerson's mum's birthday,
with Keith Emerson, Lee
Jackson and Brian Davison)

2002

APRIL
9 100 Club, London
(The Nice's first performance
in public in just over 32
years!)

OCTOBER
2 Civic Hall, Wolverhampton
3 New Tyne Theatre & Opera
House, Newcastle upon Tyne
4 Royal Concert Hall, Glasgow
6 Royal Festival Hall, London
? Other dates to be confirmed

ROYAL FESTIVAL HALL

50
Royal Festival

Mind Your Head
Keith Emerson and The Nice

SUNDAY 6 OCTOBER 2002 at 7:30 PM

LEVEL 3
STALLS   D24   £25.00   VIST

REFERENCE **SOURCES**

BOOKS

'50 Years Of Rock Music: Chambers Encyclopaedia Guide' W & R Chambers, 1992

'A–Z Of Rock Drummers' Harry Shapiro, Proteus Publishing, 1982

'A Message To Love: Isle Of Wight Festivals 1968–70'

'Bill Wyman: Stone Alone' Ray Coleman, Signet

'Bryan Ferry & Roxy Music' Barry Lazell & Dafydd Rees, Proteus Books, 1982

'Close To The Edge: The Story Of Yes' Chris Welch, Omnibus Press, 1999

'ELP: The Show That Never Ends' George Forrester, Martyn Hanson & Frank Askew, Helter Skelter, 2000

'Flying Colours: The Jethro Tull Reference' Greg Russo, Crossfire Publications, 2000

'Gong Dreaming II' Daevid Allen

'In Session Tonight' Ken Garner, BBC Books, 1993

'In The Court Of King Crimson' Sid Smith, Helter Skelter, 2001

'Interviews With Keith Emerson' (in Japanese), February 1992

'Keith Emerson: The Emergence Of Growth & Style' Blair Pethel, A Dissertation, 1988

'Listening To The Future: The Time Of Progressive Rock' Bill Martin, Open Court, 1998

'London Live' Tony Bacon, Balafon, 1999

'Lost In The Woods: Syd Barrett & Pink Floyd' Julian Palacios, Boxtree, 1998

'Mothers '68–'71: The Home Of Good Sounds' Kevin Duffy, Birmingham Council, 1997

'Revolution In The Head: The Beatles' Records & The Sixties' Ian McDonald, Pimlico, 1995

'Rocking The Classics: English Progressive Rock' Edward Macan, Oxford University, 1997

'Starmakers & Svengalis' Johnny Rogan, Futura Publications

'Stoned' Andrew Loog Oldham, 2000

'The Adventures Of The Rolling Stones' Stanley Booth, William Heinemann, 1985

'The Complete Rock Family Trees' Pete Frame, Omnibus Press, 1993

'The Great Rock Discography' M.C. Strong, Canongate Books, 1996

'The Heat Goes On: A Book About Asia' Dave Gallant

'The Music's All That Matters: A History Of Progressive Rock' Paul Stump, Quartet, 1997

'Tina Turner' Kurt Loder, Morrow Books

'Understanding Rock' Edited by John Covach & Graeme M. Boone, Oxford University Press, 1997

'Yes: Perpetual Change' David Watkinson, Plexus, 2001

'Yes: The Authorised Biography' Dan Hedges, Sidgwick & Jackson, 1981

FACE-TO-FACE INTERVIEWS

Bazz Ward: 9th June 2001, 23rd June 2001, 8th September 2001, 2nd March 2002

Brian Davison: 28th & 29th April 2001, 29th & 30th August 2001

Brian Walkley: 6th May 2001

John Mayer: 3rd December 2001

Lee Jackson: 10th March 2001, 2nd September 2001, 5th January 2002

Mike Kellie: 25th May 2001

P.P. Arnold: 31th August 2001

See acknowledgements on Page 4 for all other interviewees. Other interviews conducted variously by e-mail, written letter and telephone.

BAZZ WARD ARCHIVE

A fascinating collection of photographs, documents and tour itineraries.

PRESS ARTICLES

'1968: The Year Of The Nice' Chris Welch, Melody Maker, 13th July 1968

'A Case Of Give Booze A Chance' Chris Welch, Melody Maker, 2nd August 1969

'A Nice A Week: Brian Davison' Richard Green, NME, 8th November 1969

'A Nice A Week: Keith Emerson' Richard Green, NME, 1st November 1969

'A Nice A Week: Lee Jackson' Richard Green, NME, 15th November 1969

'Afloat With The Nice' Richard Green, NME, 21st September 1968

'American Violence Inspired The Nice' Richard Green, NME, August 1968

Andrew Loog Oldham Interview John Kearney & Barry Green, 1998

Andrew Loog Oldham Interview The Independent, 9th May 2001

'Another Victory For Repression' Melody Maker, 22 April 1972

Carl Palmer Interview Best Magazine, February 1972

'Classical Heads' Mark Plummer, Melody Maker, 19th December 1970

Cleo Odzer Night, December 1997

'Cream Declare War On Singles' Melody Maker, 18th November 1967

Davy O'List Interview Andy Wilson, May 1999

'ELP' Beat & Instrumental, January 1971

'ELP' Ian Dove, Hit Parader Annual, 1974/75

'ELP' J.P. Donlon, Fusion, 7th January 1972

'ELP: Music Scene Top 10 Series' 1974

'ELP: Here Comes Another Orgasmic Peak' Penny Valentine, Sounds, 31st October 1970

'ELP: The Group Most Likely To' Nick Logan, NME, 13th June 1970

'Every Which Way Crashes' Melody Maker, 1971

'Exit The Nice' Hit Parader, January 1971

Fanzine For The Common Man ELP Fanzine, late 1980's to present

'Give Peace A Chance' Davy O'List Interview, Chris

Welch, Melody Maker, 1973
'Giving Lee-Way' Penny Valentine, Sounds, 1973
'Groupie Grope With The Nice' Jonathan Kundra, Circus, 1969
'Hitting The Heights With Jackson' Roy Hollingsworth, Melody Maker, 29th August 1970
'Hold On, Here Come The Nice' Chris Welch, Melody Maker, 16th September 1967
Impressions ELP Fanzine 8 Editions 1996-2001
'Is The Day Of The Thinking Man's Pop Group Over?' Chris Welch, Melody Maker, 1968
'Keith Emerson: A Man And His Music' Richard Green, NME, 12th December 1970
'Keith Emerson: From Dancing Academy Of Pop' Record Mirror, 1968
'Keith Emerson: Hendrix Of The Hammond' Jonathan Glancey, The Guardian, 31st May 2002
Keith Emerson Interview – Dominic Milano, Contemporary Keyboard, September 1980
Keith Emerson Interview Bob Doerschuk, Keyboard, April 1988
Keith Emerson Interview Electronics & Music Maker, April 1985
Keith Emerson Interview Electronics & Music Maker, May 1983
Keith Emerson Interview German Keyboard, November 1994
Keith Emerson Interview Keyboard, Robert Doerschuk, October 1995
Keith Emerson Interview Keyboard (France), December 1991
Keith Emerson Interview Keyboard Player, June 1987
Keith Emerson Interview Malcolm Harrison, Home Keyboard Review, February 1989
Keith Emerson Interview Penny Valentine, Sounds, 1970
Keith Emerson Interview Tim Jones, Record Collector, September 2001
'Keith Emerson Of The Nice On Organs' Chris Hayes, Melody Maker, 15th November 1969
'Keith Emerson Speaks' Chris Welch, Melody Maker, 11th April 1970
'Lee Jackson Making Sure his Group Reaches New Heights' Melody Maker, 1972
'Me & My Music' Lee Jackson, Melody Maker, 1969
'Moog Jazz In The Garden' Bertram Stanleigh, Audio, November 1969
'Nice: Good Music & Showmanship' Richard Green, NME, 27th September 1969
'Nice Call For Freedom Of Music' Disc & Music Echo, 20th September 1969
'Nice In Paris' Richard Green, NME, 31st January 1970
'Nice Meets Moog' Charles Alverson, Rolling Stone, 16th April 1970
'Nice N America' Lon Goddard, Source Unknown, 5th July 1969
'Nice One!' Allan Jones, Melody Maker, 1971
'Nice... Very!' Melody Maker, 18th November 1967
'Out To Lunch Producer Loses Court Challenge' Sally Bolton, The Guardian, 8th February 2002
'Politics, America And The Nice' Disc & Music Echo, 28th September 1968
P.P. Arnold Interview Unknown Source – 1980s
'Refugees From A Nice Past' Richard Green, Music Scene, January 1974
'Rock Giants From A-Z' Chris Welch, Melody Maker, 1972
'Roxy Music' Classic Rock, July 2001

'Sabotage & Flag Burning' Valerie Marbs, Record Mirror, 30th August 1969
'Sound Chaser Of The '70s' Brian Rabey, Jazziz, October 1995
'Speakeasy: The Pop Star's Home-From-Home' Bob Farmer, Disc & Music Echo, 16th March 1968
Tank ELP Fanzine, 4 Editions in the late '80s
'Tear Gas & Broken Heads' Richard Williams, Melody Maker, 18th October 1969
'The 'Naughty' Nice' Chris Hodenfield, Go Magazine, 2nd May 1969
'They Came Off With Mussorgsky' Alexander Frater, 1972
'The Davy O'List Interview' Terrascope, November 1991
'The Davy O'List Story' Rock & Beat Tranquilliser, December 1976
'The English Invasion' Karl Seebacher, Trouser Press, Issue 8 1975
'The Fixer At Fifty: Bazz Ward' Jerry Gilbert, Head To Head, 1992
'The Incredible Spectrum Of Synthesizers' Martin Clifford, Circus, 22nd July 1976
'The Manticore Tapes – Interviews ELP' Keith Altham, Music Scene, 1974
'The Nice' Lita Eliscu, Crawdaddy, February 1970
'The Nice' Tony Norman, Tops Pops, 1969
'The Nice: Bernstein Is Peeved' Record Mirror, August 1968
'The Nice In Belgium' Keith Altham, Record Mirror, 7th March 1970
'The Nice In Prague' Melody Maker, 11th January 1969
The Nice Information Service Numerous Fan Club Letters
'The Refugee File' Melody Maker, 3rd August 1974
'The Sound Of The Nice' Beat Instrumental, DJM, October 1969
'The Works On ELP' Chris Welch, Melody Maker, 12th March 1977
'This Is Bazz – He Puts The Zap Into Pop' Michael Wale, Evening Standard, 16th March 1974
'Two Thirds Nice' IT/SS, 8th May 1969
'Underground Groups: The Nice' Derek Boltwood, Record Mirror, 11th November 1968
'Unsung Hero: Brian Davison' Simon Braund, Rhythm, July 2000
'Versatility Out Of Boredom' Keith Emerson Interview, Joker, 1977
'Welcome Back My Friends' Hugh Fielder, Classic Rock, May 2002
'Who Put Pretentiousness Into Pop?' David Hughes, Disc & Music Echo, 6th December 1969
'Will Nice Get Lost In The Commuters?' Chris Welch, Melody Maker, 1968

MISCELLANEOUS

Other source materials used included photocopied articles of uncertain origin and many uncredited items researched from the Internet.

CONCERT & RECORD REVIEWS

Too numerous to list!

LIFE·LINES of the NICE

The NICE (l. to r.) KEITH EMERSON, BRIAN DAVISON (bottom), DAVE O'LIST and LEE JACKSON

	Keith Emerson	Lee Jackson	Brian Davison	David O'List
Professional name:	Keith Emerson	Lee Jackson	Brian Davison	David O'List
Real name:	Keith Emerson	Keith Jackson	Brian Davison	David O'List
Birthdate:	November 2, 1944	January 8, 1943	May 25, 1942	December 13, 1948
Birthplace:	Todmorden, Lancs.	Newcastle - upon - Tyne	Leicester	Chiswick, London
Personal points:	5ft 9in; 9st 5lb; blue eyes; light brown hair	5ft 11in; 10st 8lb; grey/green eyes; brown hair	5ft 7in; 10st; brown eyes; brown hair	5ft 10½in; 10st 2lb; blue/grey eyes; brown hair
Parents names:	Dorothy and Noel	Alfred and Eve	Bella and Jack	Jennifer and Reg
Brothers and sisters:	None	Vivienne	Terry	Pauline and Suzanne
Wife's name:	None	None	Maureen	None
Children:	None	None	Julie	None
Present home:	Drayton Gardens, London	Soho	Marylebone	Fulham
Instruments played:	Organ, piano	Bass guitar	Drums	Guitar, trumpet
Where educated:	West Tarring Secondary	St. Mary's Tech. School, Newcastle	Bellfield Sec. Mod.	St. Marks, Fulham
Musical education:	Private tuition for classical piano	None	Self-taught	Royal College of Music, London Schools Symphony Orchestra
Age entered Show-business:	15	14	19	17
First public appearance as amateur:	Pier Pavilion, Worthing	Cox Lodge British Legion Night	4 Feathers Youth Club	Pub in the East End
First professional appearance:	Can't remember	Can't remember	Marquee Club	With the Attack
Biggest break in career:	Meeting Pat Arnold	Going to London	Joining the Nice	Joining the Nice
Biggest disappointment in career:	None	Many	None — but many setbacks	Haven't had one as yet
TV debut:	"Dick Clark Show"	RSG	"RSG"	Sweden
Radio debut:	"Saturday Club"	"Top Gear"	"Pop Inn"	"Top Gear"
Biggest influence on career:	My father	Keith Emerson, Oscar Wilde, Beatles, Robert The Bruce	Mark Leeman	Me
Former occupations before showbusiness:	Bank clerk	Burton's salesman	—	—
Hobbies:	Photography, music	Interior designing	—	Records, women, painting
Favourite colour:	Black, gold	Black, white, red	Blue, orange, black, every colour really	Blue, red
Favourite food:	Health foods	Indian	Fish, curries, eggs	Steak, curries
Favourite drink:	Banana, Dacquiri	Brandy, pernod	Milk	Milk
Favourite clothes:	Tight-fitting, casual, leathers, suede	Adventurous	Casual	Casual
Favourite singer:	Bob Dorough, Arthur Brown, Tiny Tim	Donovan, Julie Driscoll	Paul McCartney, Nina Simone, Dave O'List sometimes	Dionne Warwick at the moment
Favourite actor / actress:	Lee Marvin, Brando, Margaret Heald	Brando, Lee Marvin, Pat Phoenix	Lee Marvin	None
Favourite bands / instrumentalists:	Don Ellis Orchestra, Don Shinn, Keith Jarret	Keith Emerson, Jack Dejonett, Lee Morgan, Hendrix	Roland Kirk, Charles Lloyd, Beatles, Don Ellis	Charles Lloyd group, Cream, Beatles, Family, John Handy
Favourite composers:	Jim Webb, Bartok, Bach	Bach	Lennon and McCartney	Bach, Beethoven
Favourite groups:	Family, Taste, Pink Floyd	Beatles	Beatles, Canned Heat, Mothers Of Invention	John Mayall, Moby Grape
Car:	None	Rolls Royce	None	None
Miscellaneous dislikes:	Cliches, disorder, phonies	Jobsworths, messes, bad steak, frigid women, bad organisation	Driving	None
Miscellaneous likes:	Cleo, toast	Beautiful rooms, women, scenery, flying, travelling, coming home	Most people, food	None
Best friend:	Horace	None	None	None
Most thrilling experience:	Cleo	Taking off at Heathrow for America, realising a one-year dream	Playing in America	None
Tastes in music:	Anything where there is scope for free musical expression	Everything good	Wide and varied	Expanding
Origin of stage name:	Ask me parents	Changed due to surfeit of people called Keith in groups	—	—
Pets:	Cleo	Would like to own a Borzoi	Puss E. Kat	I own one-fifth of one beagle
Personal ambition:	To become more aware in my environment. To have complete control of an onslaught of musical ideas	Musical and personal acceptance for the Nice and to write a book of best-selling poetry. Ditto	To be happy. To succeed	To succeed. To become a better musician

INDEX

100 Club, The 176-178
Abrahams, Mick 76, 182
Adams, Pepper 97
Adamson, Brian 35
Advision Studios 21, 140-141
Allen, Daevid 162
Allen, Spencer 181
Allman Brothers, The 112
Ambrosian Singers, The 124
Amen Corner 44, 46, 96
Anderson, Ian 122
Anderson, Jon 49
Andrews, Bernie 43
Andrews, Eamonn 81
Animals, The 14, 17, 25
Arden, Don 27
Ardrey, John (a.k.a. Mark Leeman) 36
Arnold, Malcolm 109
Arnold, P.P. 25-26, 30-34, 42-43, 46, 61, 99, 170, 183
Ashton, Gardner & Dyke 183
Asia 74
Association, The 61
Atlantic Records 155
Atomic Rooster 130-132, 148
Attack, The 26-28, 37, 74
Atwell, Winifred 14, 96
Auger, Brian 61, 64, 87, 102
Bach, J.S. 14, 50, 80, 110, 123
Bach, J.C. 50
Baister, Mel 165
Baker, Ginger 37, 103, 132
Baker, Roy Thomas 145, 182
Baldry, Long John 12
Banks, Peter 135
Barber, Chris 21
Barenboim, Daniel 122-123
Barnard, Kenny & The Wranglers 18
Barratt, Eric 44
Barrett, Syd 45, 71, 73
Barrie, Jack 64, 68, 164-165
Basie, Count 14
Basil's Blues Band 180
BBC 31, 43, 54, 68, 70, 80, 126-127, 132, 136, 153, 161, 169, 172, 182
Beach Boys, The 117
Beatles, The 27, 30-31, 37, 42, 58, 67, 80, 88, 91, 119, 146, 174-175, 183
Beck, Jeff 20, 28, 30, 88

Beethoven, Ludwig Van 14
Beggars Opera 27
Bell, Graham 143, 145
Berlioz, Hector 108
Bermondsey Boys Club 35
Bernstein, Leonard 59, 67-69, 87-88, 138
Berry, Chuck 27
Berry, Robert 155
Betjeman, Sir John 164
Blackwell, Chris 23
Blakey, Art 35
Block, Derek 116, 130
Blood Sweat & Tears 54, 163
Blue Jays, The 26
Bodast 76
Bond, Graham 12, 24, 36, 102
Bonham, John 102, 132
Bonzo Dog Doo Dah Band, The 91-94
Bowie, David 37
Boy George 183
Boyle, Gary 146
Bracewell, Fred 146
Brando, Marlon 64
Brewer, Don 79
British Lions, The 180
Brown, Arthur 20, 184
Brown, James 66
Brown, Joe & The Bruvvers 37
Browne, Duncan 96
Brubeck, Dave 15, 48-49
Bruce, Jack 111
Bruford, Bill 37
Burman, Greg 103
Burns, John 160
Byrds, The 113
Cale, John 182
Canned Heat 88
Cannonball Adderley 57
Carlos, Walter/Wendy 117-118
Carr, Roy 134
Cartwright, Alan 144
Chairman Mao 49
Chambers Brothers, The
Chandler, Chas 25, 44
Chapman, Graham 165
Charisma Records 59, 74, 99, 110, 127, 135-137, 141, 143-144, 158, 164
Charles, Ray 37, 122
Chatton, Brian 142-143
Chicken Shack 103
Chopin, Frédéric 168
Churchill, Chic 86

City Of London Ensemble, The 110
Clapton, Eric 18, 22, 32, 69, 74, 88, 161, 180, 183
Cody's Glider 182
Collins, Phil 132
Colosseum 88, 175
Coltrane, John 145
Conway, Russ 14
Copland, Aaron 153
Coryell, Larry 73
Coulson (née Munt), Gail 59, 125-126, 137, 158, 164-165
Craddock, Steve 183
Cramer, Floyd 14, 88
Crazy World of Arthur Brown, The
Cream 43, 69-70, 132, 182
Cronley, Arthur 30
Crosby, David 57, 71
CTS Studios 153
D'Abo, Mike 51
Dali, Salvador 56
Dankworth, John 64
Dauner, Wolfgang 146
Davidson, Jim 171-172
Davis Jr, Sammy 64
Davison, Brian 15, 34-39, 42-48, 50, 52, 54-57, 61-62, 64-71, 77-81, 84-85, 87-88, 90-91, 96-97, 100, 103, 106, 108-109, 111, 118, 122, 124-125, 127, 130-133, 135, 137-138, 140-146, 158, 160-165, 168-172, 176-178, 180-181
Davison, Maureen 158
Debussy, Claude 168
Deep Purple 106, 109, 126, 150-151, 168, 171
Delaney & Bonnie 183
Derek & The Dominoes 180
Deutsch, Herb 117
Dickens, Barry 71, 134
Doud, Earl 88
Downliners Sect 27
Driscoll, Julie 12, 87
Dr John 151
Dunbar, Aynsley 28
Dunne, Bill 100, 102
Du Pré, Jacqueline 122
Dvorak, Anton 60
Dylan, Bob 22, 30, 50, 54, 77, 90, 97, 103, 110, 123, 137, 170-171, 175
Dynamics, The 17
EG Management 113, 182
Eger, Joseph 99, 108-109,

116, 123-124, 127
Eire Apparent 44
Elkind-Toure, Rachel 118
Ellington, Duke 14
Ellis, Don 88
Emerson, Aaron 163, 172
Emerson, Dorothy 12, 22, 171
Emerson, Elinor 116, 125, 148, 168
Emerson, Keith 12-16, 20-26, 28, 30-35, 43-52, 54-57, 59-60, 62, 64-65, 67-74, 76-80, 82, 84-88, 90-91, 93-94, 96-100, 102-104, 106-113, 116-120, 122, 124-127, 130-138, 140-143, 148-155, 158, 161-165, 168-172, 174-178, 180
The Albums:
'Night Hawks' 155
'Emerson Plays Emerson' 176, 180
Emerson, The Keith Trio 12, 14, 80
Emerson, Lake & Palmer 30, 49, 74, 106, 130-134, 137-138, 141-142, 148-155, 158, 163, 168-171, 174-175
The Albums:
'Emerson Lake & Palmer' 148
'Tarkus' 149-150, 175
'Pictures At An Exhibition' 106, 137, 149-150
'Trilogy' 163
'Brain Salad Surgery' 151
'Welcome Back My Friends...' 152-153
'Works Volume 1' 153-155
'Works Volume 2' 154
'Love Beach' 155
'In Concert' 155
'Black Moon' 168
'In The Hot Seat' 168
Emerson, Lake & Powell 155, 181
The Album:
'Emerson Lake & Powell' 155
EMI Classics 180
Emmerson, Michael 81
English, Scott 27
Epstein, Brian 42
Ertegun, Ahmet 154
Et Cetera 146

Etheridge, John 177
Every Which Way 70, 141-143-146, 180
The Album:
'Every Which Way' 144-146
Fairfield Hall 70, 107, 124-125, 171
Faithful, Marianne 42, 104, 123
Fallon, B.P. 92
Fame, Georgie 12, 14, 24, 36, 102
Family 86
Farlowe, Chris 25-26, 51
Farr, Gary & The T-Bones 12, 14-16, 18, 20-24, 50, 61, 103, 148, 171
Farr, Rikki 20, 148
Ferry, Bryan 182
Fillmore East 85-86, 97, 99, 111-112, 136
Fillmore West 57, 112-113, 136
Fleetwood Mac 31, 62, 106, 111
Flock 122
Flynn, Roy 91
Four Just Men 17
Franklin, Aretha 30
Free 126
Fripp, Robert 113
Fugs, The 62
Funkadelic 66
Gabriel, Peter 164
Garland, Judy 56, 65
Gee, Jon 67
Genesis 74
Gentle Giant 58
Gerry & The Pacemakers 12
Gibb, Barry 183
Giger, Hans Rudi 151
Giles, Michael 113, 175
Ginestera, Alberto 151
Ginger Pig Boogie Band, The 180
Goddard, Lon 98
Goff, Jim 37
Goins, Herbie 184
Goldberg, Terry 36
Gomelsky, Giorgio 12, 15, 16, 22, 61
Gong 125, 162
Good, Jack 122
Goodman, Jerry 122
Golding, William 49
Graham, Bill 57, 86-87, 113
Grant, Julie 36
Granz, Norman 35
Greatest Show On Earth, The 126
Green, Mick 36
Green, Peter 28, 74
Green, Richard 'The Beast' 77, 90, 96, 98, 116, 119, 130, 132, 137-138, 165

Griffiths, Mark 180
Grosvenor, Luther 23-24, 26
Habits, The 36-37
Hague, Ian 26, 32-35, 49, 184
Haley, Bill 16
Hammill, Peter 165
Hammond Organ 12, 14-15, 20-21, 23-24, 32, 37, 39, 43-44, 46, 49-50, 52, 55-57, 62, 70, 78-80, 84, 86, 97, 100-102, 106-108, 110, 116, 135-136, 149, 161, 170, 176
Harcourt, Charlie 140-141
Hardin & York 126
Hardin, Tim 96, 137
Harper, Roy 68, 78, 88, 103, 158, 170
Harriott, Joe 97, 108
Harrison, George 27, 119
Hawes, Hampton 14
Hedgehoppers Anonymous 18
Hedley, John 144-146
Henderson, 'Piano' Joe 14
Hendrix, Jimi 25, 43-46, 48, 70, 111, 144
Henry, Richard 27
Henshaw, Jim 23
Hilbourne, Phil 176-177
Hillage, Steve 162
Hinton, Brian 103
Hipgnosis 135
Hiseman, Jon 42, 132
Hitler, Adolf 12
Hollies, The 57
Hooker, John Lee 36
Hough, Bill 84, 102, 106
House Of Usher 25
Howe, Steve 76-77
Howlin' Wolf 14
Hugg, Mike 84
Humble Pie 23
Hunter, Ian 182
Hyde, David 36
IBC Studios 140
Immediate Records 25-26, 42, 46, 49, 51, 61, 67, 74, 79, 81, 87, 98-99, 123, 130, 135, 137, 141, 175, 181, 184
Impressions, The 20
Incredible String Band, The 158
Invaders, The 17
Island Records 148
Island Studios 160
Isley Brothers, The 113
Jackson, J.J. 184
Jackson, Lee 16-18, 30, 32, 34-35, 42, 45-52, 54, 56-60, 64, 67-68, 70-71, 73-74, 76-81, 84-85, 87-88, 90-91, 93, 96-100, 103-104, 106, 108-

113, 117, 119-120, 122-125, 127, 130-133, 135-138, 140-146, 158-165, 168-172, 176-178, 180-181
Jackson Heights 140-144, 146, 158, 163
The Albums:
'King Progress' 140-143
'The 5th Avenue Bus' 142
'Ragamuffin's Fool' 142-143
'Bump'N'Grind' 142
Jagger, Mick 25-26, 42, 47, 57
Jankel, Chaz 183
Jensen, Arne 46
Jet 182
Jethro Tull 74, 76, 122, 168, 175, 182
Jobim, Antonio Carlos 58
John Brown's Bodies 12
John Henry's 177, 181
Johns, Glyn 47-48
John Mayall's Bluesbreakers 18, 22, 64
Jones, Paul 37
Joplin, Janis 88
Joy, Don 91
Juicy Lucy 182
Junco Partners, The 140
Kellie, Mike 23-25
Kennedy, John F 61, 64
Kennedy, Robert 60-61, 64, 66
Keylock, Tom 36
King Bees 20
King Crimson 74, 107, 111-113, 130-132, 144, 148, 151, 175
King, Jonathan 18
King, Martin Luther 60-61, 64, 84
Kingsway Hall 153-154
Kinks, The 36, 37, 183
KLF 183
Knowler, Stuart 180
Koobas, The 44
Kooper, Al 163
Korner, Alexis 18, 106
Kossoff, Paul 23
Kotcheff, Ted 64-65
Kramer, Eddie 87
Kubrick, Stanley 124
Kylastrons, The 80
Laine, Cleo 64
Lake, Greg 48, 107, 111-113, 131-134, 148-150, 154-155, 163, 170
Lalo, Eduardo 84
Lane, Brian 162
Langstaff, Malcolm 73, 80
Langston, David 'Cyrano' 18, 20-22
LA Philharmonic, The 122
Led Zeppelin 12, 90, 102,

175, 182
Lemmy 44
Lennon, John 94
Lewis, Jerry Lee 14, 68
Ligeti 124
Lindh, Par 108, 169
Little Boy Blue 27
Little Richard 17
Logan, Nick 113, 150
London Philharmonic Orchestra, The 153, 180
Lord, Jon 109
Loussier, Jacques 80
Lyceum, The 88, 110, 116-117, 180
McBurnie, John 142-143
McCarthy, Bob 151
McCaskill, Bruce 180
McDonald, Ian 113
McDonald, Ranald 180
McEwan, Rory 16
McLaughlin, John 184
McQueen, Steve 160
McVie, John 18
Mabel Greer's Toyshop 54
Macduff, Brother Jack 21, 37, 43, 102
Mackay, Andy 182
Maharishi Mahesh Yogi 42
Mahavishnu Orchestra 122
Mainhorse 143
Man 146
Mandela, Nelson 64
Manfred Mann 15, 30, 37, 58, 67, 84, 144
Mankowitz, Gered 26, 52, 81
Manticore Records 151
Manzanera, Phil 182
Mark Leeman Five, The 15, 33-34, 36-37
Marlow, Andrew 169
Marmalade 68
Marquee, The 12, 15, 21, 23-24, 31, 37, 52, 54, 58-59, 64, 66-68, 71, 134, 159, 163-165
'Marquee 12', The 15, 125-126, 174
Martyn, John 71
Matthew, Brian 43
Mayall, John 17-18, 28, 74
Mayer, John 84, 97, 110-111, 153-154
Medicine Head 180
Mehta, Zubin 122-123
Mickey O 26
Mike Cotton Band, The 37
Misunderstood 182
Mitchell, Mitch 88
Mitchell, Warren 64-65
Monty Python 164-165
Mott The Hoople 181
Moody Blues, The 109, 141
Moog Synthesiser 116-120, 124, 142, 148, 151, 155
Moog, Dr Robert 117-118,

148, 151
Moon, Keith 132
Moore, Dudley 14
Moraz, Patrick 110, 143, 158, 160-162
Morricone, Ennio 30
Morrow, Jeff 36
Mountain 57
Mountain Studios 153
Move, The 44, 61
Mozart, Wolfgang Amadeus 49
Mrs Mills 14
Munday, Frank 64-66
Munt, Fred 93
Mussorgsky, Modeste 27, 148
My Little Candle 27
NEMS 145
Neville, John 124
Newton, Isaac 78
Newman, Joe 97
New Seekers, The 66
Nice, The
The Albums:
'The Thoughts Of Emerlist Davjack' 47-52, 70, 74,
'Ars Longa Vita Brevis' 77-81
'Nice' 96-99
'Five Bridges' 90, 107-110, 127, 135-137, 181
'Elegy' 137-138, 148
'Autumn 67-Spring 68' 143
'America (BBC Sessions)' 169, 172
'Swedish Radio Sessions' 46, 172
The Tracks:
'America' 59-62, 64-65, 67-69, 71, 77, 87, 97, 112, 120, 124, 138, 140, 163, 170-171, 177
'Aries' 43, 170
'Ars Longa Vita Brevis' 70-71, 77-80, 82, 99, 136
'Azrial (Angel Of Death)' 51
'Azrael Revisited' 96
'Better Than Better'
'Bonnie 'K'' 49
'Brandenburger' 77, 99
'Country Pie / Brandenburg Concerto No.6' 90, 110, 123, 126, 136
'The Cry Of Eugene' 50, 141, 143
'Daddy Where Did I Come From' 54, 77-78, 80, 143

'Dawn' 50-51, 60
'The Diamond Hard Blue Apples Of The Moon' 62, 159
'Diary Of An Empty Day' 84, 97
'Don Edito El Gruva' 79
'The Five Bridges Suite' 106, 110, 116, 120, 126, 135-136, 143, 170
'Flower King Of Flies' 43, 49
'For Example' 108
'Hang On To A Dream' 96-97, 110, 119, 137
'Happy Freuds' 78
'Intermezzo From The Karelia Suite' 78, 90, 99, 103, 108, 120, 136
'Little Arabella' 67-68, 77-78, 171
'Lt. Kije (The Troika)' 99, 108, 124, 135
'Man In The Long Black Coat' 170
'My Back Pages' 126, 137
'One Of Those People' 136
'Pathetique Symphony' 103, 124, 126, 136-137
'Rondo' 42, 46, 48-49, 52, 60, 67-68, 77, 82, 104, 108, 124, 126, 148, 153, 163, 169, 171, 177
'Rondo (69)' 97
'Sampler for 'The Thoughts Of Emerlist Davjack' 52
'She Belongs To Me' 54, 90-91, 97-99, 108, 110, 119, 159
'Sombrero Sam' 43, 170, 172
'St. Thomas' 88, 170
'Tantalising Maggie' 43, 50
'The Thoughts Of Emerlist Davjack' 43-44, 49, 51
'War & Peace' 43, 50-51, 77, 96
Nicholls, Billy 49, 181
Niforos, Maria 124-125, 145, 158, 162
Oasis 183
Ocean, Billy 183
Ocean Colour Scene 183
Ochs, Ed 87
Offord, Eddie 140-141
Oldham, Andrew Loog 25, 31, 33-34, 44, 47-

48, 50, 54, 57-59, 61-62, 64, 66, 74, 81, 98, 123, 127, 137, 184
O'List, Davy 26-28, 30-32, 34, 36, 39-40, 45-50, 52, 56-57, 61-62, 64, 67, 70-74, 76-80, 84, 96-97, 100, 164, 169-170, 172, 176, 182-183
The Album:
'Flight Of The Eagle' 183
O'List, Pauline 32, 73, 125
O'List, Suzie 32, 73, 125
Olympic Studios 47
O'Neill, Cpt. Terence 82
O'Neill, Eugene 57
Ono, Yoko 104
Opal Butterfly 182
Orbison, Roy 14
Outer Limits 44
Page, Jimmy 90, 158
Paisley, Rev Ian 91
Palmer, Carl 20, 130, 132-133, 135, 148-149, 154, 163
Parker, Charlie 80
Parks, Stuart 16, 171
Patton, John 21
Paul, Steve 54
Peach, Geoff 144
Peacock, Roger 36
Peel, John 28, 43, 52, 134
Pendleton, Harold 31, 165
Pentangle 32
Peterson, Oscar 14
Phonogram Studios 143
Pine, Chris 97, 108, 136
Pink Floyd 44-45, 61, 106, 183
Pirates, The 36
Pitt, Ken 37
Plastic, Johnny 46
Poe, Edgar Allen 96
Polydor Records 127
Powell, Cozy 155
Presley, Elvis 14, 16, 154
Preston, Billy 30
Pretty Things, The 67, 103
Previn, André 14
Price, Alan 17
Prokofiev, Sergei 99, 108, 135
Pye Studios 37, 47, 50, 78
Quaye, Caleb 42
Rachmaninov, Sergei 96
Rare Bird 110
Ravel, Maurice 169
Refugee 132, 158-162
The Album:
'Refugee' 160-162

Reid, Terry 84
Richard, Cliff 14
Richards, Keith 26
Ridley, Greg 23
Rimell, Pete 100
Roach, Max 35
Robertson, Keith 163, 176
Robson, John 70
Rocker Shakes, The 36
Rolling Stones, The 12, 25-27, 47, 67, 70, 132, 175
Rollins, Sonny 88
'Rondo' Dave 125-126
Ronson, Mick 182
Roskams, Alan 36
Roundhouse, The 159
Roxy Music 182
Royal Albert Hall, The 25, 44-45, 64-66, 84, 109
Royal Festival Hall, The 27, 116, 119, 123-124, 163
Rubettes, The 25
Russel, Leon 182
Ryan, John 15
Ryan, Paul & Barry 15
Saint-Marie, Buffy 111
Salmon, Godfrey 153
Sanctuary Records 172, 175-176
Sanders, Pharoah 145
Santana 122, 134, 180
Sargeant, Bob 88
Sarjeant, Sandy 32-34
Satellites, The 17
Scaffold, The 15
Schaffer, Myron 117
Scott, Ronnie 68, 153
Searchers, The 35
Secunda, Tony 16
Sex Pistols, The 180
Shaw, Damon Lyon 140
Sheppard, Godfrey 15
Shinn, Don 24, 36
Shirman, Richard 27-28, 37
Shrieve, Mike 122
Sibelius, Jean 78, 110
Simon, Paul 135
Sinfield, Peter 151
Sinfonia Orchestra, The
Skidmore, Alan 97, 108
Skip Bifferty 143
Slee, Bert 180
Sloane, Tommy 140-141
Small Faces, The 27, 33, 81, 183
Smith, Alan 70, 85, 124-125, 144-145
Smith, Jimmy 14, 43
Soft Machine 177
Soul System, The 27
Speakeasy, The 34, 59, 143, 158

Spear, Roger Ruskin 93
Spector, Phil 23
Spencer Davis Group,
  The 23, 37, 67, 180
Spencer, Don 26
Spirit 54
Spooky Tooth 25
Squire, Chris 97, 111
Stanshall, Vivian 91, 93-
  94, 111
Status Quo 181
Steppenwolf 88
Stevens, Cat 26
Stewart, Rod 12, 103
Storey, Mike 145
Stratton-Smith, Tony
  44, 58-59, 66-68,
  70-74, 77-80, 82,
  84-86, 91, 93, 96,
  109-113, 124,
  127, 130, 136-137,
  140, 142-143, 145-
  146, 162, 164-165,
  168-169, 184
Strauss, Richard 124
Stringfellow, Peter 30,
  37
Surman, John 97
Sweet Sensation 180
Talmy, Shel 59
Tapia, Mario 140
Taste 106
Taylor, Bob 27
Taylor, Chip 183

T-Bones, The (see Farr,
  Gary & The T-Bones)
Tchaikovsky, Peter 103,
  110, 124, 136-137
Temptations, The 12
Ten Years After 61-62 ,
  68, 86
Third Ear Band 103
Thompson, Paul 182
Three 155
  The Album:
  'To The Power Of...' 155
Thunderclap Newman
  103
Timperley, John 154
Toft, Malcolm 145
Toogood, Johnny 142
Townshend, Pete 22, 76
Traffic 23, 67
Trendsetters Ltd. 175
Trident Studios 137, 144
Trojan Records 169-170
Turner, Alan 21
Turner, Ike & Tina 25
Tyrannosaurus Rex 68
Ustinov, Peter 123
Vagrants, The 57
Valiants, The 17
Vangelis 161
Velvet Underground,
  The 56, 87, 182
Vickers, Mike 118-119,
  124
V.I.P.s, The 23-26

Von/Van Dykes, The 17
Voorman, Klaus 58
Wakeman, Rick 161
Walker, T-Bone 14-15,
  21
Walkley, Brian 12, 15-
  16, 20, 103, 171
Wallace, Ian 163
Waller, Fats 14
Ward, Bazz 32-33, 35,
  42-44, 46, 50, 54-59,
  68, 70-71, 78, 80, 82,
  84-87, 90, 93, 100-
  102, 106-107, 112,
  116, 124-127, 134,
  136, 138, 145, 163-
  165, 176-178, 163-
  165, 176-178, 180-
  181, 184
Warhol, Andy 37, 56
Washington, Kenneth 21
Waters, Muddy 106
Waters, Roger 44, 183
Watkins, Charlie 107,
  124
Watts, Charlie 25, 124
Weatherall, Winston 16,
  20, 171
Weathers, John 58
Webber, Andrew Lloyd
  183
Weber, Eberhard 146
Weedon, Bert 16
Welch, Chris 26, 31-34,

37, 58, 62, 68, 73, 80,
  91-94, 110, 132, 136,
  153, 158, 162, 174-
  176, 182
Welles, Orson 90, 174
Wessex Studios 77-79
Westrop, David 125
Wheeler, Kenny 97, 108
Who, The 22, 57, 59, 67,
  70, 150
Wilde, Oscar 49-50
Williams, Andy 122
Williams, Richard 106,
  182
Winter, Johnny 134, 180
Winwood, Stevie 23,
  102
Wonder, Stevie 12
Wyman, Bill 25
Yamaha GX1 153
Yardbirds, The 12, 15,
  22, 28, 31
Yes 49, 54, 74, 77, 88,
  91-92, 97, 132, 134-
  135, 161, 175
Young, Bob 181
Zappa, Frank 66, 149
Zuckerman, Pinkas 122

COMING SOON...

Steve Marriott: The Definitive Biography
by Paolo Hewitt and John Hellier £18.99
Marriott was the prime mover behind '60s chart-toppers
The Small Faces. Longing to be treated as a serious
musician, he formed Humble Pie with Peter Frampton
where his blistering rock 'n' blues guitar playing soon
saw him take centre stage in the US live favourites. After
years in seclusion, Marriott's plans for a comeback in
1991 were tragically cut short when he died in a house
fire. He continues to be a key influence for generations
of musicians from Paul Weller to Oasis and Blur.

Pink Floyd: A Saucerful of Secrets
by Nicholas Schaffner £12.99
Long overdue reissue of the authoritative and detailed
account of one of the most important and popular bands
in rock history. From the psychedelic explorations of the
Syd Barrett-era to '70s superstardom with 'Dark Side of
The Moon', and on to triumph of 'The Wall', before
internecine strife tore the group apart. Schaffner's
definitive history also covers the improbable return of
Pink Floyd without Roger Waters and the hugely
successful 'Momentary Lapse Of Reason' album and tour.

**The Dark Reign of Gothic Rock: In The
Reptile House with The Sisters Of Mercy,
Bauhaus and The Cure**
by Dave Thompson £12.99
From Joy Division to Nine Inch Nails and from Siouxsie
and the Banshees to Marilyn Manson, gothic rock has
endured as the cult of choice for the disaffected and the
alienated. The author traces the rise of '80s and '90s
goth from influences such as Hammer House of Horror
movies and schlock novels, through post-punk into the
full blown drama of Bauhaus, The Cure and the Sisters
of Mercy axis.

Marillion: Separated Out
by Jon Collins £14.99
From the chart hit days of Fish and 'Kayleigh' to the
Steve Hogarth incarnation, Marillion have continued to
make groundbreaking rock music. Collins tells the full
story, drawing on interviews with band members,
associates, and the experiences of some of the band's
most dedicated fans.

Psychedelic Furs: Beautiful Chaos
by Dave Thompson £12.99
Psychedelic Furs were the ultimate post-punk band -
combining the chaos and vocal rasp of the Sex Pistols
with a Bowie-esque glamour. The Furs hit the big time
when John Hughes wrote a movie based on their early
single 'Pretty In Pink'. Poised to join U2 and Simple
Minds in the premier league they withdrew behind their
shades, remaining a cult act, but one with a hugely
devoted following.

Bob Dylan: Like The Night (Revisited)
by C.P. Lee £9.99

Fully revised and updated B-format edition of the hugely
acclaimed document of Dylan's pivotal 1966 show at
the Manchester Free Trade Hall where fans called him
'Judas' for turning his back on folk music in favour of
rock 'n' roll.

Marc Bolan and T Rex: A Chronology
by Cliff McLenahan £13.99
Bolan was the ultimate glam-rock icon; beautiful, elfin,
outrageously dressed and capable of hammering out
impossibly catchy teen rock hits such as 'Telegram Sam'
and 'Get It On'. With their pounding guitars and three
chord anthems, T Rex paved the way for hard rock and
punk rock.

**Back To The Beach: A Brian Wilson and
The Beach Boys Reader**
Edited by Kingsley Abbott £12.99
Revised and expanded edition of the Beach Boys
compendium Mojo magazine deemed an 'essential
purchase'. This collection includes all of the best articles,
interviews and reviews from the Beach Boys' four
decades of music, including definitive pieces by Timothy
White, Nick Kent and David Leaf. New material reflects
on the tragic death of Carl Wilson and documents the
rejuvenated Brian's return to the boards.
"Rivetting!" **** Q
"An essential purchase." Mojo

Serge Gainsbourg: A Fistful Of Gitanes
by Sylvie Simmons £9.99
Rock press legend Simmons' hugely acclaimed biography
of the French genius.
"I would recommend 'A Fistful Of Gitanes' [as summer
reading] which is a highly entertaining biography of
the French singer-songwriter and all-round scallywag."
JG Ballard
"A wonderful introduction to one of the most overlooked
songwriters of the 20th century." The Times (No.3, Top
Music Books of 2001)
"The most intriguing music-biz biography of the year."
The Independent
"Wonderful. Serge would have been so happy." Jane
Birkin

Blues: The British Connection
by Bob Brunning £12.99
Former Fleetwood Mac member Bob Brunning's classic
account of the impact of Blues in Britain, from its
beginnings as the underground music of '50s teenagers
like Mick Jagger, Keith Richards and Eric Clapton, to the
explosion in the '60s, right through to the vibrant scene
of the present day.
"An invaluable reference book and an engaging personal
memoir." Charles Shaar Murray

On The Road With Bob Dylan
by Larry Sloman £12.99
In 1975, as Bob Dylan emerged from 8 years of
seclusion, he dreamed of putting together a travelling
music show that would trek across the country like

a psychedelic carnival. The dream became a reality, and 'On The Road With Bob Dylan' is the ultimate behind-the-scenes look at what happened. When Dylan and the Rolling Thunder Revue took to the streets of America, Larry 'Ratso' Sloman was with them every step of the way.

"The War and Peace of Rock 'n' Roll." Bob Dylan

CURRENTLY AVAILABLE FROM HELTER SKELTER...

Emerson Lake & Palmer: The Show That Never Ends
by George Forrester, Martyn Hanson and Frank Askew £14.00
Drawing on years of research, the authors have produced a gripping and fascinating document of the prog-rock supergroup who remain one of the great rock bands of the seventies.

King Crimson: In The Court of King Crimson
by Sid Smith £14.99
King Crimson's 1969 masterpiece 'In The Court Of The Crimson King' was a huge U.S. chart hit. The band followed it with 40 further albums of consistently challenging, distinctive and innovative music. Drawing on hours of new interviews, and encouraged by Crimson supremo Robert Fripp, the author traces the band's turbulent history year by year, track by track.

Gram Parsons: God's Own Singer
by Jason Walker £12.99
Brand new biography of the man who pushed The Byrds into country-rock territory on Sweethearts Of The Rodeo, and quit to form the Flying Burrito Brothers. Gram lived hard, drank hard, took every drug going and somehow invented country rock, paving the way for Crosby, Stills & Nash, The Eagles and Neil Young. Parsons' second solo LP, Grievous Angel, is a haunting masterpiece of country soul. By the time it was released, he had been dead for 4 months. He was 26 years old.
"Walker has done an admirable job in taking us as close to the heart and soul of Gram Parsons as any author could." **** Uncut, Book Of The Month

Ashley Hutchings: The Guvnor and The Rise of Folk Rock - Fairport Convention, Steeleye Span and The Albion Band
by Geoff Wall and Brian Hinton £14.99
As founder of Fairport Convention and Steeleye Span, Ashley Hutchings is the pivotal figure in the history of folk rock. This book draws on hundreds of hours of interviews with Hutchings and other folk-rock artists and paints a vivid picture of the scene that also produced Sandy Denny, Richard Thompson, Nick Drake, John Martyn and Al Stewart.

Al Stewart: True Life Adventures of A Folk Troubadour
by Neville Judd £25.00
Authorised biography of the Scottish folk hero behind US Top Ten hit 'Year of The Cat'. This is a vivid insider's account of the pivotal '60s London coffee house scene that kickstarted the careers of a host of folkies including Paul Simon - with whom Al shared a flat in 1965 - as well as the wry memoir of a '60s folk star's tribulations as he becomes a chart-topping star in the US in the '70s. Highly limited hardcover edition!

Rainbow Rising: The Story of Ritchie Blackmore's Rainbow
by Roy Davies £14.99
Blackmore led rock behemoths Deep Purple to international multi-platinum, mega-stardom. He quit in '75, to form Rainbow, one of the great live bands, with Ronnie James Dio and enjoyed a string of acclaimed albums and hit singles, including 'All Night Long' and 'Since You Been Gone' before the egos of the key players caused the whole thing to implode. A great rock 'n' roll tale.

ISIS: A Bob Dylan Anthology
Edited by Derek Barker £14.99
Expertly compiled selection of rare articles which trace the evolution of rock's greatest talent. From Bob's earliest days in New York City to the more recent legs of the Never Ending Tour, and his new highly acclaimed album, Love and Theft, the ISIS archive has exclusive interview material - often rare or previously unpublished - with many of the key players in Dylan's career: his parents, friends, musicians and other collaborators.

The Beach Boys' Pet Sounds: The Greatest Album of The 20th Century
by Kingsley Abbott £11.95
Pet Sounds is the 1966 album that saw The Beach Boys graduate from lightweight pop like 'Surfin' USA et al into a vehicle for the mature compositional genius of Brian Wilson. The album was hugely influential, not least on The Beatles. This the full story of the album's background, its composition and recording, its contemporary reception and its enduring legacy.

A Journey Through America With The Rolling Stones
by Robert Greenfield UK Price £9.99
Featuring a new foreword by Ian Rankin, this is the definitive account of their legendary 1972 tour.
"Filled with finely-rendered detail... a fascinating tale of times we shall never see again." Mojo

Razor Edge: Bob Dylan and The Never Ending Tour
by Andrew Muir £12.99
Respected Dylan expert Andrew Muir documents the ups and downs of this unprecedented trek, and finds time to tell the story of his own curious meeting with Dylan. Muir also tries to get to grips with what exactly it all means - both for Dylan and for the Bobcats: dedicated Dylan followers, like himself, who trade tapes of every show and regularly cross the globe to catch up with the latest leg of The Never Ending Tour.

Calling Out Around The World: A Motown Reader
Edited by Kingsley Abbott £13.99

With a foreword by Martha Reeves, this is a unique collection of articles which tell the story of the rise of a black company in a white industry, and its talented stable of artists, musicians, writers and producers. Included are rare interviews with key figures such as Berry Gordy, Marvin Gaye, Smokey Robinson and Florence Ballard as well as reference sources for collectors and several specially commissioned pieces.

I've Been Everywhere: A Johnny Cash Chronicle
by Peter Lewry £14.99
A complete chronological illustrated diary of Johnny Cash's concerts, TV appearances, record releases, recording sessions and other milestones. From his early days with Sam Phillips in Memphis to international stardom, the wilderness years of the mid-sixties, and on to his legendary prison concerts and his recent creative resurgence with the hugely successful 2000 release, 'American Recordings III: Solitary Man'.

Sandy Denny: No More Sad Refrains
by Clinton Heylin £13.99
Paperback edition of the highly acclaimed biography of the greatest female singer-songwriter this country has ever produced.

Animal Tracks: The Story of The Animals
by Sean Egan £12.99
Sean Egan has enjoyed full access to surviving Animals and associates and has produced a compelling portrait of a truly distinctive band of survivors.

Like A Bullet of Light: The Films of Bob Dylan
by C.P. Lee £12.99
Studying in-depth an often overlooked part of Bob Dylan's *oeuvre*.

Rock's Wild Things: The Troggs Files
by Alan Clayson and Jacqueline Ryan £12.99
Respected rock writer Alan Clayson has had full access to the band and traces their history from '60s Andover rock roots to '90s covers, collaborations and corn circles. Also features the full transcript of the legendary 'Troggs Tapes'.

Waiting for the Man: The Story of Drugs and Popular Music
by Harry Shapiro UK Price £12.99
Fully revised edition of the classic story of two intertwining billion dollar industries.
'Wise and witty.' The Guardian

Dylan's Daemon Lover: The Tangled Tale of a 450-Year Old Pop Ballad by Clinton Heylin £12.00
Written as a detective story, Heylin unearths the mystery of why Dylan knew enough to return 'The House Carpenter' to its 16th century source.

Get Back: The Beatles' Let It Be Disaster
by Doug Sulpy & Ray Schweighardt £12.99
No-holds barred account of the power struggles, the

bickering, and the bitterness that led to the break-up of the greatest band in the history of rock 'n' roll.
"One of the most poignant Beatles books ever." Mojo

XTC: Song Stories – The Exclusive And Authorised Story by XTC and Neville Farmer £12.99
"A cheerful celebration of the minutiae surrounding XTC's music with the band's musical passion intact... high in setting the record straight anecdotes. Super bright, funny and commanding." Mojo

Born In The USA: Bruce Springsteen and The American Tradition by Jim Cullen £9.99
"Cullen has written an excellent treatise expressing exactly how and why Springsteen translated his uneducated hicktown American-ness into music and stories that touched hearts and souls around the world." Q****

Bob Dylan
by Anthony Scaduto £10.99
"The best book ever written on Dylan."
Record Collector
"Now in a welcome reprint it's a real treat to read the still-classic Bobography." Q*****

COMING SOON FROM FIREFLY PUBLISHING...
(AN ASSOCIATION OF HELTER SKELTER AND SAF)

The Nirvana Recording Sessions
by Rob Jovanovic £14.99
Drawing on years of research and interviews with many who worked with the band, the author has documented details of every Nirvana recording, from early rehearsals to 'In Utero'. A fascinating account of the creative process of one of the great bands.

Marty Balin: Full Flight – A Tale of Airplanes and Starships
by Marty Balin & Bob Yehling £20.00
Marty Balin founded Jefferson Airplane, as the male half of American rock's greatest vocalist duo, Marty Balin & Grace Slick. A key figure at Woodstock, Monterey and famously beaten up onstage by Hell's Angels at Altamont, Balin wrote many of the band's key songs. He also took Airplane's successor, Jefferson Starship, to the top of the '70s singles and albums charts with self-penned hits like 'Miracles'. Balin left Airplane with 17 scrapbooks containing memorabilia and photos of the band's history, which form the basis for this heavily illustrated book.

The Music of George Harrison: While My Guitar Gently Weeps
by Simon Leng £18.99
Often in Lennon and McCartney's shadow, Harrison's music can stand on its own merits. Santana biographer Leng takes a studied, track by track look at both Harrison's contribution to The Beatles and the solo work

that started with the release in 1970 of his epic masterpiece 'All Things Must Pass'. 'Here Comes The Sun', 'Something' (covered by Sinatra who considered it the perfect love song) and 'While My Guitar Gently Weeps' are just a few of Harrison's classic songs. Originally planned as a celebration of Harrison's music, this is now sadly a commemoration.

CURRENTLY AVAILABLE FROM FIREFLY...

The Pretty Things: Growing Old Disgracefully
by Alan Lakey £20
First biography of one of rock's most influential and enduring combos. Trashed hotel rooms, infighting, rip-offs, sex, drugs and some of the most remarkable rock 'n' roll, including land mark albums like the first rock opera, SF Sorrow, and Rolling Stone's album of the year, 1970's 'Parachute'.
"They invented everything, and were credited with nothing." Arthur Brown, 'God of Hellfire'

The Sensational Alex Harvey
by John Neil Murno £20
Part rock band, part vaudeville, 100% commitment, SAHB were one of the greatest live bands of the era. But behind his showman exterior, Harvey was beset by alcoholism and tragedy. He succumbed to a heart attack on the way home from a gig in 1982, but he is fondly remembered as a unique entertainer by friends, musicians and legions of fans.

U2: The Complete Encyclopedia
by Mark Chatterton £14.99

Poison Heart: Surviving The Ramones
by Dee Dee Ramone and Veronica Kofman £9.99

Minstrels In The Gallery:
A History of Jethro Tull
by David Rees £12.99

Soul Sacrifice: The Santana Story
by Simon Leng UK Price £12.99

Opening The Musical Box:
A Genesis Chronicle
by Alan Hewitt UK Price £12.99

Blowin' Free: 30 Years of Wishbone Ash
by Gary Carter and Mark Chatterton UK Price £12.99

CURRENTLY AVAILABLE FROM SAF PUBLISHING...

The Zombies: Hung Up On A Dream
by Claes Johansen (limited edition hardback) £16.99

Gentle Giant – Acquiring The Taste
by Paul Stump (limited edition hardback) £16.99

Free At Last: The Story of Free and Bad Company
by Steven Rosen £14.99

Necessity Is... The Early Years of Frank Zappa and The Mothers Of Invention by Billy James £12.95

Procol Harum: Beyond The Pale
by Claes Johansen £12.99

No More Mr Nice Guy: The Inside Story of The Alice Cooper Group
by Michael Bruce and Billy James £11.99

An American Band: The Story of Grand Funk Railroad by Billy James £12.99

Wish The World Away: Mark Eitzel and American Music Club by Sean Body £12.99

Go Ahead John! The Music of John McLaughlin by Paul Stump £12.99

Lunar Notes: Zoot Horn Rollo's Captain Beefheart Experience
by Bill Harkleroad and Billy James £11.95

Digital Gothic: A Critical Discography of Tangerine Dream by Paul Stump £9.95

Plunderphonics, Pataphysics and Pop Mechanics: The Leading Exponents of Musique Actuelle
by Andrew Jones £12.95

Kraftwerk: Man, Machine and Music
by Pascal Bussy £12.95

All Helter Skelter, Firefly and SAF titles are available by
mail order from the world famous **Helter Skelter Bookshop**.

You can either phone or fax your order to Helter Skelter
on the following numbers:

Telephone: +44 (0)20 7836 1151
Fax: +44 (0)20 7240 9880

Email: helter@skelter.demon.co.uk
Website: http://www.skelter.demon.co.uk

Office hours: Monday-Friday 10.00am - 7.00pm,
Saturday: 10.00am - 6.00pm, Sunday: Closed.

Postage prices per book worldwide are as follows:
UK & Channel Islands £1.50,
Europe & Eire (Air Mail) £2.95, USA, Canada (Air Mail) £7.50,
Australasia, Far East (Air Mail) £9.00,
Overseas (Surface Mail) £2.50

You can also write enclosing a cheque, International Money Order
or cash by Registered Post. Please include postage.
Please DO NOT send cash. Please DO NOT send foreign currency
or cheques drawn on an overseas bank.
Send to: Helter Skelter Bookshop, 4 Denmark Street, London,
WC2H 8LL, United Kingdom.

If you are in London, why not come and visit us and
browse the titles in person!